WAVERLY® at home windows

Meredith® Books
Des Moines, Iowa

Meredith® Press
An imprint of Meredith® Books

WAVERLY® At Home: Windows

Editor: Vicki L. Ingham
Writer: Dondra Green Parham
Designer: Marisa Dirks
Copy Chief: Terri Fredrickson
Book Production Managers: Pam Kvitne, Marjorie J. Schenkelberg
Contributing Copy Editor: Carol Boker
Contributing Proofreaders: Becky Danley, Susan Sanfrey, Kathy Roth Eastman
Illustrator: Michael Burns
Indexer: Elizabeth T. Parson
Electronic Production Coordinator: Paula Forest
Editorial and Design Assistants: Kaye Chabot, Mary Lee Gavin, Karen Schirm

Meredith® Books
Editor in Chief: J ames D. Blume
Design Director: Matt Strelecki
Managing Editor: Gregory H. Kayko
Executive Decorating and Home Design Editor: Denise L. Caringer

Director, Retail Sales and Marketing: Terry Unsworth
Director, Sales, Special Markets: Rita McMullen
Director, Sales, Premiums: Michael A. Peterson
Director, Sales, Retail: Tom Wierzbicki
Director, Book Marketing: Brad Elmitt
Director, Operations: George A. Susral
Director, Production: Douglas M. Johnston

Vice President, General Manager: Jamie L. Martin

Meredith Publishing Group
President, Publishing Group: Stephen M. Lacy
Vice President, Finance and Administration: Max Runciman

Meredith Corporation
Chairman and Chief Executive Officer: William T. Kerr

Chairman of the Executive Committee: E. T. Meredith III

WAVERLY®
President: Christiane Michaels
Vice President, Marketing and Licensing: Carolyn A. D' Angelo
Director, Design, Licensed Product: Christina Angelides
Design Director, Licensing: Kristin Osterberg

Library of Congress Control Number: 200113018
ISBN: 0-696-21294-3
Manufactured and distributed by Meredith Corporation.
All of us at Meredith® Press are dedicated to providing you with information and ideas to enhance your home. We welcome your comments and suggestions. Write to us at: Meredith Press, Decorating and Home Design Editorial Department, 1716 Locust St., Des Moines, IA 50309-3023. If you would like to purchase any of our books, check wherever quality books are sold. Visit us online at meredithbooks.com

Making your own window treatments gives you the freedom to choose exactly the right fabrics, colors, and patterns for your home. It also opens up a world of creative possibilities for combining fabrics, trims, and hardware to produce a look that is uniquely your own.

The projects in this book have been assigned skill levels and time requirements based on the following definitions:

Beginner: One who is familiar with basic sewing terms, such as seamline, seam allowance, grainline of fabric, and selvage edge. Experience with a sewing machine includes making seams, hems, and gathering. The beginner can work precisely from illustrations.

Intermediate: One who is comfortable with basic sewing terms and uses sewing techniques such as understitching and top stitching; can make custom paper patterns for projects such as scallops; has constructed a simple garment and can make facings, install zippers, and make button holes.

Advanced: One who completely understands sewing terms and measurements; feels confident with the complexity of multiple treatments for individual windows; easily makes paper pattern shapes from illustrations. Sewing experience includes dresses or jackets, which may include pleating and piping.

Some of the window treatments, such as building a cornice box, involve working with lumber; lumber companies will make simple cuts for a small fee, but you will need to be able to use a jigsaw or table saw to cut shaped edges.

The time required for each project is a general guide only; actual time required will depend on individual skill level and individual circumstances.

Please read all instructions carefully before beginning a project. If you encounter unfamiliar sewing terms in the instructions, please check the glossary on pages 124 and 125 for help. On pages 126 and 127, you will find a complete listing of the Waverly fabrics shown in the photos of each project.

table of contents

table of contents

Sheer fabrics filter the light, bringing a luminous quality to a room.

Using unlined cotton drapery fabric for a roller blind softens harsh sun but lets in as much light as possible on gray days. Sheer fabric is ideal for a knotted swag that drapes loosely across the window and falls to the floor, gracefully softening the architecture.

roller blind & knotted swag

The roller blind offers tailored and traditional style along with the ease of no-sew construction. Fusible tapes take the place of needle and thread in this project. The blind is named for its form: The lower edge rolls up when you pull the cords, which are similar to those found in a Roman shade. This is the reverse of an old-fashioned roller blind, which snaps in a roll at the top.

The semitranslucence of unlined cotton fabric makes it a fresh choice for a blind, bringing an airy look to a room. If privacy at night is a concern, however, choose a more opaque fabric that will block light.

To soften the architecture, opt for unstructured, knotted swags made from a sheer that coordinates with the scrim. These easily assembled valances are also no-sew. The variety of sheers available now lets you choose a fabric to suit your style. A windowpane check offers traditional elegance, polka dots suggest whimsy, and sleek swirls create a contemporary look.

FAST FACTS ON FUSIBLE WEB

- Paper-backed fusible adhesive tapes and an iron can take the place of thread and a sewing machine in many home decorating projects. The side hems of the roller blind (pages 8–9) are just one example.

- Not only can you fuse fabrics together, but you can also use the paper-backed fusibles to bond fabric to other porous materials, such as wood or cardboard.

- It generally takes two steps to fuse fabrics. First, apply the paper-backed fusible adhesive material to one fabric with a hot iron. Remove the paper backing. Next, place the fabric as desired—turn the hem, for example—and fuse the layers together.

- Read the manufacturer's instructions for fabric suitability. Some recommend different weights of fusible material depending on the fabric. Always test on a scrap first.

materials

54"-wide decorator fabric
⅞"-wide paper-backed fusible adhesive tape
Shade-and-blind cord
1×2 pine board
½"-diameter dowel
Cleat with fasteners
2 (2") No. 8 wood screws
3 screw eyes

tools

Handsaw (or have the lumber supply shop cut the wood for you)
Electric drill and drill bits
Screwdriver
Staple gun and ¼" staples

sewing tools

Iron and ironing board
Scissors
Tape measure

skill level: beginner
time required: ½ day

making the roller blind:

1 This blind mounts inside the window frame. Measure the height and width of the window inside the frame. To determine yardage for one blind, add 2" to the width and 10" to the length. For Roman blind cord yardage, multiply 7 times the measured height of the window. The 1×2 board (the mounting board) and the dowel (to weight the blind's lower edge) must equal the window width. Purchase materials after taking the window measurements.

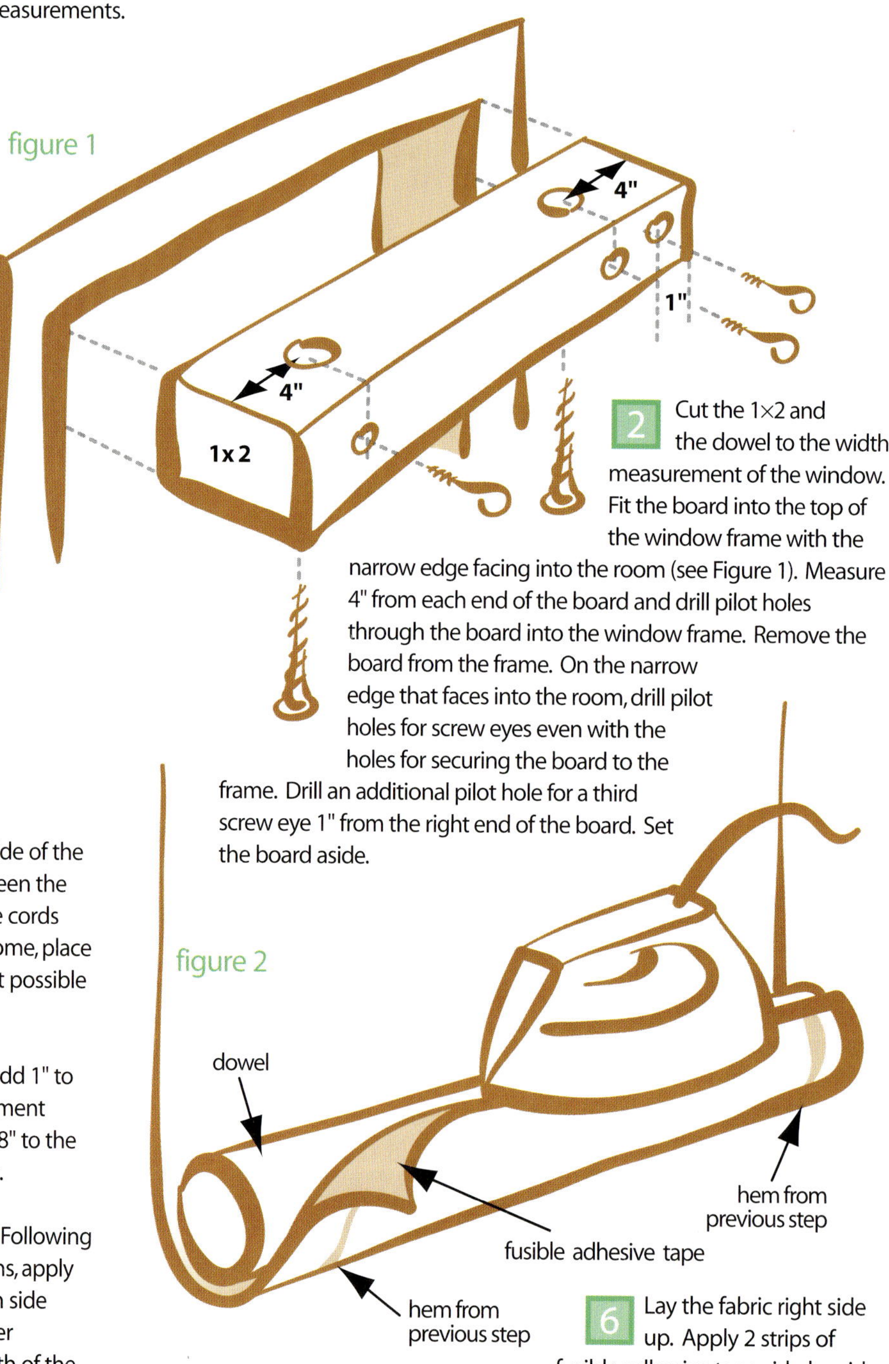

2 Cut the 1×2 and the dowel to the width measurement of the window. Fit the board into the top of the window frame with the narrow edge facing into the room (see Figure 1). Measure 4" from each end of the board and drill pilot holes through the board into the window frame. Remove the board from the frame. On the narrow edge that faces into the room, drill pilot holes for screw eyes even with the holes for securing the board to the frame. Drill an additional pilot hole for a third screw eye 1" from the right end of the board. Set the board aside.

3 Install the cleat on the right side of the window frame midway between the top and bottom. The cleat holds the cords taut. If you have small children at home, place the cleat closer to the top to prevent possible entanglement with the cords.

4 For the cut size of the fabric, add 1" to the window's width measurement (from Step 1) for the side hems and 8" to the length measurement. Cut the fabric.

5 Lay the fabric wrong side up. Following the manufacturer's instructions, apply the fusible adhesive tape along each side edge of the fabric. Remove the paper backing. Fold each edge by the width of the fusible tape to the wrong side and finger press. Follow the manufacturer's instructions to fuse the hems in place. Apply one strip of fusible adhesive tape to the top edge of the fabric, but do not remove the paper backing.

6 Lay the fabric right side up. Apply 2 strips of fusible adhesive tape side-by-side to the bottom edge of the fabric. Remove the paper backing. Center the dowel on the edge of the fabric over the fusible surface. Begin rolling the dowel inside the lower edge of the fabric. Fuse the fabric to the dowel as you roll (see Figure 2).

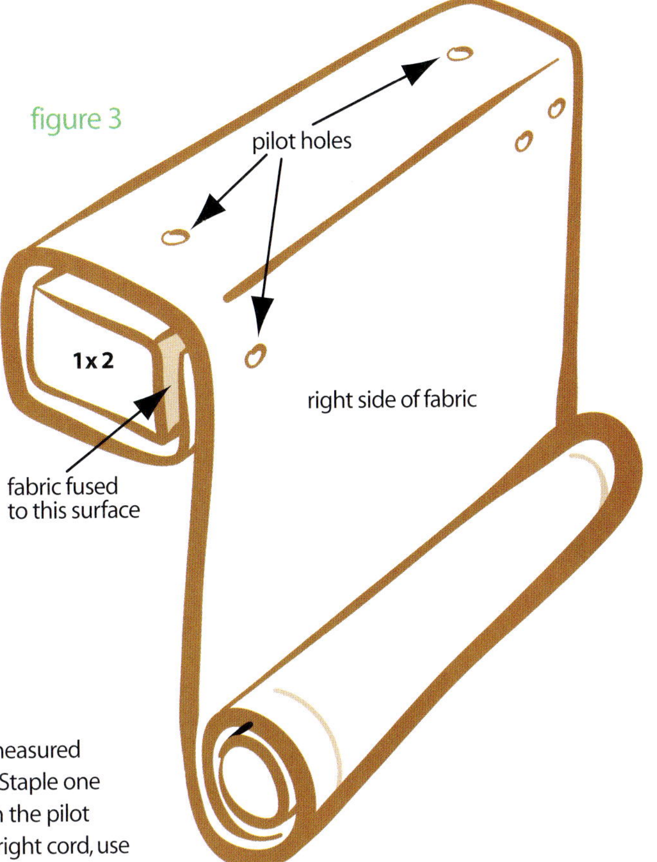

7 Remove the paper backing from the fusible adhesive tape at the top edge of the fabric. Center the narrow edge of the board with the pilot holes on the fusible surface. Fuse the fabric to the board. Wrap the fabric smoothly around the board, overlapping the fused edge (see Figure 3). Punch a small hole through the fabric into each pilot hole.

8 For the left cord, cut a length 3 times the measured window length plus the measured width. Staple one end of the cord to the top of the board even with the pilot hole for the left screw eye (see Figure 4). For the right cord, use the remaining length and staple one end to the top of the board even with the pilot hole that is 4" from the right end of the board.

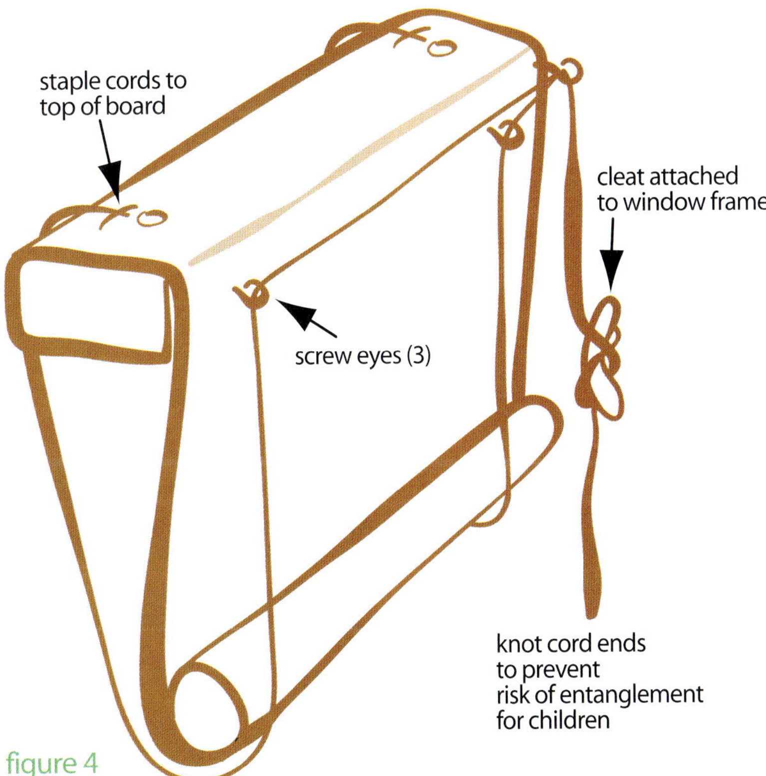

9 Install the board in the top of the window frame with wood screws. Install screw eyes in the front. Take each cord down the back of the blind, under the dowel at the bottom edge to the front of the blind, and through the screw eye at the top. Thread both cords through the extreme right screw eye (see Figure 4). Begin rolling the blind from the dowel edge. Pull up the cord snugly along the blind. Trim cord ends even. To raise the blind, gently pull the cords together, causing the fabric to continue rolling around the dowel. At the desired height, secure the cords to the cleat with a figure-eight motion.

materials

54"-wide decorator fabric
⅞"-wide paper-backed fusible adhesive tape
Covered wire twist ties, as for kitchen or trash bags
2 screw eyes

tools

Electric drill and drill bits

sewing tools

Iron and ironing board
Pressing cloth
Scissors
Tape measure
Large safety pins
Sewing machine

skill level: beginner
time required: ½ day

making the knotted swag:

1 Mount this swag with screw hooks directly into the window frame. One continuous length of fabric spans the top of the window, knots at each corner, and falls to the floor. Twist ties hold the knots. Measure the height from the top of the window frame to the floor. Measure the window width. For the swag, you need a length of 54"-wide fabric two times the height plus the width plus an additional yard for the knots and puddles. Purchase materials after taking measurements.

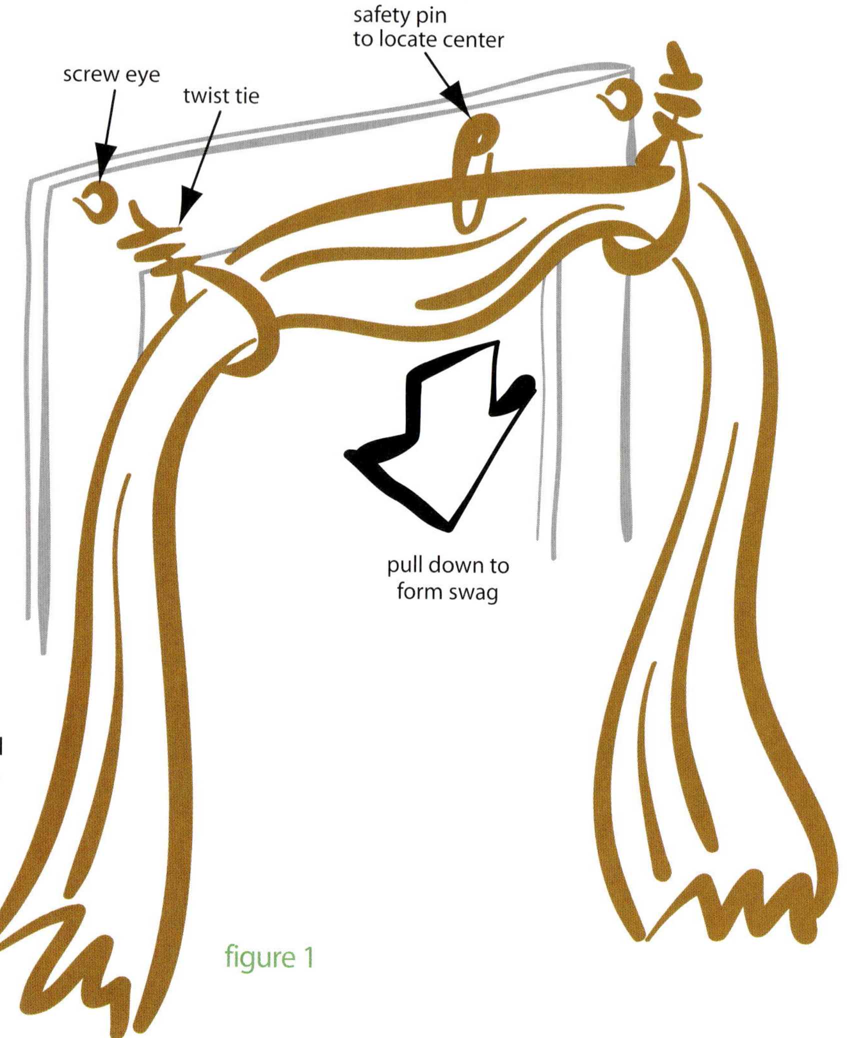

figure 1

2 Drill pilot holes in the window molding at each top corner. Install one screw eye in each (see Figure 1).

3 Trim the selvage edges from the fabric. Test a small scrap of fabric for use with fusible adhesive. If the fabric is compatible, fuse the hems in place. Lay the fabric wrong side up. Following the manufacturer's instructions, apply fusible adhesive tape to the long edges of the fabric. Remove the paper backing. Fold each edge to the wrong side by the width of the fusible surface and finger-press. Fuse the hems in place. Repeat to fuse the hems on each short edge of the fabric.

4 If the fabric cannot be fused, machine stitch ½" from each raw edge of the fabric. Turn the raw edge to the wrong side along the stitches. Finger-press. Turn again to make a double hem and press with an iron. Machine stitch through all layers close to the first line of stitches.

5 Find the center of one long edge of the fabric. Mark with a large safety pin. Measure one-half the window width on either side of the center mark. Use additional pins to mark these as corners. Holding one marked corner in your hand, loosely fold the width of the fabric back and forth in accordion pleats. Gather the pleats with a twist tie. Repeat at the opposite marked corner. Remove the pins at the corners, but leave the center pin for reference.

6 Place the fabric at the window by hanging the twist ties on the screw eyes. Gently pull the top edge of the fabric outward to make the top of the drape taut. Redress the pleats along the center section as needed. Gently pull down the lower edge of the fabric to make the swag.

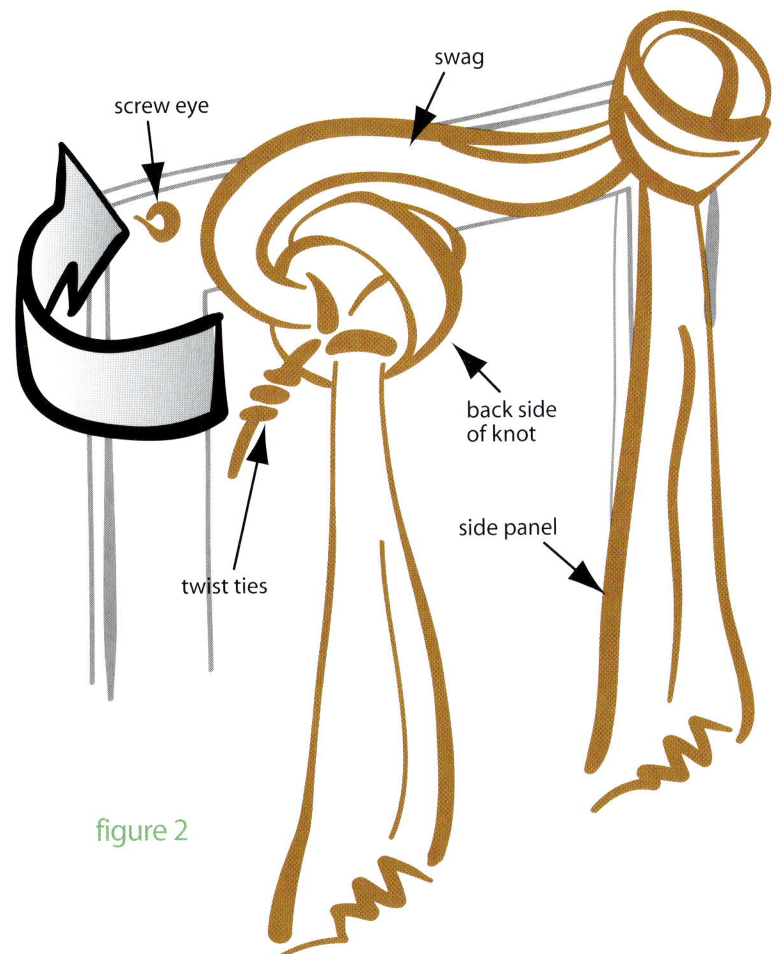

figure 2

7 Remove the fabric from the window. Make a knot (see box below) beyond each twist tie. Both the swag center and side panel will appear to come from the back of the knot.

8 Return the swag to the window to check fit. Adjust each knot as needed. Gather the fabric for each side panel into a twist tie, hiding the tie behind the knot. To keep the knot from pulling apart, twist together the tie from the swag with the tie from the side panel (see Figure 2). Secure the twist ties to the screw eyes.

secrets of a great knot: Tying a great decorative knot is easy when you take it step by step.

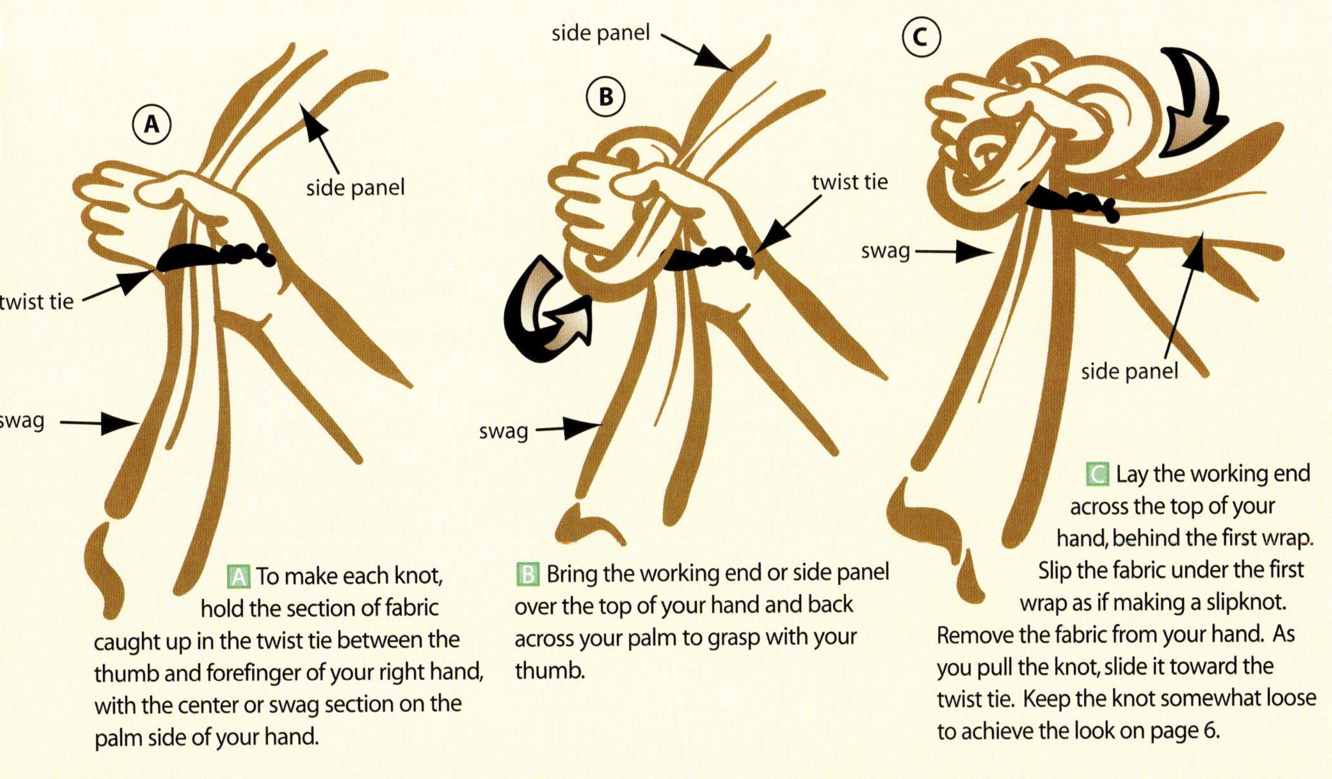

A To make each knot, hold the section of fabric caught up in the twist tie between the thumb and forefinger of your right hand, with the center or swag section on the palm side of your hand.

B Bring the working end or side panel over the top of your hand and back across your palm to grasp with your thumb.

C Lay the working end across the top of your hand, behind the first wrap. Slip the fabric under the first wrap as if making a slipknot. Remove the fabric from your hand. As you pull the knot, slide it toward the twist tie. Keep the knot somewhat loose to achieve the look on page 6.

JAMES RIVER

One of the easiest and most versatile window treatments you can sew is unlined tab-top panels. Pair them with stationary roller blinds to add the effect of a cornice behind the panels.

roller blind & tab-top panels

Layered window treatments offer lots of decorating options. The unlined tab-top panels bring softness, color, and pattern to a room, while the stationary reverse roller blind, mounted inside the window frame, functions like a valance, dressing the top third of the window. The blind doesn't raise or lower, but in a variation of this treatment, you can make the blind long enough to roll up manually, if you like, and secure it at the desired level with the ties.

To enlarge the apparent height of the window, install the curtain rod above the window frame. Let the rod ends extend beyond the frame to enhance the apparent width of the window.

Layered window treatments give you an opportunity to mix and match fabrics. This is a good way to link two adjoining rooms, using the same palette of colors and patterns in varying amounts from one room to the next. To guarantee success in mixing patterns, remember the rule of three: Choose three scales—small, medium, and large.

materials

54"-wide decorator fabric
1×2 pine board
3/4"-diameter dowel
2 (2") No. 8 wood screws

tools

Handsaw
Electric drill and drill bits
Screwdriver
Staple gun and 1/4" staples

sewing tools

Sewing machine
Iron and ironing board
Scissors
Tape measure
Thread
Pins

skill level: beginner
time required: 1/2 day

making the stationary reverse roller blind:

1 This blind mounts inside the window frame. Measure the height and width of the window inside the frame. Determine the desired finished length of the blind: This is generally one-third the window height. For yardage, add at least 4" to the measured window width and 16" to the desired finished length to make sure you have enough fabric. For the ties, decide whether the ties will be cut on the bias (as shown in the photograph, page 10) or on the straight grain. Sketch a diagram of the layout to determine how much fabric you need to create the desired look. The 1×2 board is the mounting board at the top of the blind. The 3/4" dowel weights the lower edge. Both the board and dowel must be as long as the window width. Purchase materials after taking window measurements and making calculations.

2 Cut the 1×2 and the dowel to the width measurement of the window. Fit the board into the top of the window frame with the narrow edge facing into the room. Measure 4" from each end of the board. Drill pilot holes through the board into the frame (see Figure 1, page 6). Remove the board from the frame.

3 To determine the cut size of the fabric, add 2" for side hems to the window width measurement from Step 1. Add 14" to the desired finished length measurement. Cut the fabric. For the ties, cut four 8"-wide strips that are 12" longer than the desired finished length measurement.

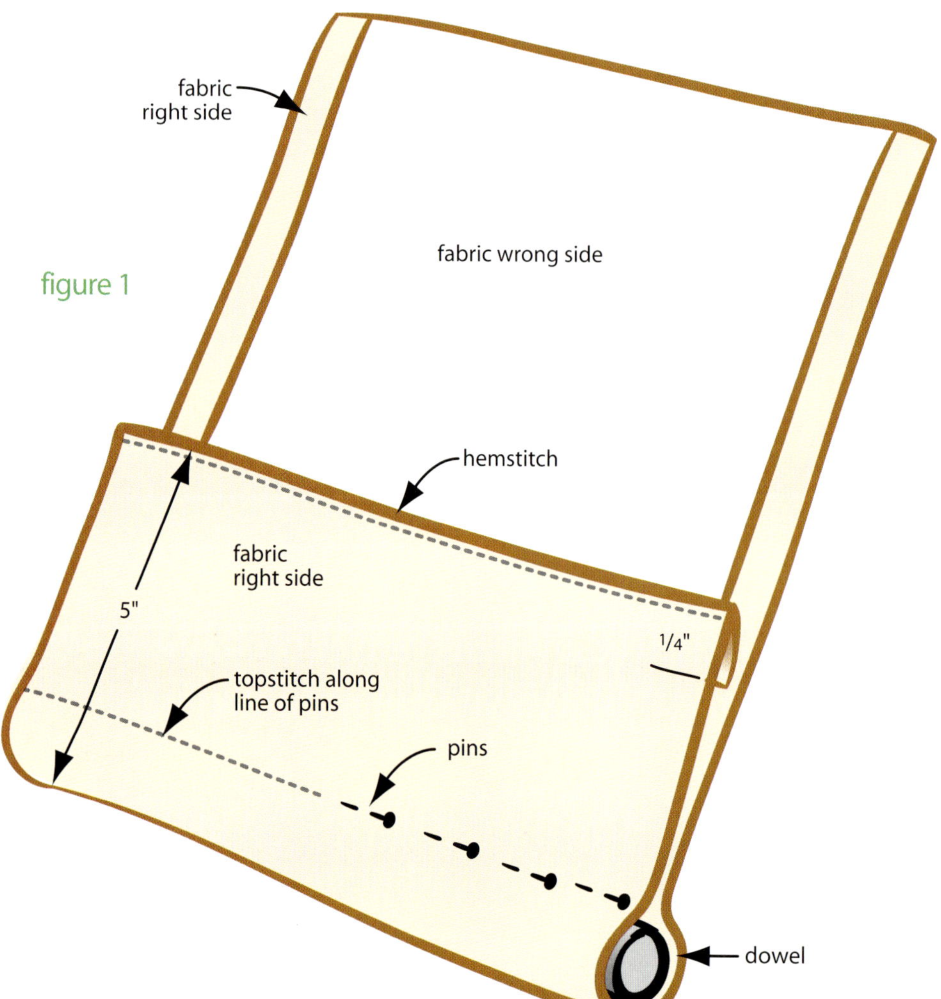

figure 1

4 On each side edge of the blind, fold a 1/2" hem twice. Press. With the wrong side of the blind faceup, edgestitch the hem in place (see Figure 1). On the lower edge of the blind, turn under 1/2". Press. Turn under 5" to form a deep hem and hemstitch. Insert the dowel into the hem along fold. Pin a line close to the dowel to form a casing (see Figure 1). Remove the dowel. Topstitch along the line of pins. Replace the dowel in the pocket.

figure 2

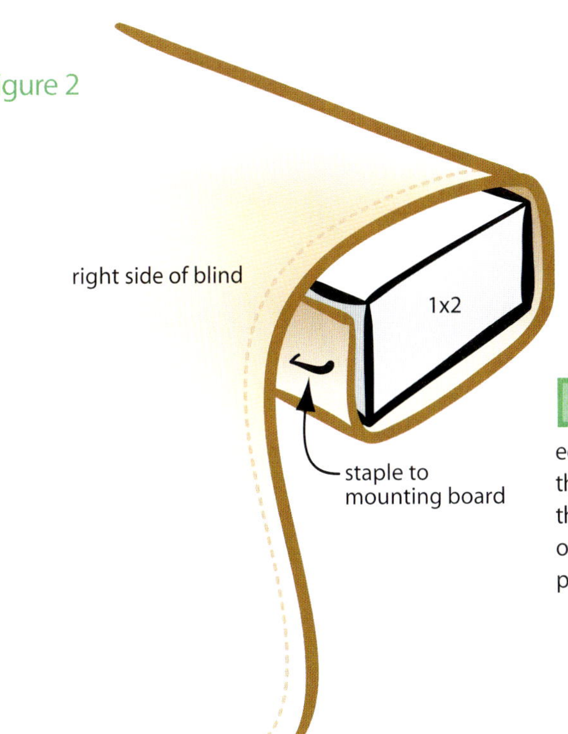

5 With the wrong side of the fabric facing the wood, center the top edge of the blind on the narrow front edge of the mounting board (see Figure 2). Staple the fabric to the board. Smoothly wrap the board with the fabric. Conceal the staples behind the blind as it falls from the front top edge of the board. Punch small holes through the fabric into each pilot hole.

6 For each tie, fold one strip lengthwise with right sides facing. Cut one short end at an angle. Using a ½" seam allowance, stitch the long edges and angled edges together. Pivot the stitching line at the corner. Clip the corner. Press the seam open as far as possible. Turn to the right side. Place the seam on the edge and press flat.

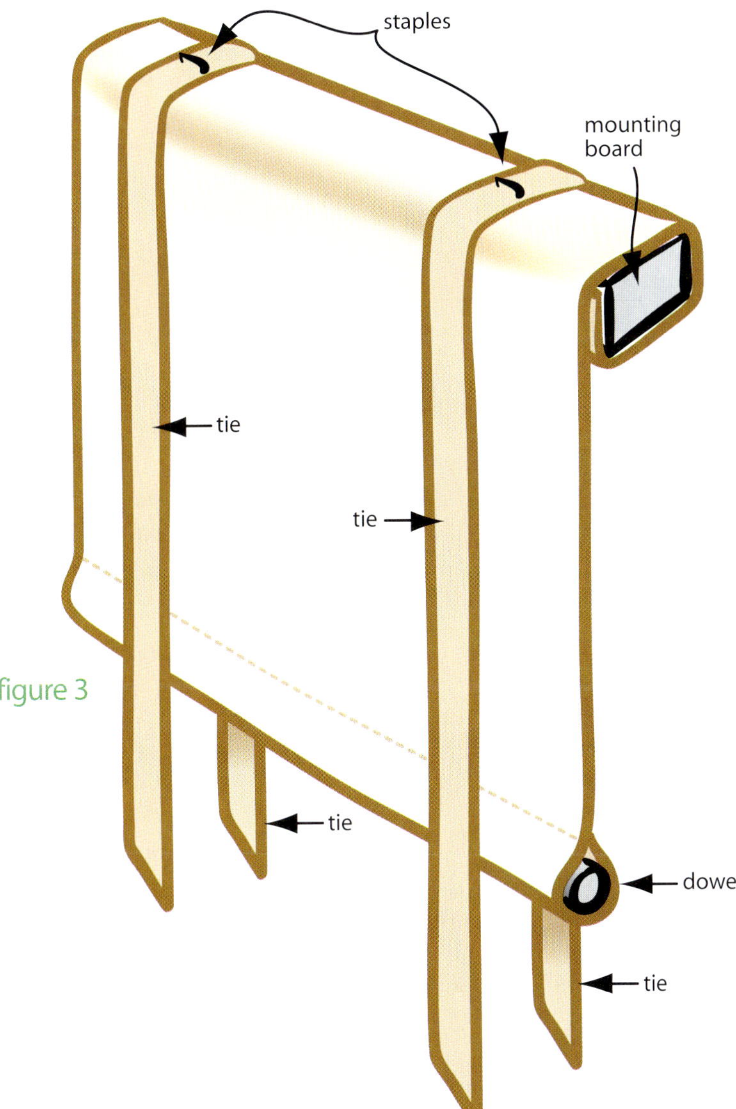

figure 3

7 Make 4 ties. Position the ties in pairs on the front and back of the blind with the open raw ends on top of the mounting board. Staple the ends to the top of the mounting board (see Figure 3).

8 Install the board in the top of window frame with wood screws. Roll the dowel to the right side of the blind, taking care not to expose the wrong side of the fabric above the hem. Temporarily pin the roll in place. Knot together pairs of ties under the roll and remove the pins.

materials

54"-wide decorator fabric
54"-wide complementary decorator fabric (optional)
Medium-weight fusible interfacing
Iron curtain rod and mounting hardware

tools

Electric drill and drill bits
Screwdriver

sewing tools

Sewing machine
Iron and ironing board
Tape measure
Pins
Thread
Scissors

skill level: beginner
time required: 1 day

making the unlined tab-top panels:

1 Install the curtain rod. The iron rods shown in the photograph (page 10) are mounted above and outside the window moldings.

2 These unlined panels are cut from a full width of 54"-wide drapery fabric. The tabs are stitched into the seam between the curtain front and the curtain facing. For each curtain panel you need a length of fabric equal to the distance from the rod to the floor plus 10". Consider the length of the fabric repeat before you purchase fabric. For the contrast tabs, which are cut on the bias in the photograph on page 12, you need ½ yard of complementary fabric.

3 Trim the selvages from the curtain panel fabric. Cut 2 curtain fronts the measured length from the rod to the floor plus 6". Be sure each piece begins at the same point in the fabric repeat. Also cut 2 4"-wide curtain facings.

4 On the long side edges of each curtain front, turn under 1½" twice. Press. Working on the wrong side, edgestitch the hem in place.

5 Following the manufacturer's instructions, fuse interfacing to the wrong side of the fabric for the tabs. Cut 3"-wide bias strips and cut the strips into 6" lengths.

baste in place
tabs (6)
right side
seams centered on inside of tab

figure 1

6 With right sides together, fold each tab lengthwise. Using a ½" seam allowance, stitch the long edges together. Press the seam open. Turn each tab to the right side. Center the seam on the back of the tab. Press flat. When all tabs are complete, fold each in half widthwise, with the seam inside and the raw edges matching. Lay one curtain front right side up. Place 1 tab at each edge of the curtain front and evenly space the remaining tabs between these, using 6 tabs per curtain (see Figure 1). Using a ½" seam allowance, baste the tabs in place. Repeat for each remaining curtain panel.

7 Insert the curtain rod through the tabs. Hang the curtain to check the length of the tabs. If the top of the curtain hangs too low, you can shorten the length of the tabs at this time.

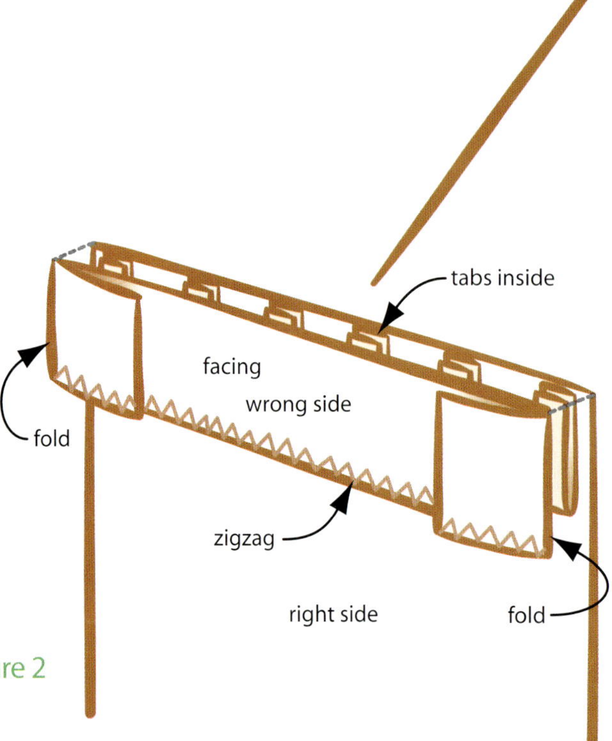

figure 2

8 Finish one long edge of the curtain facing with a row of zigzag stitches. With right sides together, align the raw edge of the curtain facing over the tabs (see Figure 2). Turn back the facing ends so they don't extend beyond the side edges of the front. Press the folds.

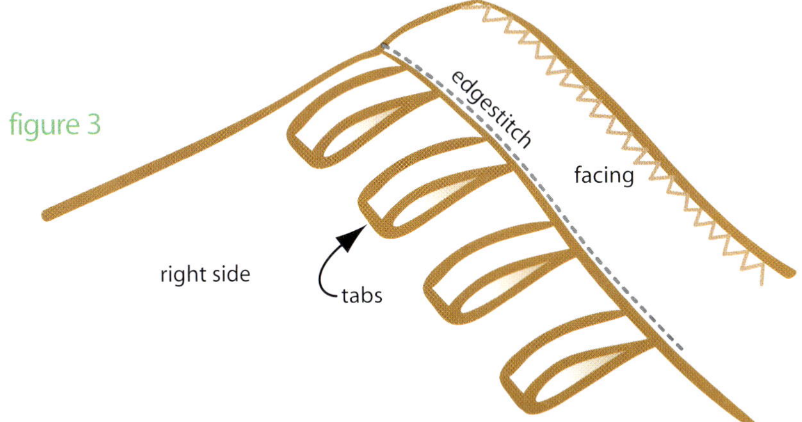

9 Using a 1/2" seam allowance, stitch the facing to the curtain front. Press the seam open, with the tab ends toward the facing and the loops toward the curtain front. Working from the right side of the fabric, understitch the facing 1/8" from the seam, catching the seam allowance of the tabs in the stitching (see Figure 3). Turn the facing to the wrong side of the curtain front, allowing tabs to pop up. Press.

10 Following the stitches from the side hems and working from the right side of the curtain front, topstitch through all layers, catching the facing in the stitches.

11 Insert the curtain rod through the tabs. Hang the curtain. Turn under the hem so the edge meets the floor. Pin. Remove the curtain from the rod. Press the fold. Turn under the raw edge to meet the crease. Press. Hemstitch the folded edge.

HARDWARE MADE EASY

IRON AND METAL POLES

Iron and metal poles look at home in almost every decorating style. The trick is finding a finish to suit your room. Antique brass and wrought iron hardware suggest traditional settings. Verdigris, black, or pewter suits a cottage style. Chrome, polished brass, and copper strike a contemporary chord in modern settings.

Metal rods are usually mounted in one of two ways. A straight rod may clip into a standard bracket that's attached to the wall or molding. The rod may also bend at the ends and mount directly to the wall.

In either case, to make sure the mounting is secure, fasten the hardware directly into the molding or a wall stud. If you mount the rod off the window to achieve a special effect, you should use wall anchors or a similarly designed fastener to attach the rod securely to the wall. For help in selecting the best type of anchor for your home, ask for assistance in the "fasteners" area of your local hardware store.

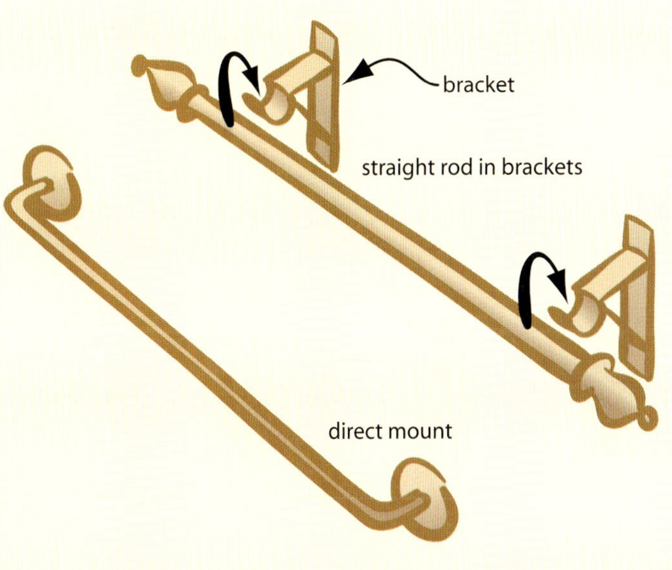

When you need a tailored, functional window treatment, choose Roman shades. Because they're usually installed inside the window frame, they don't hide the architecture, providing privacy and light control with a minimum of fuss. Dress them up with contrast edging and special valances or play them down by using neutral fabrics that blend with your woodwork.

basic roman shade & flat valance

With clean, uncluttered lines, Roman shades control light and privacy. Normally the shade fits inside the window frame. As you raise the shade, it pleats, forming flat accordion-like folds that stack at the top of the window. In the window-seat niche shown opposite, however, the shade and valance are mounted outside the frame to cover the whole window wall. This makes the area look larger by downplaying the small strip of wall on each side of the window.

If you have a window set into a small nook, such as a dormer window, this approach to installing a Roman shade may work for you. Very large windows, however, are not suited for Roman shades. The weight of large shades makes it difficult to raise and lower them. As a rule, consider covering any window or set of windows wider than 7 feet with two or more narrow shades.

Plan for the valance to be one-fourth to one-third the height of the window, but no shorter than 8 inches.

materials

54"-wide decorator fabric
Loop shade tape
Shade-and-blind cord
Flat braid or ribbon
1×2 pine board
1/2"-diameter dowel
Cleat with fasteners
8 (2") No. 8 wood screws
8 (1") No. 8 wood screws
5 screw eyes
4 (3") inside corner braces

tools

Handsaw
Electric drill and drill bits
Screwdriver
Staple gun and 1/2" staples

sewing tools

Iron and ironing board
Pressing cloth
Scissors
Tape measure

skill level: intermediate
time required: 1 day

making the basic roman shade:

1 Measure the height and width of the window inside the window recess or frame. For the shade, you will need a piece of fabric at least 2" wider and 16" longer than this measurement. You will also need loop tape 4 times the measured height plus 24", cord 8 times the measured height plus 4 times the measured width, and braid 2 1/2 times the measured window height. The 1×2 board serves as the mounting board at the top of the shade. The 1/2" dowel will weight the lower edge of the shade. Both the board and dowel must be as long as the measured width. Purchase materials after taking measurements.

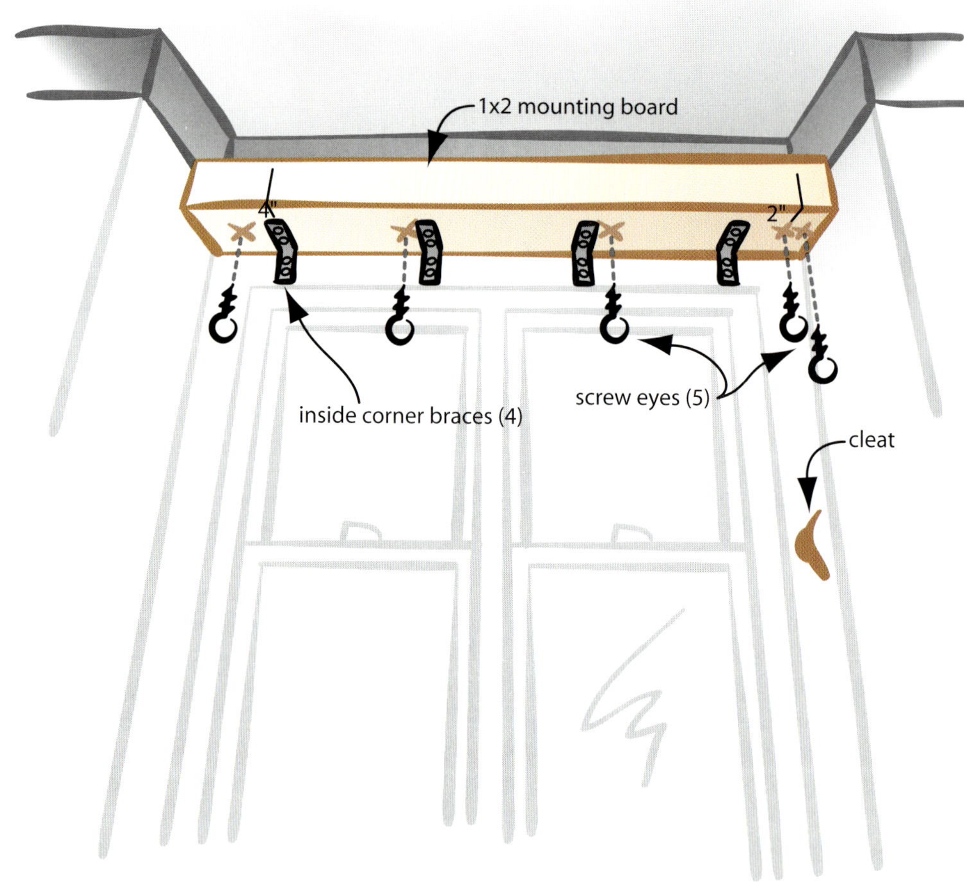

figure 1

2 Cut the 1×2 and dowel to the width measurement. Referring to Figure 1, fit the board into the top of the window frame (or to the wall below the crown molding) with the narrow edge facing into the room. Install one inside corner brace to the wall above the window at each end of the board, using 2" wood screws. Space the remaining 2 braces evenly between the first two. Place the mounting board on top of the braces and drill pilot holes through the braces into the board. Remove the board. Mark points 2" from each end of the board for screw eyes. Measure even segments and mark 2 more points along the board for screw eyes. Drill shallow pilot holes. Drill one additional pilot hole for a fifth screw eye 1" from the right end of the board. Set the board aside.

3 Place the cleat on the right side of the frame about midway between top and bottom. The cleat holds the cords taut. If you have small children in your home, place the cleat closer to the top of the frame, lowering the risk of possible entanglement. Drill pilot holes in the frame. Mount the cleat.

4 Find the cut size of the fabric for the shade. Add 3" to the width measurement. Add 13" to the length measurement. Cut the fabric. For the shade shown in the photograph (page 20), fabric lengths were seamed together to make the required width. For the most attractive panel, arrange lengths so that you have a wide center panel flanked by two narrower side panels. If applicable, be sure to match pattern repeats across seams. In most cases, you will use a full fabric width for the center panel because fabric patterns are easier to match with full widths. Remember to include 1/2" seam allowances on each section in your calculations. If you wish, topstitch braid or ribbon to the shade front to cover seams (see Figure 2).

5 Turn under each side edge 1 1/2". Press. On the bottom edge, turn under 1/4". Press. Turn under 3/4" for dowel casing. Press. Working from the wrong side, edgestitch the casing on the bottom edge close to the folded edge.

6 On the wrong side, measure and mark a line 2" from each side edge. Also measure and mark 2 more lines to match the spacing of additional pilot holes for screw eyes in the mounting board. Center the loop shade tape along each line, having the first loops at the casing (see Figure 3). Tapes also cover the raw edge of the side edges. Turn under the raw ends of the tape. Edgestitch the tapes in place. Work each line of stitches from the casing to the top.

7 Center the top edge of the shade, wrong side down, on the narrow, front edge of the board with the pilot holes. Staple the fabric to the board. Wrap the fabric smoothly around the board, overlapping the first edge. Punch a small hole through the fabric into each pilot hole. Install the board in the window frame or ceiling with wood screws. (If using the shade with the flat valance, assemble and staple the valance over the shade before installing the mounting board in the window frame.) Install screw eyes. Insert the dowel into the casing.

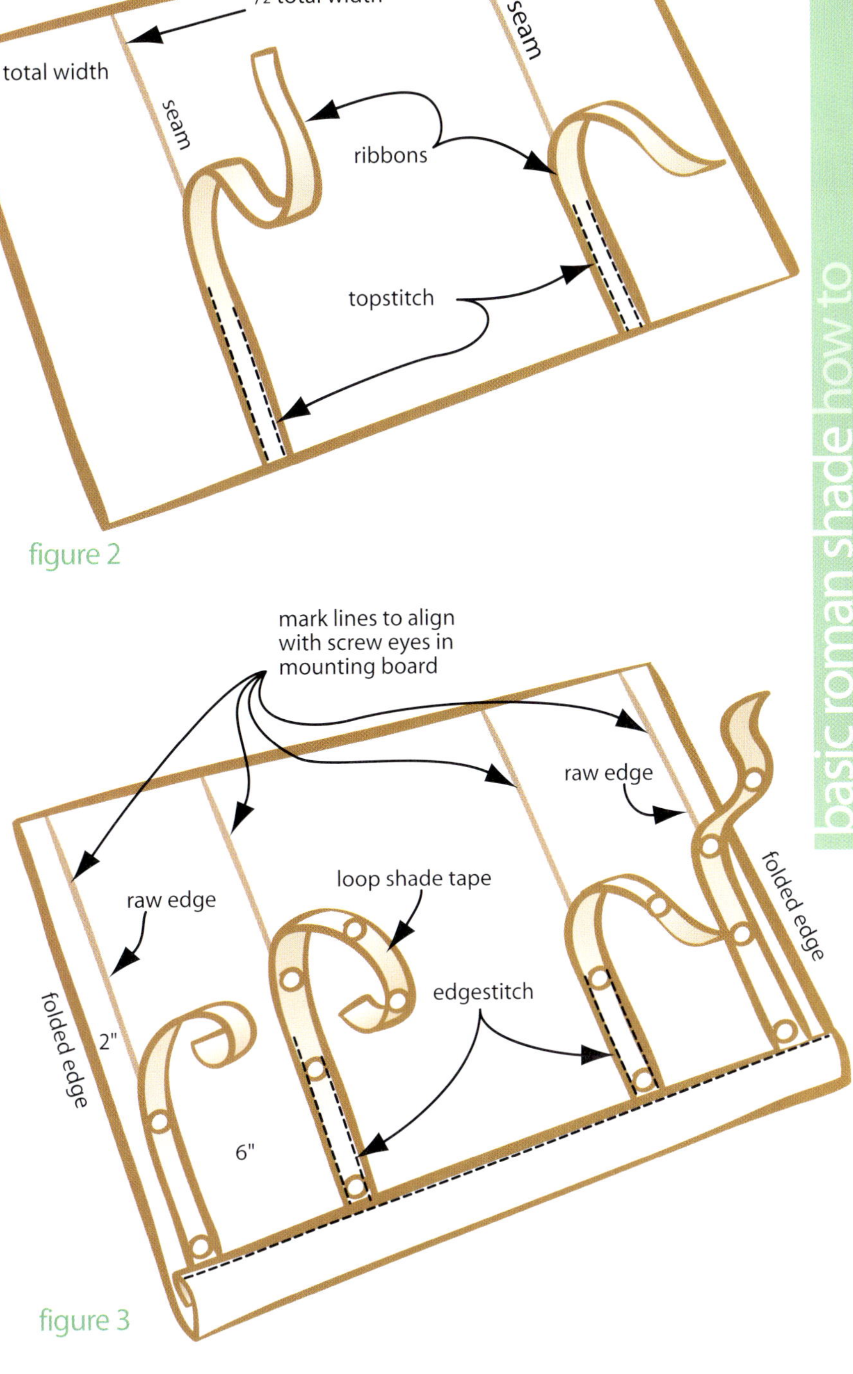

figure 2

figure 3

8 For the left cords, cut a length 2 times the measured window length plus the measured width. Tie one end of each cord to the lowest rings on the left side of the blind. For the right cords, halve the remaining length. Tie one end of each cord to the lowest rings on right side of the shade. Thread the cords through the column of rings and through the screw eye at the top. Thread all cords through the extreme right screw eye. Pull the cords to take up the slack. Trim the cord ends even. To raise the shade, gently pull the cords, causing the fabric to pleat. At the desired height, secure the cords to the cleat with a figure-eight motion.

9 To set the pleats, raise the shade to the highest position and secure the cords. Arrange the pleats by hand and leave in place for one week.

materials

54"-wide decorator fabric
Lining fabric
Flat braid
Frog and tassel
1×1 pine board (see Step 2)
2 (2") No. 8 wood screws

tools

Handsaw
Electric drill and drill bits
Screwdriver

sewing tools

Sewing machine
Thread

skill level: intermediate
time required: 1 day

making the flat valance:

1 Measure the window height and width inside the window recess or frame. The valance should be one-fourth to one-third the measured window height, but no shorter than 8". The finished width is as wide as the measured width. You need a piece of fabric and lining 1" wider and 6" longer than the measurements.

2 If you use the flat valance with the shade as shown on page 18, you will attach the valance to the same mounting board as the shade, layering it over the shade. If you use the flat valance alone, without the roman shade, it mounts inside a window recess on a mounting board or inside the window frame on a tension rod. To prepare the mounting board, cut the 1×1 to the width measurement. Fit the board into the top of the window frame or window recess. Measure 4" from each end of the board and drill pilot holes through the board into the frame or ceiling. Take the board down.

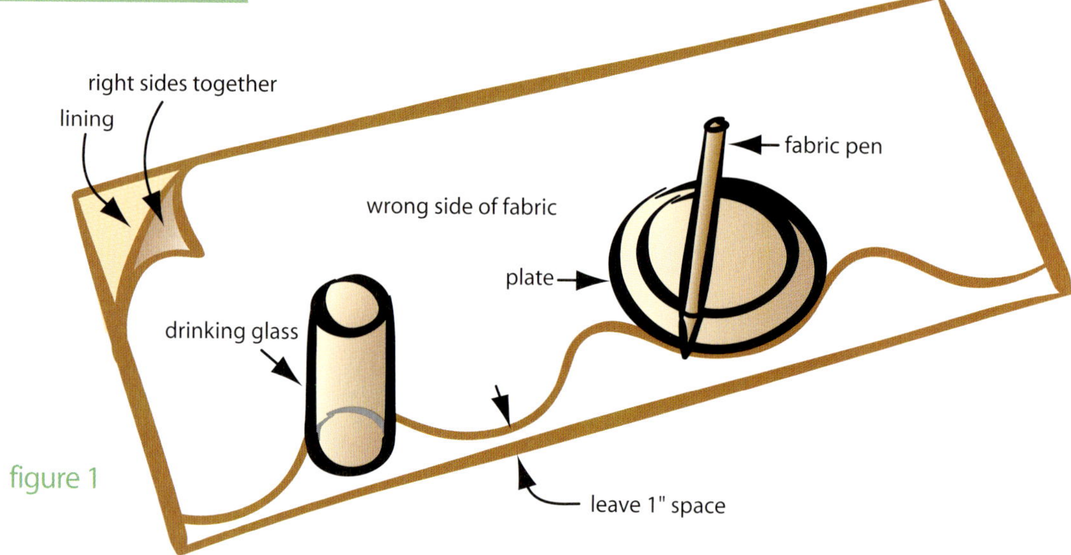

figure 1

3 Plan the pattern placement on the valance. If necessary, seam together fabric lengths and lining lengths to make up the required valance width. Plan the shaped edge. From the fabric and lining, cut one each the measured window width plus 1" by the finished valance length plus 6". With right sides together, stack the fabric and lining, having the wrong side of the fabric on top so you can see the pattern. On the lower edge, draw a shaped edge by tracing around a plate, a bowl, or a drinking glass (or some combination of these). Leave a 1" seam allowance below each curve (see Figure 1).

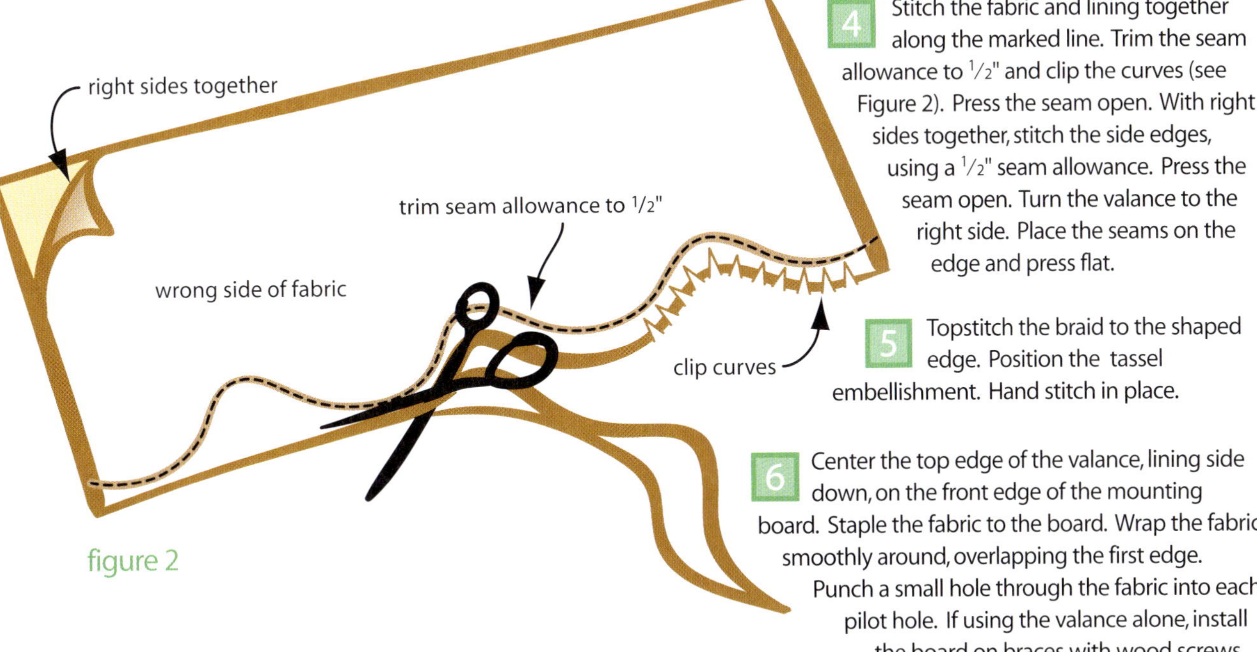

figure 2

4 Stitch the fabric and lining together along the marked line. Trim the seam allowance to 1/2" and clip the curves (see Figure 2). Press the seam open. With right sides together, stitch the side edges, using a 1/2" seam allowance. Press the seam open. Turn the valance to the right side. Place the seams on the edge and press flat.

5 Topstitch the braid to the shaped edge. Position the tassel embellishment. Hand stitch in place.

6 Center the top edge of the valance, lining side down, on the front edge of the mounting board. Staple the fabric to the board. Wrap the fabric smoothly around, overlapping the first edge. Punch a small hole through the fabric into each pilot hole. If using the valance alone, install the board on braces with wood screws.

TECHNIQUES MADE EASY

PLANNING A SHAPED EDGE

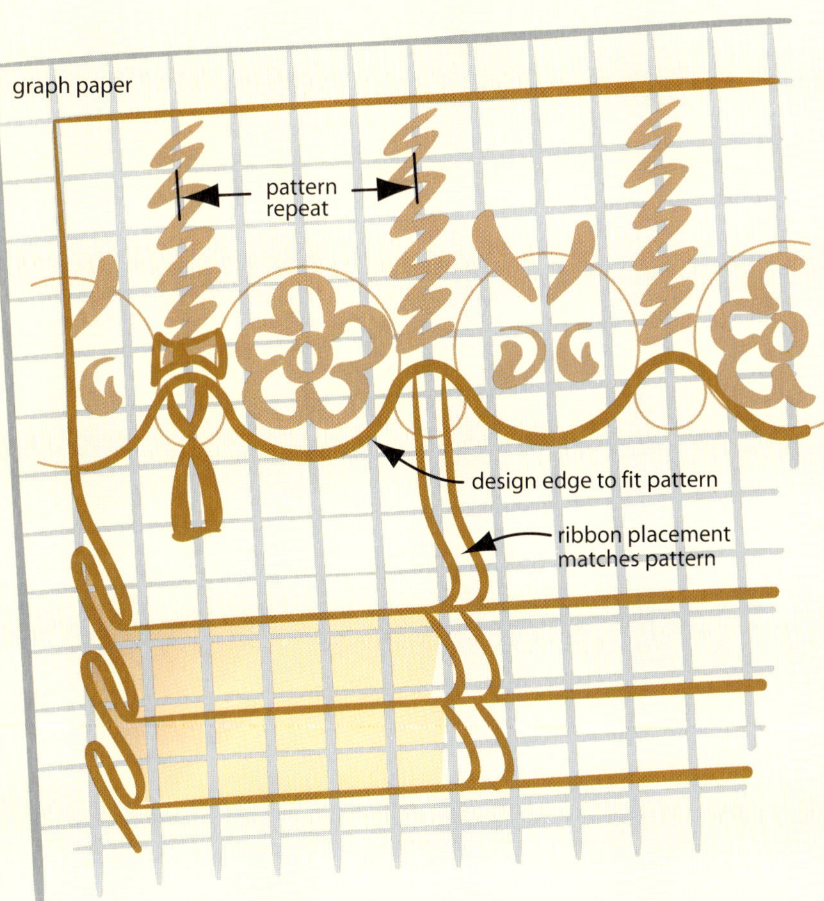

While the elements of this window treatment are simple individually, the combination of valance and shade takes some planning.

- First, the striped fabric is centered on the valance so each end has a similar stripe.
- Second, the scalloped edge of the valance rises at each dark stripe and falls below the dominant flower in every other light stripe. To make these curves, look for plates, bowls, and glasses with differing diameters.
- Third, the trim placement further highlights the shaped edge, defining the curve with the braid and highlighting the dark stripe with a frog and tassel embellishment.
- Fourth, note that the ribbon-covered seam in the Roman shade is directly below a dark stripe and tassel.
- To create a well-planned window treatment, make sketches, loosely penciling in the fabric patterns to help you see what the overall design will look like. Use 1/4" graph paper to help you keep the drawings in proportion. Buy trims and tassels *after* you have finalized a shaped edge.

THE NEW DECORATING BOOK
A SENSE OF THE COUNTRY
Modern

When you need a working cover for a window but can do without billows of curtain fabric, a Roman shade is the perfect answer. The flat shade lifts into neat folds to let in light and views and easily lowers at night to provide privacy. If you wish to ensure that the shade blocks light completely when lowered, choose blackout lining.

tucked roman shade & scarf

Roman shades traditionally mount inside the window frame, so when the shade is lowered, it fits tidily inside the window frame or recess. If you wish to cover the window opening completely, as shown here, you can install it outside the window opening. The mounting board rests on 2"-long, inside corner braces installed above the window.

Whether you install the shade inside the window frame or outside it, soften the treatment by pairing it with a softly pleated scarf. The topper extends two-thirds of the way down the window so it doesn't interfere with seated guests. The scarf is a classic no-sew design. (You could also team the scarf with blinds and shades or curtain panels.)

Customize the fabric to fit the room design. With parallel rows of tucks, the semitransparent solid fabric used for this Roman shade appears to be a subtle stripe. Strips of the striped fabric used for the window scarf become custom tapes on the shade.

materials

54"-wide decorator fabric
Strips cut from contrast fabric (see instructions)
Small O-rings
Roman shade cord
2 (2") inside corner braces
1×2 pine board
$1/2$"-diameter dowel
Cleat with fasteners
4 (1") No. 8 wood screws
4 (2") No. 8 wood screws
4 screw eyes

tools

Handsaw
Electric drill and drill bits
Screwdriver
Staple gun and $1/4$" staples

sewing tools

Sewing machine
Iron and ironing board
Scissors
Tape measure
Pins
Fabric marking pen or pencil

skill level: intermediate
time required: 1 day

making the tucked roman shade:

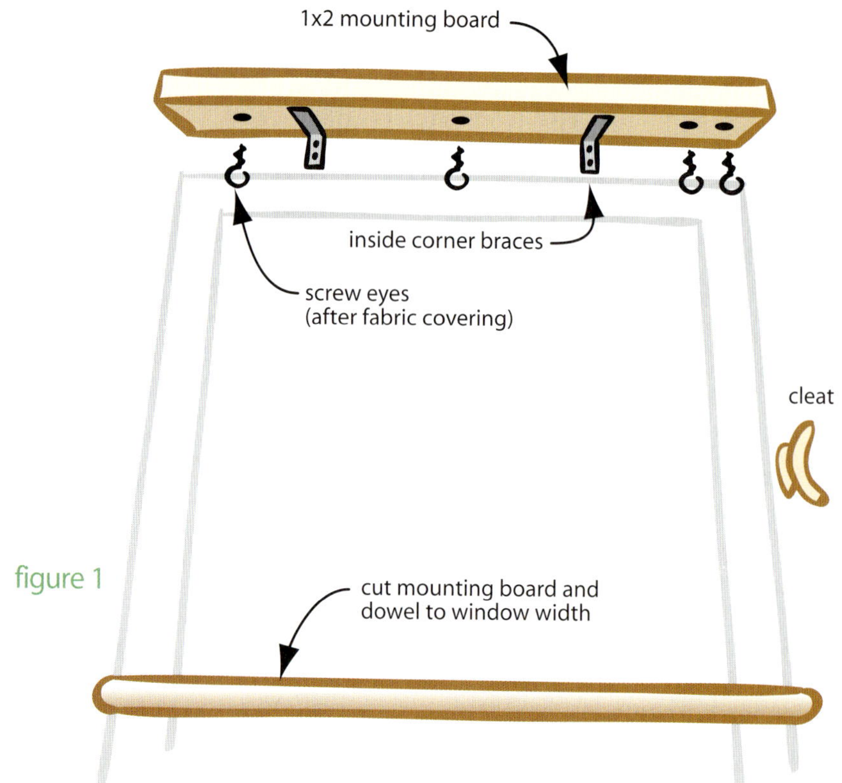

figure 1

1 Install the inside corner braces with 2" wood screws. Measure the window width and cut the 1×2 and dowel to this measurement. Set the dowel aside (it will weight the lower edge of the shade). Center the board on the corner braces with the narrow edge of board facing into the room (see Figure 1). Mark the pilot holes to attach the board to the braces. Mark additional points for screw eyes 2" from each end and at the center. Mark a pilot hole for a fourth screw eye 1" from the right end of the board. Drill the pilot holes, then set the board aside.

2 Place the cleat on the right side of the window frame about midway between the top and bottom. The cleat holds the cords taut. If you have small children in your home, place the cleat closer to the top of the frame, lowering the risk of possible entanglement. Drill pilot holes in the frame or wall and mount the cleat.

3 Measure the window height from the top of the board. Divide the length by 6, dropping any remainder, to find the number of pleats in the finished shade. For the additional length needed to make a 2" tuck at each pleat, multiply the number of pleats in finished shade by 4.

4 Cut a length of fabric the measured window height plus 7" for the mounting and casing and 4 times the number of pleats. Measure the window width. Add 3" to the measured width for the cut width of fabric. To determine the number of O-rings you need, multiply the number of pleats in the finished blind by 3. You will need cord 6 times the measured height plus 2 times the measured width. Purchase materials after taking measurements.

5 From the contrast fabric, cut a strip to be used as an accent on the Roman shade, adding a $3/8$" allowance on each long edge of the strip to turn under. (A striped fabric was used on page 26. The striped section is $2\,1/4$" wide and was cut 3" wide to allow the small blue stripe on the outer edges to show.) Measure the length needed against the length of the blind. Turn under $1/4$" on each long edge. Press. Place the strip $3\,1/2$" from each long edge. Topstitch the strip to the shade, stitching each edge in the same direction, from the lower edge of the shade to the top edge.

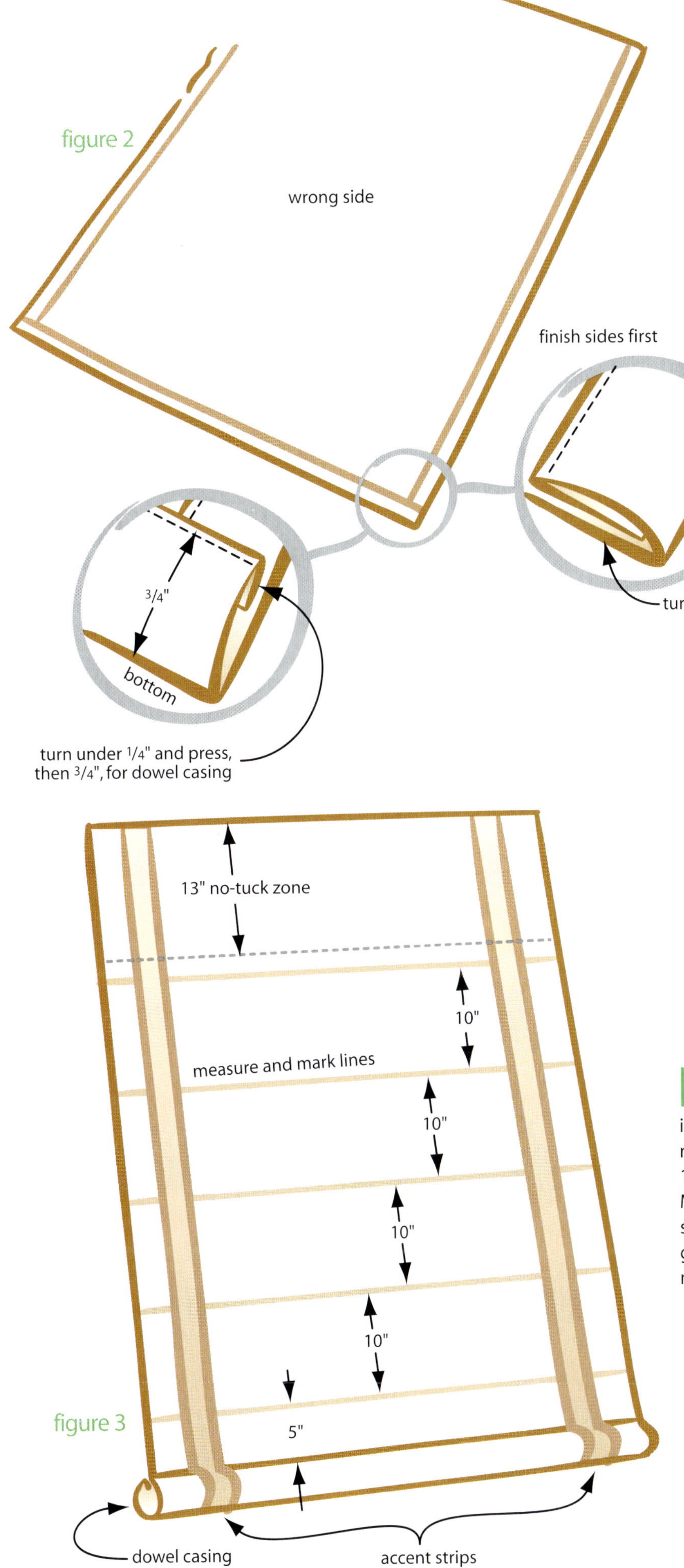

6 On the shade, turn under each side edge 3/4" twice. Press. Working on the wrong side, edgestitch close to the folded edge. On the bottom edge, turn under 1/4". Press. Turn under 3/4" for the dowel casing and press. Working from the wrong side, edgestitch the casing on the bottom edge close to the folded edge (see Figure 2).

7 On the right side of the shade, measure and mark a line 5" from the casing. This is the fold line for the first tuck. From this line, measure and mark lines every 10" to within 13" of the top of the shade (see Figure 3). Mark as many lines as pleats in the finished shade calculated in Step 1. There may be a gap between the uppermost line and the 13" margin at the top of the blind.

making the tucked roman shade (continued)

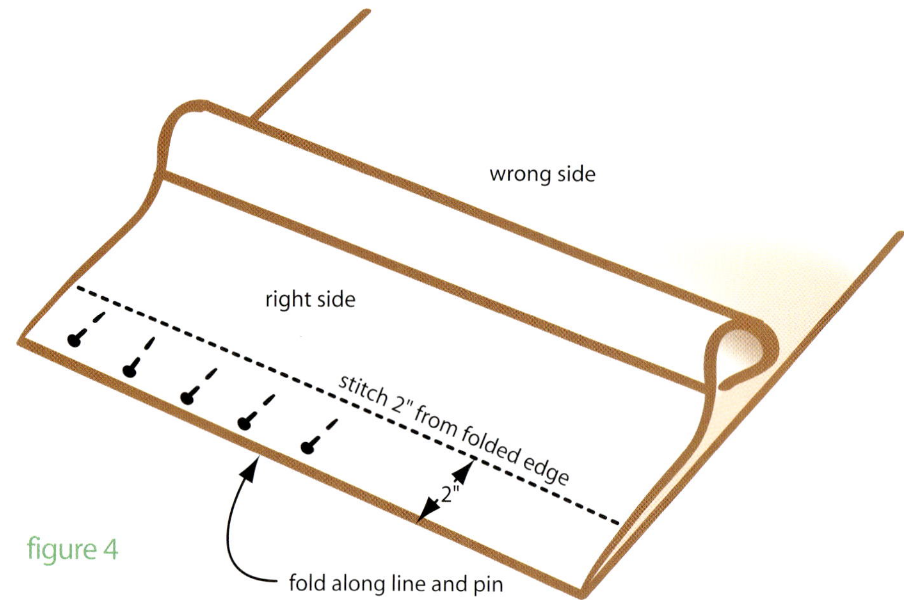

figure 4

8 Fold the shade along the first line. Pin the layers together. Stitch 2" from the folded edge, forming a tuck (see Figure 4). Be sure the stitching line is no more than 2" from the fold: If the tucks are stitched too deeply, the shade will be too short. Fold each line in turn and stitch the tucks. Remove the marks from the fabric. Press each tuck flat, creasing the fold. Lay each tuck to the bottom of the shade. Press the shade on the front and back.

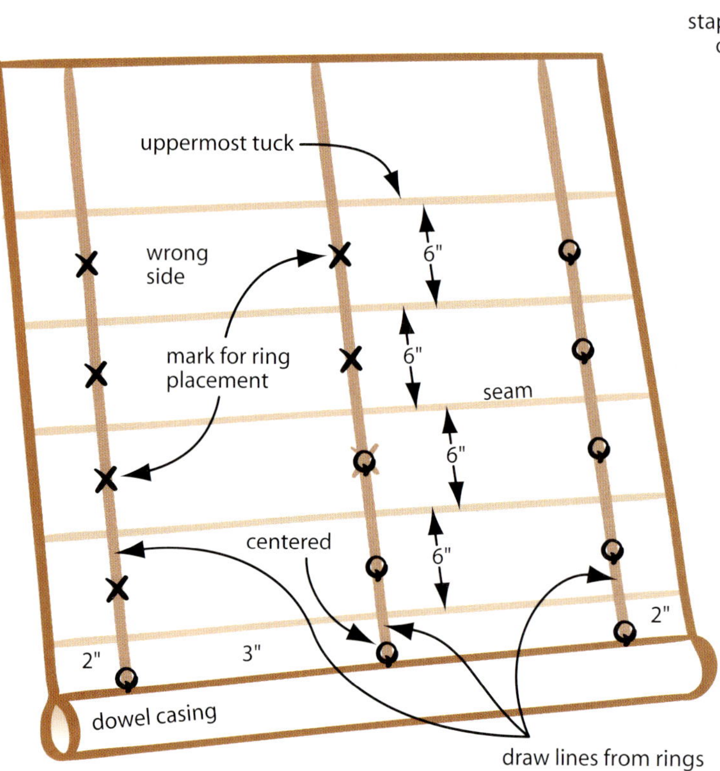

figure 5

9 On the wrong side of the shade, use a needle and thread to stitch one ring to the dowel casing 2" from each side edge and at center of shade. Draw lines straight up the shade from each ring. Mark placements for additional rings halfway between each tuck along each line. Place the final ring 3" above the uppermost tuck (see Figure 5). Stitch the rings to the shade at each mark.

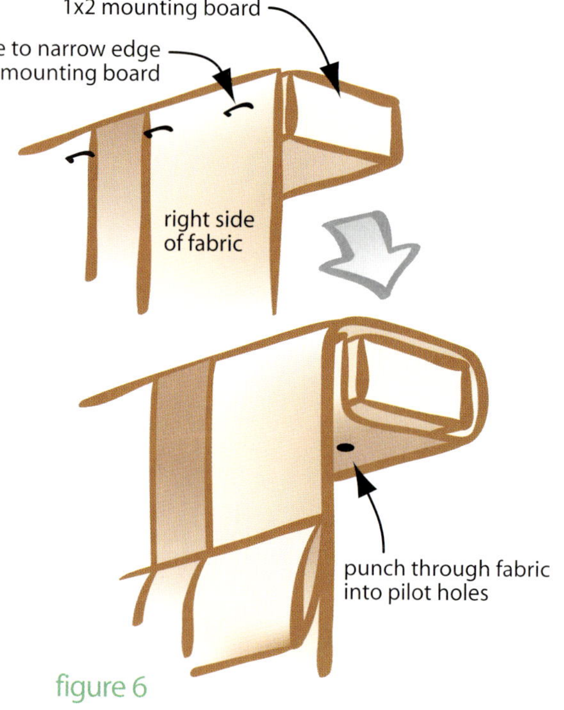

figure 6

10 Center the top edge of the shade, wrong side down, on the narrow, front edge of the mounting board. Staple the fabric to the board. Wrap the fabric smoothly around the board, overlapping the first edge (see Figure 6). Punch a small hole through the fabric into each pilot hole. Set the board on the corner braces. Install with 1" wood screws. Install screw eyes in the pilot holes and insert the dowel into the casing.

11 For the left cord, cut a length of cord equal to the window width plus 2 times the window length. Tie one end of the cord to the lowest ring on the left side of the shade, opposite the cleat. For the center cord, cut a length $^{1}/_{2}$ the width plus 2 times the length. Tie one end of this cord to the lowest ring in the center of the shade. Tie one end of the remaining cord to the lowest ring on the right side of the shade. Thread each cord through the column of rings to the screw eye at the top of the column. Thread the cords to the right toward the cleat. Thread all cords through the extreme right screw eye. Pull the cords to take up the slack. Trim the cord ends even. To raise the shade, gently pull the cords together.

figure 7

12 To set (or dress) the pleats, raise the shade to the highest position and wrap the cords around the cleat in a figure-eight pattern (see Figure 7). Arrange the pleats by hand and leave them in place for one week.

HARDWARE MADE EASY

THE INSIDE CORNER BRACE

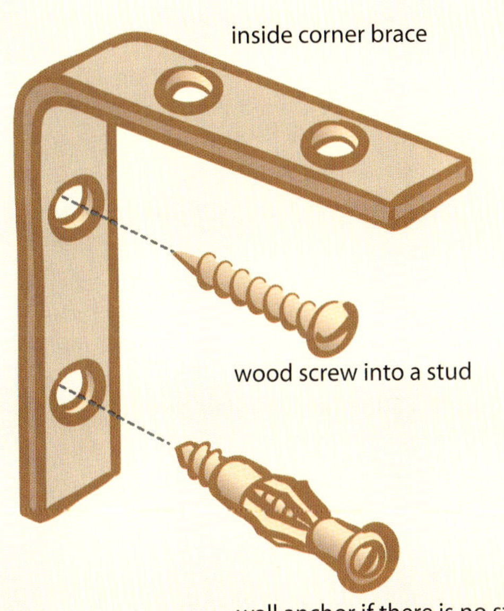

Many blinds or shades are designed to be mounted inside the window frame or window recess. If that positioning is impossible because of construction techniques used in the house or the type of window being covered, you have an option: Mount the board on L-shaped inside corner braces.

- Metal inside corner braces come in sizes from 1" to 4". They are often mistakenly called "L-brackets" because their shape resembles the letter L. Ask for inside corner braces at your local hardware store.

- Choose the brace size based on the weight load you expect it to carry. In most applications, a 2" brace will do the job. Attach the brace to the wall with wood screws into a stud. Use wall anchors where there is no wall stud. Set the board on top of the braces and attach it with wood screws.

- If you mount the board outside the window frame, adjust the window measurements. Instead of measuring the window height inside the frame, measure from the top of the board to the windowsill or floor, depending on the curtain style. Use the length of the mounting board as the window width measurement.

materials

54"-wide decorator fabric
⅞"-wide fusible adhesive tape
2 wooden pegs or curtain tiebacks
Hardware to mount pegs

tools

Electric drill and drill bits
Screwdriver

sewing tools

Iron and ironing board

skill level: beginner
time required: ½ day

making the window scarf:

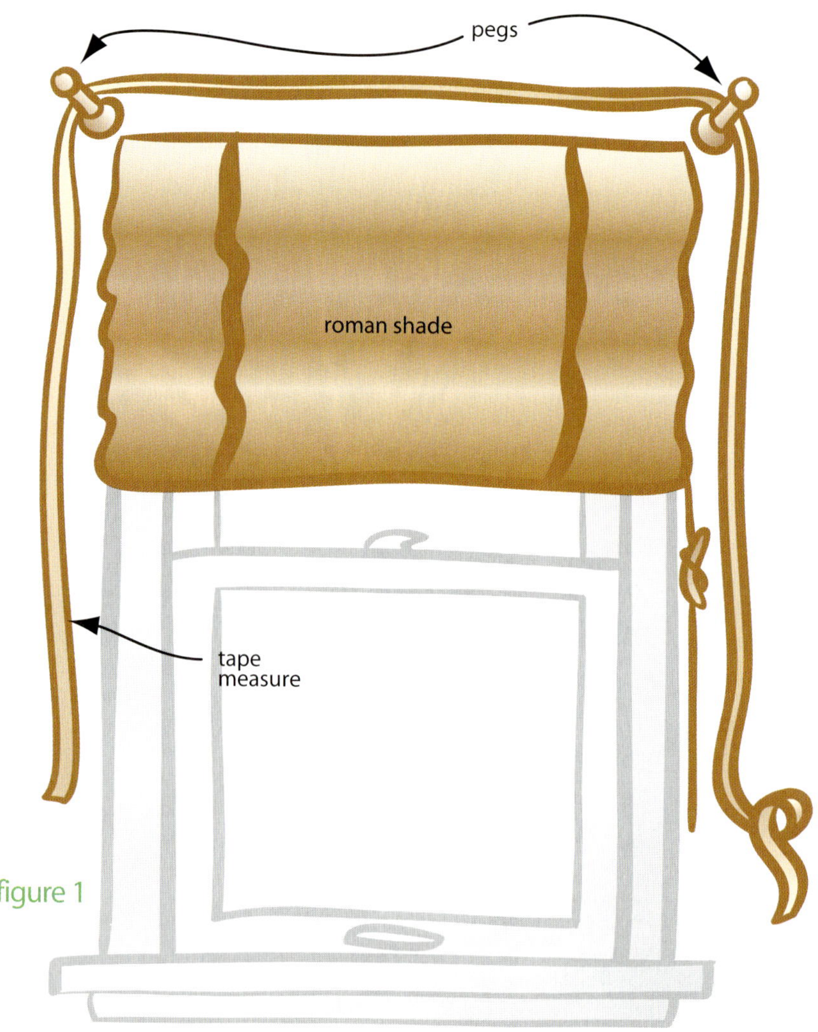

figure 1

1 Install the wooden pegs or tiebacks slightly above and outside the Roman shade. Drape a tape measure or a length of string or ribbon over the pegs to find the desired length of the scarf (see Figure 1). In general, a symmetrically placed window scarf should extend two-thirds of the way down the window.

2 From a single width of decorator fabric, cut a piece the measured length plus 2". Trim the selvages. On 1 long edge, measure 12" in from each corner. Cut diagonally from this point to the corner of the opposite long edge.

3 On the wrong side, following the manufacturer's instructions, apply fusible tape to each raw edge. Remove the paper. Turn under each edge by the width of the fusible surface. Trim the fabric in the corners for a neat application (see Figure 2). Fuse the hems in place.

figure 2

4 Fold the scarf accordion-style to make casual pleats. Drape the scarf over the pegs. Pull down the center to form a drape. Arrange the pleats at the sides.

TECHNIQUES MADE EASY

THERE'S MORE THAN ONE WAY TO DRAPE A WINDOW SCARF

Change the style of your window dressing by rearranging the scarf.

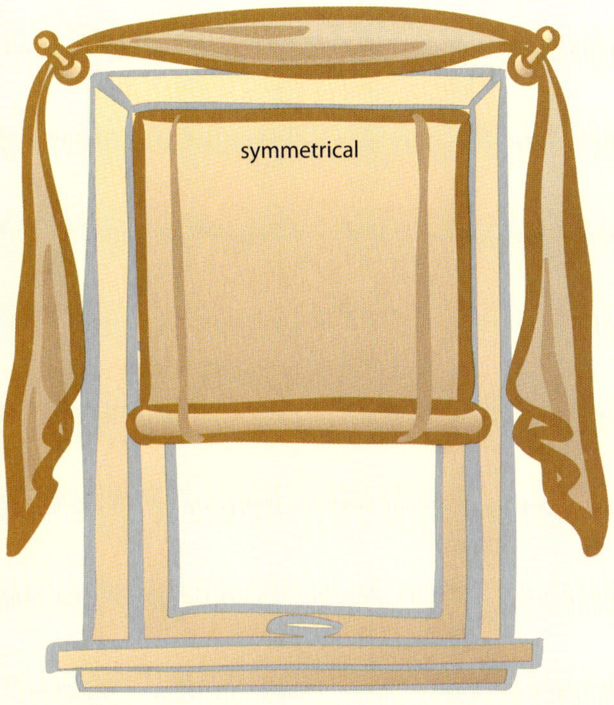

asymmetrical

When the scarf hangs lower on one side than on the other, the drape is asymmetrical. Asymmetry creates a feeling of energy and movement in a window treatment. If you are draping a pair of tall, narrow windows, pull each scarf lower on the outside of the pair.

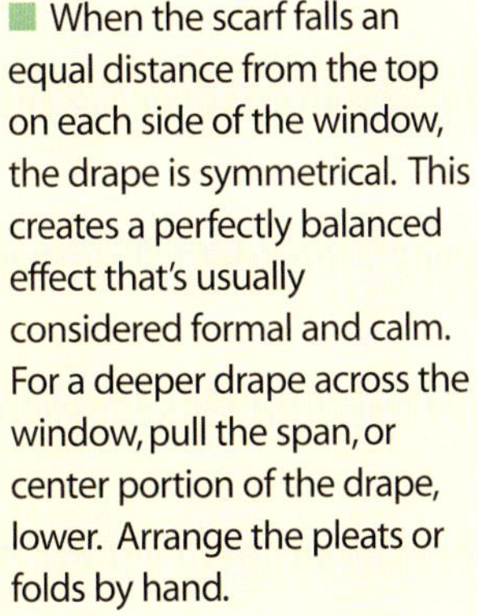

When the scarf falls an equal distance from the top on each side of the window, the drape is symmetrical. This creates a perfectly balanced effect that's usually considered formal and calm. For a deeper drape across the window, pull the span, or center portion of the drape, lower. Arrange the pleats or folds by hand.

For a casual, off-the-shoulder look, cut a long scarf to drape and swirl over a wooden pole. Fold, scrunch, and knot the fabric to create a soft and pleasing presentation.

You may not need to cover patio doors for privacy, but a simple valance across the top, paired with a bracket-mounted shelf, gives you a chance to soften and dress up a functional architectural feature. The shelf is easy to make using wooden brackets and lumber from a home-improvement center. Cable wire, the high-tech version of a tension rod, holds the valance.

patio door valance

The shelf offers an ideal opportunity to add color and personality to a room by showcasing a favorite collection. In a breakfast area, for example, choose bowls, plates, pitchers, and vases in a variety of shapes and sizes. Select colors that coordinate with the fabrics used in the room and let one color dominate, such as tints and shades of blue as shown opposite. Add a few items in such accent colors as yellow and lime green to enliven the blues by contrast. If you prefer a clean, monochromatic look, choose vessels in a single color, such as an arrangement of ironstone vases and pitchers, or a collection of identical objects, such as transferware plates.

Although this valance-and-shelf treatment is designed for sliding glass doors, you also can adapt it to an ordinary window in any room. In a nursery or child's room, use the shelf to display stuffed toys or dolls. If your child is an athlete, showcase trophies from sporting events. See page 35 for tips on mounting the shelf securely on your wall.

materials

2 (6") decorative wooden shelf brackets
1 sanded pine, oak or maple 1×6
1"-wide edge molding
1 1/4" wood screws and wall anchors
1" finishing nails or wire brads
Paint
Curtain wire
O-rings with clips
54"-wide decorator fabric*
54"-wide decorator lining fabric*

tools

Electric saw and blades or handsaw
Miter box and backsaw
Electric drill and drill bits
Screwdrivers
Hammer
Carpenter's level
Carpenter's square
Paintbrush

sewing tools

Sewing machine
Iron and ironing board
Fabric marking pen or pencil
Pins
Needles
Thread
Scissors
Tape measure
Liquid ravel preventer

*(Note: Yardage estimate does not allow for matching patterns. Compare cut size of panels to fabric design to find how much fabric you will need.)

skill level: intermediate
time required: 1 day

making the patio door valance:

1 Measure the door or window width outside the frame. Determine the desired length of the shelf to obtain the cut length of the board. Most lumber is sold in cut lengths of 4', 6', 8', and 10', but a home improvement center or lumberyard will also cut the board for you. Purchase edge molding to fit 1 long edge and 2 short ends of the board plus 12" for miter cuts.

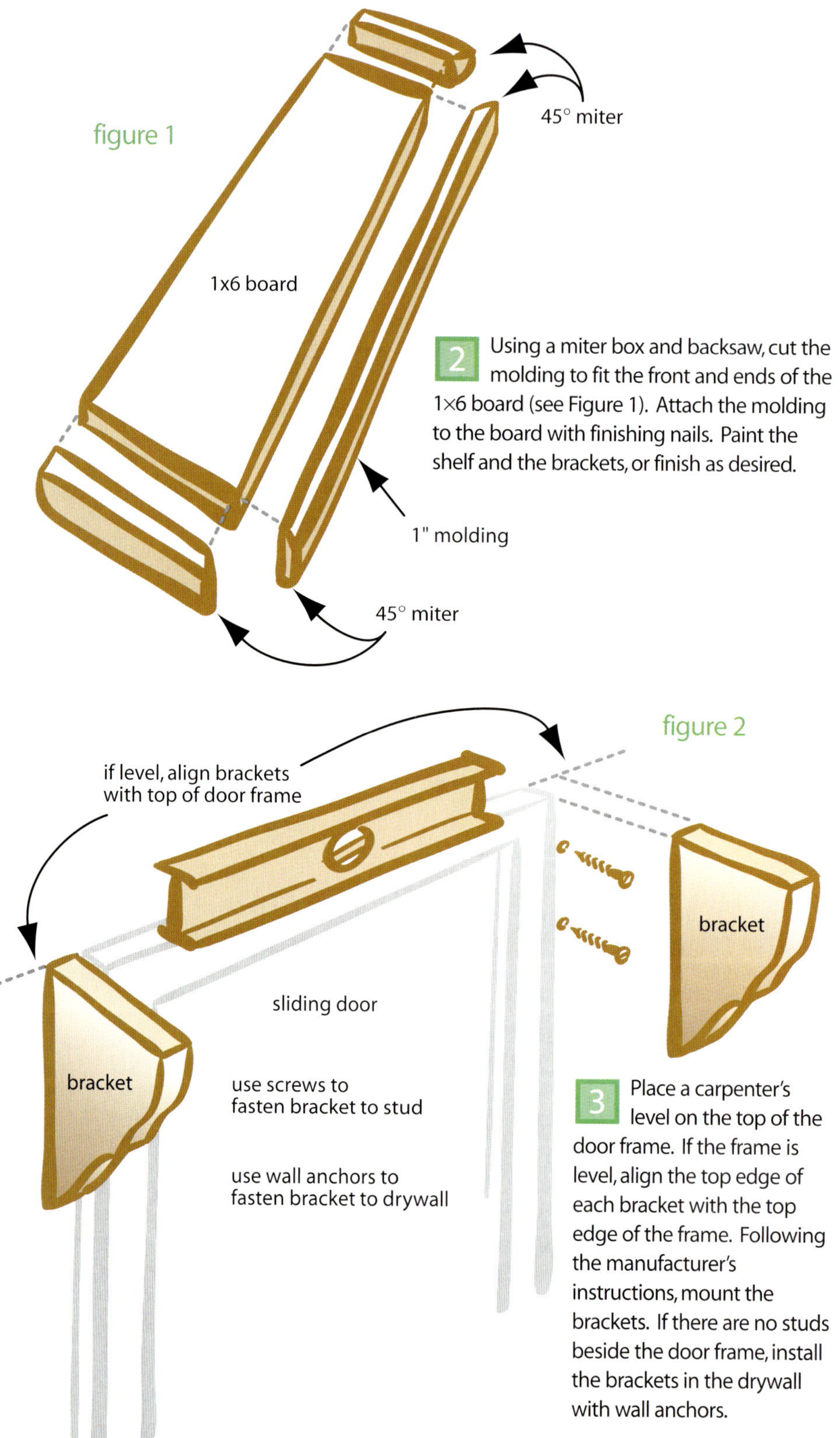

2 Using a miter box and backsaw, cut the molding to fit the front and ends of the 1×6 board (see Figure 1). Attach the molding to the board with finishing nails. Paint the shelf and the brackets, or finish as desired.

3 Place a carpenter's level on the top of the door frame. If the frame is level, align the top edge of each bracket with the top edge of the frame. Following the manufacturer's instructions, mount the brackets. If there are no studs beside the door frame, install the brackets in the drywall with wall anchors.

HARDWARE MADE EASY

WALL ANCHORS

The walls in your home probably are constructed on a 2×4 frame with drywall covering the structure. In the frame, boards that run from floor to ceiling are called studs. These studs, by industry standards, are placed in the frame every 16½" on center. To hang a picture, mirror, or shelf on a wall, drive the nail or screw into a stud to ensure that the mounting will be secure.

Small devices known as stud finders can help you locate the position of studs in your wall. You can purchase one at your local hardware store.

Sometimes, however, the stud isn't where you need it to be. To mount the brackets safely, you need to use wall anchors. Install the anchor in the drywall into which you can then install the screws. The wall anchor distributes the weight over a larger area in the drywall and holds the screw in place. Screws used alone in drywall, sooner or later, will pull out of the drywall, bringing your shelf crashing down.

Anchors are rated for the total weight they will support. Determine what you will display and approximate the combined total weight of the items. Include the weight of the fabric valance. Because the shelf shown on page 32 has two brackets, it needs anchors that will support half the total weight. For a securely mounted shelf, err on the side of larger wall anchors or ones with a higher rating.

Manufacturers develop different types of anchors to be used on different types of walls. Some can only be used on drywall while others can be used to anchor screws in wood paneling or masonry. Read the packages to find the anchor ideal for the specific job.

universal expanding anchor

As implied by the name, this wall anchor is suitable for use in a wide variety of materials, including masonry. The universal expanding anchor accepts a range of screw sizes. To mount a valance shelf, use at least No. 8 screws.

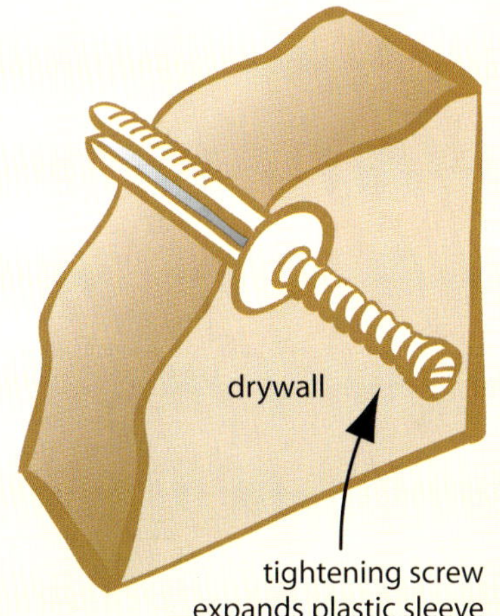

self-drilling wall anchor

This is only for use in drywall. The only tool you need is a screwdriver, and no pilot hole is required. The anchor accepts specific-size screws, and anchors and screws are packaged together.

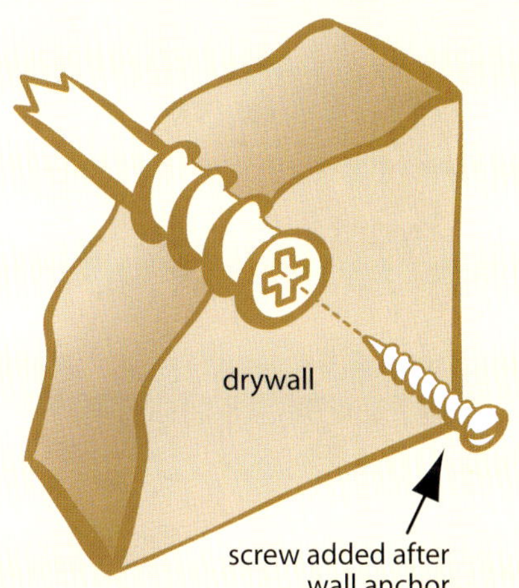

molly® bolt

The screw and sleeve in a Molly bolt, also called an expansion bolt, are in a single unit. The sleeve spreads out behind the wall to anchor the screw. Use in drywall only. Blunt-tip expansion bolts require a pilot hole; refer to the packaging for the appropriate-size drill bit to use. A self-tapping expansion bolt has a nail-like point and does not require a pilot hole. Simply drive the screw and sleeve through the wall with a hammer, then tighten the screw to expand the sleeve behind the wall.

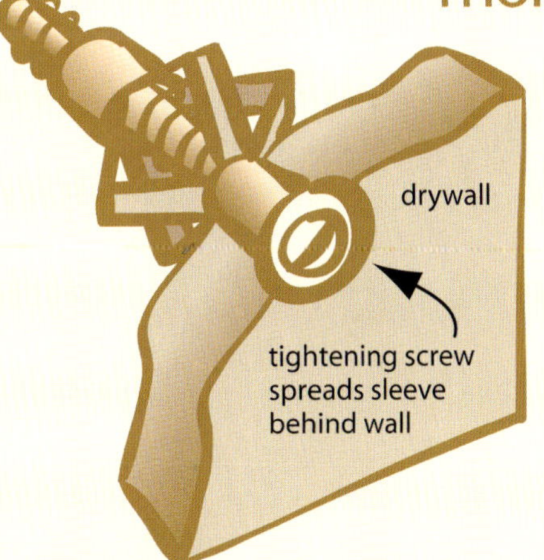

making the patio door valance (continued)

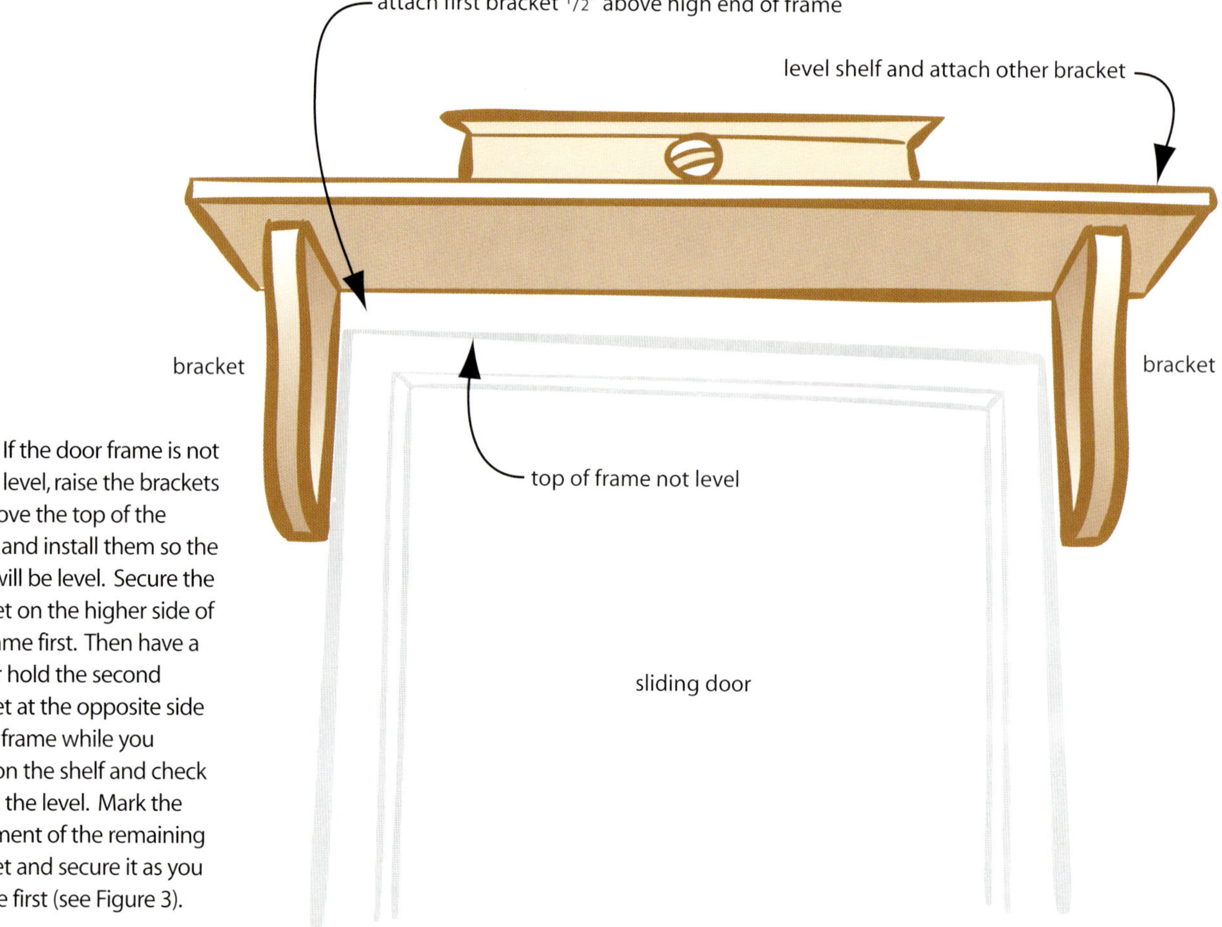

figure 3

4 If the door frame is not level, raise the brackets ½" above the top of the frame and install them so the shelf will be level. Secure the bracket on the higher side of the frame first. Then have a helper hold the second bracket at the opposite side of the frame while you position the shelf and check it with the level. Mark the placement of the remaining bracket and secure it as you did the first (see Figure 3).

5 Center the shelf on the brackets. Using an electric drill, make pilot holes through the shelf into the top edge of each bracket. Secure the shelf to the brackets with screws.

6 Follow the manufacturer's instructions to install the cable wire. (If necessary for easier access to the brackets, remove the shelf while you install the wire.) If you're using closed O-rings, be sure to thread them onto the wire before installation. The rings used on this valance have an opening that allows them to be placed on the wire after it has been installed.

7 For the valance, double the width of the measurement between the shelf brackets and add 1". Determine the desired drop of the valance and add 1". (The drop should be no less than 8".) From the fabric, cut a piece to this size. If necessary, piece fabric to obtain the required size, matching motifs or patterns in the fabric repeat. To join sections, with right sides together and raw edges aligned, pin the edge, matching the fabric design across the seam. Using a ½" seam allowance, stitch the edges together. Press the seam open, then turn and press on the right side as well. Cut and piece fabric for the lining in the same manner.

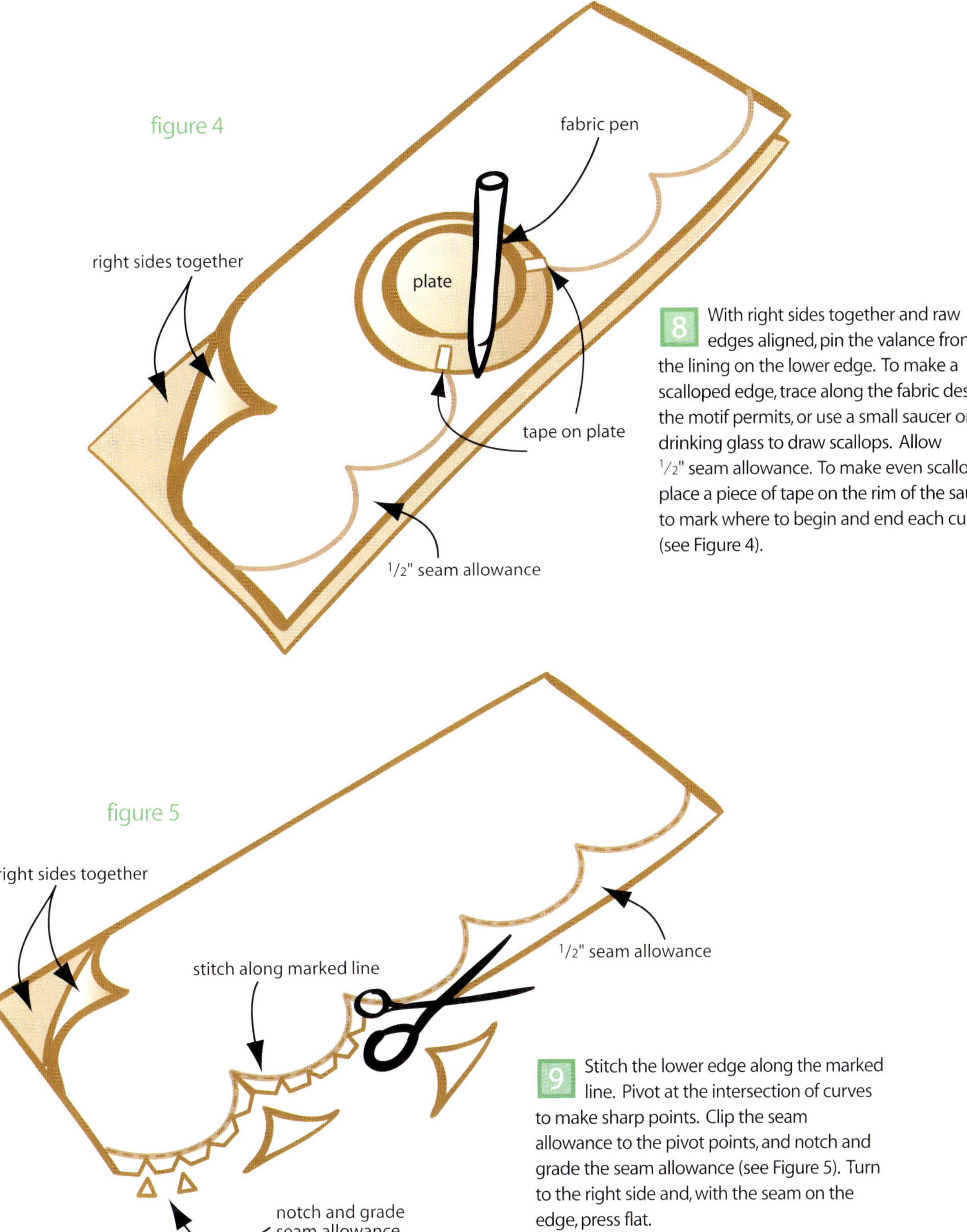

8 With right sides together and raw edges aligned, pin the valance front to the lining on the lower edge. To make a scalloped edge, trace along the fabric design if the motif permits, or use a small saucer or drinking glass to draw scallops. Allow ½" seam allowance. To make even scallops, place a piece of tape on the rim of the saucer to mark where to begin and end each curve (see Figure 4).

9 Stitch the lower edge along the marked line. Pivot at the intersection of curves to make sharp points. Clip the seam allowance to the pivot points, and notch and grade the seam allowance (see Figure 5). Turn to the right side and, with the seam on the edge, press flat.

10 Turn the valance again so right sides are facing. With raw edges aligned, pin the remaining edges. Leave a long opening in the top edge for turning. Using a ½" seam allowance, stitch the edges, pivoting at the corners. Clip the corners and grade the seam allowances. Press the seams open. Turn the valance to the right side through the opening in the top edge. Place the seams on the edges and press flat. Turn the raw edges at the opening to the inside and press. Using a needle and thread, stitch the opening closed by hand. Clip the O-rings to the top edge of the valance, spacing them evenly.

You've invited guests for the weekend, but that bare window in the guest room keeps you from feeling your best about the house. Solution? Drape the window with a sheer scarf that's easy to sew and offers lots of style for very little money and time. Use textured and patterned sheers or opt for plain white or ivory and add your own embellishments, such as seashells or ribbons.

bordered sheer valance

If you need to dress a window quickly but you don't want to sacrifice style, try this sheer scarf. The filmy fabric diffuses light and filters direct views into the room. The mitered border gives the casual, unstructured treatment a professional finish and offers an opportunity to accent or reinforce your room's color scheme.

To dress a large window with this scarf, make multiple squares, arranging them along the width of the window.

The sheer scarf also offers lots of opportunities for creative additions that make the window treatment uniquely yours. For a little girl's room, make small bows from organdy ribbon and scatter them over the scarf, attaching each with a stitch or two. For a bathroom window, sew small and medium-size vintage buttons around the edges, or collect seashells with holes worn in them and tack them randomly over the fabric.

PATTERNED SHEERS

- Shift the focus of this unstructured valance with a printed or patterned sheer. Shop the fabric store and you will find your choices in sheer fabrics are no longer limited to white or ivory. These translucent and opaque fabrics now come in a wide array of tints, textures, and patterns.

- Choose one of the new sheers to deliver subtle pattern, color, or interest in a window treatment. You will still enjoy that wonderful quality of soft, diffused light for which traditional sheers are known.

- Work with contemporary sheers in the same way you would any other fabric when choosing a border. The classic white shown here allows the border to claim all the attention: Simplicity is the charm. To emphasize sheer fabric itself, you may want to choose a plainer fabric for the border. Or pair an interesting sheer with an equally strong border for extra impact in the room.

materials

1 1/2 yards 54"-wide sheer fabric
1 yard 54"-wide contrast fabric
3 O-rings
3 small cup hooks
Pushpins

sewing tools

Sewing machine
Iron and ironing board
Tape measure
Pins
Thread
Scissors

skill level: beginner
time required: 1/2 day

making the bordered sheer valance:

1 For the best proportions, begin with a 54" square of sheer fabric. Trim the selvages off the fabrics. Measure the sheer to confirm the fabric is square. Trim if necessary.

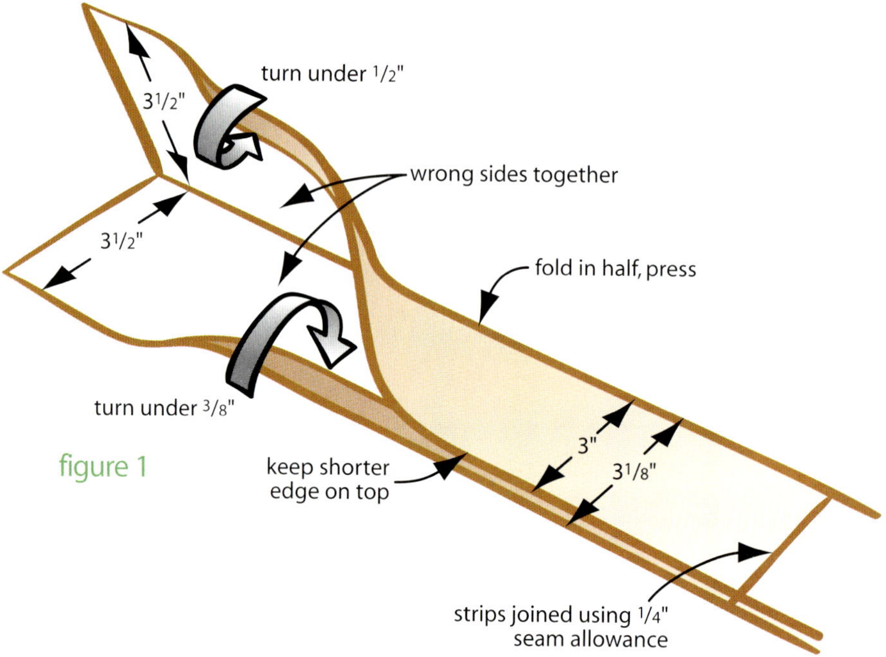

figure 1

2 From the contrast fabric cut 5 (7"-wide) strips from selvage to selvage. Trim off the selvages. With right sides together, join the strips at the short ends with a 1/4" seam allowance to make one long strip. Press seams open. With wrong sides together, fold the strip in half, matching the long edges. Press. Open the fold. On one long edge, turn under 1/2". Press. On the remaining raw edge, turn under 3/8". Press. Refold the center crease. The edge turned 1/2" will be slightly shorter than the edge turned 3/8". Keep the shorter edge on top (see Figure 1).

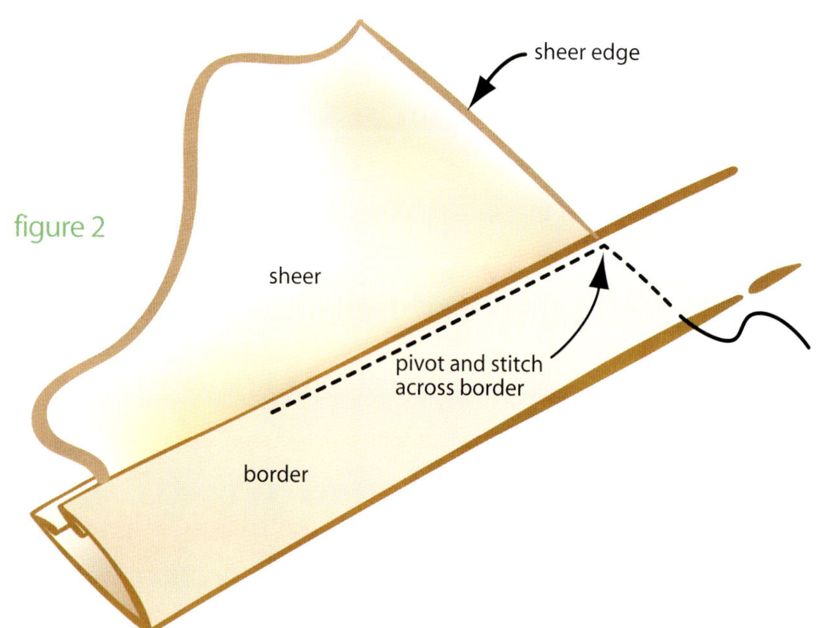

figure 2

3 Insert one edge of the sheer into the border, aligning the raw edge of the sheer with the center crease. Beginning at the middle of the border, edgestitch through all layers. When you reach the edge of the sheer, pivot the fabric and stitch straight across the border (see Figure 2). Cut the thread.

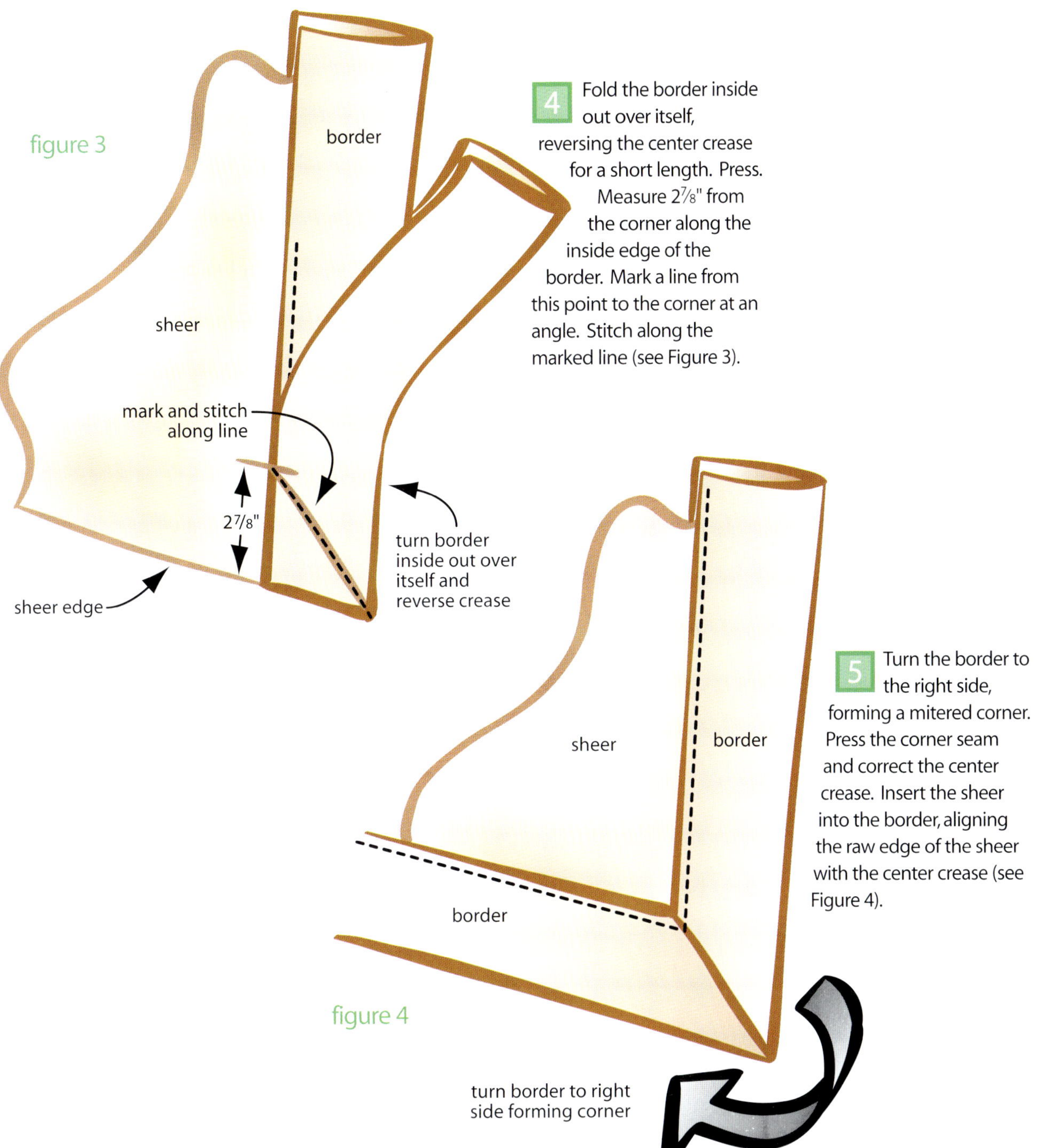

4 Fold the border inside out over itself, reversing the center crease for a short length. Press. Measure 2⅞" from the corner along the inside edge of the border. Mark a line from this point to the corner at an angle. Stitch along the marked line (see Figure 3).

5 Turn the border to the right side, forming a mitered corner. Press the corner seam and correct the center crease. Insert the sheer into the border, aligning the raw edge of the sheer with the center crease (see Figure 4).

6 Beginning in the corner, edgestitch through all layers. At the end of the sheer, pivot the fabric and stitch straight through the border as in Step 3. Cut the thread. Repeat Steps 4, 5, and 6 until all corners have been mitered.

7 Where the beginning and end of the border meet, turn under the working end to overlap the stitched end ¼" to ½". Press. Insert the sheer into the border, aligning the raw edge of the sheer with the center crease. Beginning in the corner, edgestitch through all layers, catching the beginning of the border in the stitches. Use a needle and thread to invisibly stitch the ends of border together by hand.

8 Press the border well. Temporarily secure the scarf to the window frame with pushpins to determine placement. When you are satisfied, stitch small O-rings to the corners and center of the scarf. Slip the O-rings over cup hooks screwed into the wall or window frame.

This window treatment proves that you can warm a room and soften the architecture without having to do a lot of complicated cutting and sewing. Flat panels on curtain rings simply hang on knobs in the window frame. A bamboo pole or plain dowel keeps the lower edge rigid so you can pull back the panel to let in light.

lined flat panels

Privacy and light control provide two excellent reasons to cover windows with wood blinds or shutters. But stop there and the window looks cold and unfinished. This fabric treatment, layered over blinds, softens the effect and gives you a chance to reinforce a room's palette of color and texture. Two flat panels hang by rings along the top edge of the window frame.

Why settle for white lining when you are layering treatments this way? Blinds or shutters provide a uniform street-side look, freeing you to play with different linings for indoor effects. The combination of stripes and checks plays up the vintage charm of the setting opposite, for example.

Bamboo poles weight the hem edge of these panels. You could also use custom-finished dowel rods or clean woodsy branches, depending on whether your room is traditional or rustic.

FABRICS WITH PERSONALITY

- This window treatment works well using a variety of decorator fabrics, provided they have enough body or weight. Sheers are too flimsy, but you don't want a stiff upholstery fabric either. A suitable fabric should drape nicely in your hand yet have enough weight to stay in place along the bottom edge.

- Adapt the window dressing to suit the season with a change of fabrics. Consider using a light-colored cotton print for summertime and a darker or heavier fabric for winter. For a child's room, try colorful polar fleece for a cozy winter look and a cotton novelty print for summer.

- "Found" fabrics, such as chenille bedspreads, quilts, quilt tops, or vintage tablecloths, could be adapted to this design as well. To protect the textiles from the sun, back with lining; consider adding interlining as well, to enhance the fabric's light-blocking quality.

materials

54"-wide decorator fabric
54"-wide contrast decorator fabric for lining
Clip rings
Decorative knobs
Dowel screws
Bamboo poles
Drapery tiebacks

tools

Electric drill and drill bits
Pliers

sewing tools

Sewing machine
Iron and ironing board
Thread
Scissors
Tape measure
Hand-sewing needle
Pins

skill level: beginner
time required: 1 day

making lined flat panels:

1 These curtains mount on the window frame without hiding the decorative molding. To cover one large window as shown on page 44, measure the window width and halve this figure; then add 1" to each measurement to obtain the needed width of each curtain panel. For the panel length, measure the window length and add 10". You may need to seam fabric lengths together to achieve the desired width for the fabric panel and lining. Consider the length of the fabric repeat before you purchase fabrics. For the tabs, you will need an additional ¼ yard of fabric or contrast fabric. Purchase materials after taking window measurements and performing calculations.

(*Note: If you have multiple closely set windows, make one curtain panel for each window. Measure the window width and length inside the frame. The fabric panel width should equal the measured window width plus 1". The panel length should equal the measured window length plus 10".)

2 Trim the selvages off the fabrics and cut curtain fabric and lining to the size determined in Step 1. Be sure each piece of the curtain fabric starts at the same point in the repeat. With right sides together and using a ½" seam allowance, stitch the fabric and lining together along the side edges. Press the seams open. Stitch the top edge. Press the seam open. Turn the curtain to the right side. Place the seams on the edge and press flat.

3 Temporarily catch each top corner of the curtain in the clip ring. Evenly space the remaining clips between the corners (5 clips per curtain). With help from a friend, hold the curtain in the window to mark the placement of the knobs on the molding (see Figure 1).

4 Drill pilot holes at the marks. Using pliers, screw one end of the dowel into the knob. Screw the opposite end of the dowel screw into the molding. Hang the rings on the knobs.

5 At the hem edge of the curtain, position the bamboo pole to find the finished length of the curtain. Mark the stitching line on the curtain. Remove the curtains from the window. Leaving a ½" allowance, trim the excess length from the curtain front and lining. Remove the clips from the curtains. Set the curtains and the clips aside.

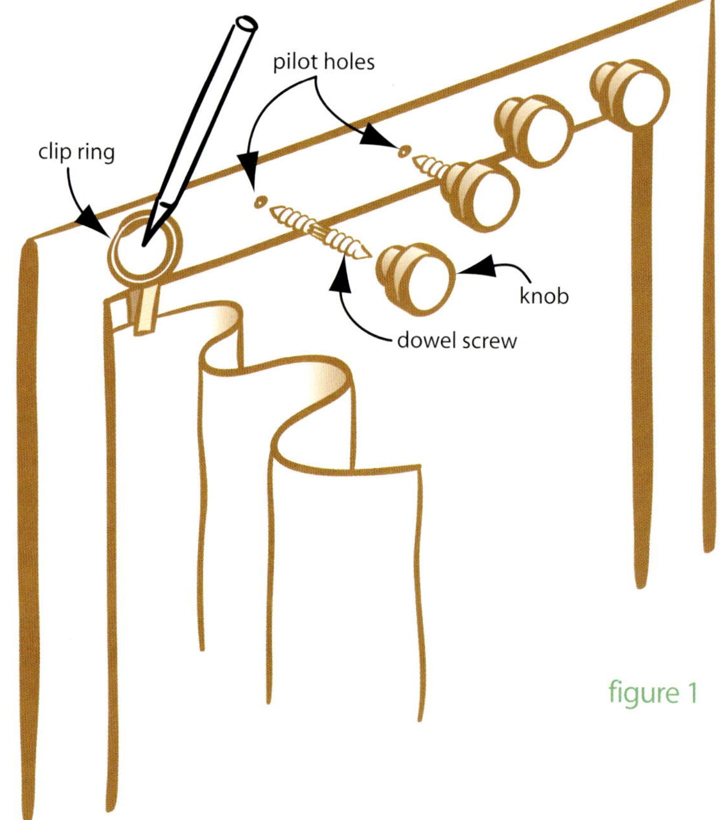

figure 1

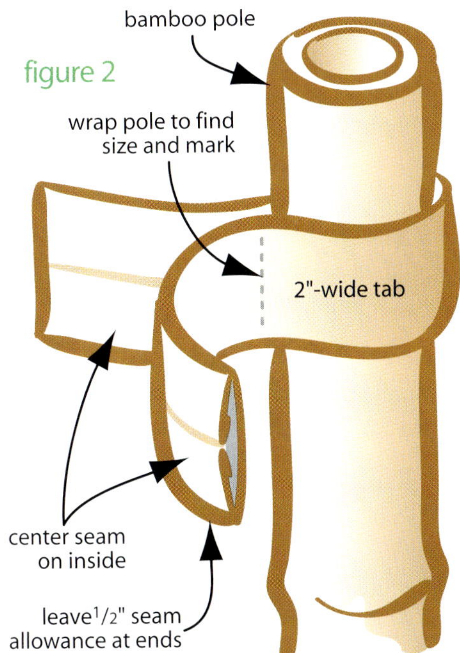

6 From the remaining fabric or lining, cut 4 (5"×8") pieces for the tabs. Fold the tabs in half, right sides together, matching the long edges. Using ½" seam allowance, stitch the long edges together. Press the seam open. Turn the tab to the right side. Center the seams on the back and press flat. Wrap the tab around the bamboo or other pole to determine the required size (see Figure 2). The tab should fit snugly but allow the bamboo to be removed. Trim the tabs to size, leaving ½" seam allowance at each end.

7 Fold the tabs in half, matching the raw edges with the seam inside. Turn the curtain inside out. On the right side of the curtain at the lower edge, place one tab at each corner and evenly space the remaining tabs. Match the raw edges. Place the lining over the tabs. Stitch the edges together, using ½" seam allowance and leaving an opening in the seam between 2 of the tabs. Press the seam open.

8 Turn the curtain to the right side. Position the seams on the edges and press flat. Turn the seam allowances at the opening to the inside. Press flat. Hand-stitch the opening closed. Insert the bamboo pole.

9 At each top corner, catch the edge of the curtain in a clip ring. Evenly space the remaining clips between the corners (5 clips per curtain). Hang the rings on the knobs. Lift the bottom edge of the curtain to find the placement of the drapery tieback. Install the tieback.

HARDWARE MADE EASY

clip rings are trendy as well as vintage-inspired, at home in both contemporary and cottage-style settings. Their straightforward function is easy to see. A small and somewhat decorative clip hangs below a metal ring. The clip catches the curtain fabric, eliminating the need to sew on rings or place drapery hooks. The ring glides over metal poles or hangs on knobs or hooks. For the flat panels in this project, the rings can hang over the knob or hang behind the knob, depending on the size of the knob compared to the diameter of the ring.

O-rings, made of metal or plastic, provide a less expensive option for hanging window treatments like these flat panels. Because there is no metal clip dangling from the ring, add an extra 1" to the curtain length before you cut the fabric. Sew the O-rings to the top edge of the curtain. Hang each ring over a knob.

knobs or drawer pulls let you show your personality in window dressings. Visit your local hardware store to see the options. Many specialty home shops also sell an eclectic range of knobs. To mount most knobs directly into the window molding you will need a double-ended screw called a dowel screw. Ask for these in the "fasteners" aisle at the hardware store. Take the knob along to help in finding the right size screw.

tiebacks do just as the name states, hold back curtains. Generally, you will use a tieback when you would like a curtain panel to drape across the window, as do these flat panels (page 42). Look for decorative tiebacks in wood or metal alongside curtain rods in the window-treatment section of department stores and home decorating shops. When installing a tieback, remember that they will need to bear some pressure or weight from the fabric. If the drapery fabric is heavy and the curtains are full, consider installing the tieback in a wall stud or using wall anchors to secure the screws.

Traditional pleated panels offer a timeless yet versatile way to dress your windows. For a casual, cottage-style room, catch the top edge of the fabric with curtain clips that slip over the drapery rod. For more formal rooms, fix the pleats with pleating tape and pins (see page 115 for more information).

easy pleated panels

Whether you choose the formal or the casual option, line the panels to protect the fabric from damaging sunlight. Lining not only helps the curtains hang better, but also provides some additional insulation when you draw the curtains closed on a chilly winter night.

Workrooms often interline curtains with a thin, flannel-like layer between the curtain front and the lining. The British call this fabric "bump." This interlining gives added weight to the curtain, making it hang more elegantly.

The pleats in these easy pleated panels are secured when the fabric is folded before you catch the top edge in clip rings.

materials

54"-wide decorator fabric
Lining fabric
Interlining
18 clip rings
Iron rods with mounting hardware

tools

Electric drill and drill bits

sewing tools

Sewing machine
Iron and ironing board
Scissors
Tape measure
Pins
Thread

skill level: intermediate
time required: 2 days

making easy pleated panels:

1 Measure the width of the window frame from outside edge to outside edge and mount the rod just outside the frame. Each finished curtain panel should be as wide as the measured window width. It may be necessary to seam together fabric lengths to achieve the desired fullness. Measure the window height from the top of the rod to the floor. Add 10" to the measured height to find the cut length of the panels for the curtains. Purchase fabrics after taking measurements and making calculations. Consider the length of the fabric repeat before you purchase fabrics.

2 Trim the selvages off the fabric, interlining, and lining. From the fabric, cut 2 front panels the measured window length plus 10". Be sure each piece starts in the same point in the fabric repeat. From the interlining, cut 2 panels the measured window length. From the lining, cut 2 panels the measured window length plus 4". (If covering a wide window, cut additional panels of each fabric to seam together for the required width. To join lengths, with right sides together and raw edges aligned, pin the edge, matching the fabric design across the seam. Using a 1/2" seam allowance, stitch the edges together. Press the seam open. Turn and press on the right side as well.)

3 Lay each front panel flat, wrong side up. Place the top edge of one interlining panel 4" from the top edge of the front panel. Smooth the interlining down the length of the panel. If necessary, trim the width of the interlining so that it is 1 1/2" narrower on each side than the front panel. Beginning near the top edge of the interlining, use a needle and thread to tack the interlining to the front panel down each side. Use tiny stitches so they are barely visible on the right side of the fabric. Space the stitches 4" to 6" apart. Do not tack the last 12" of the interlining to the front panel.

4 Lay each front panel right side up. Place the top edge of the lining 3" from the top edge of the panel. Smooth the lining down the length of the panel. If necessary, trim the lining so that it is 1" narrower on each side than the front panel. Slide the lining to one side edge. Measure and mark 8" from the top edge and 12" from the bottom edge. Using a 1/2" seam allowance, stitch the front and the lining together between the marks. Slide the lining to the opposite side edge of the curtain front. Stitch the front and lining together in the same manner. Press the seams open.

5 Turn the curtain to the right side. Lay the curtain with the lining side up and center the lining over the front panel so there is 1" of curtain fabric turned to the lining side on each side. Press the folds and seams.

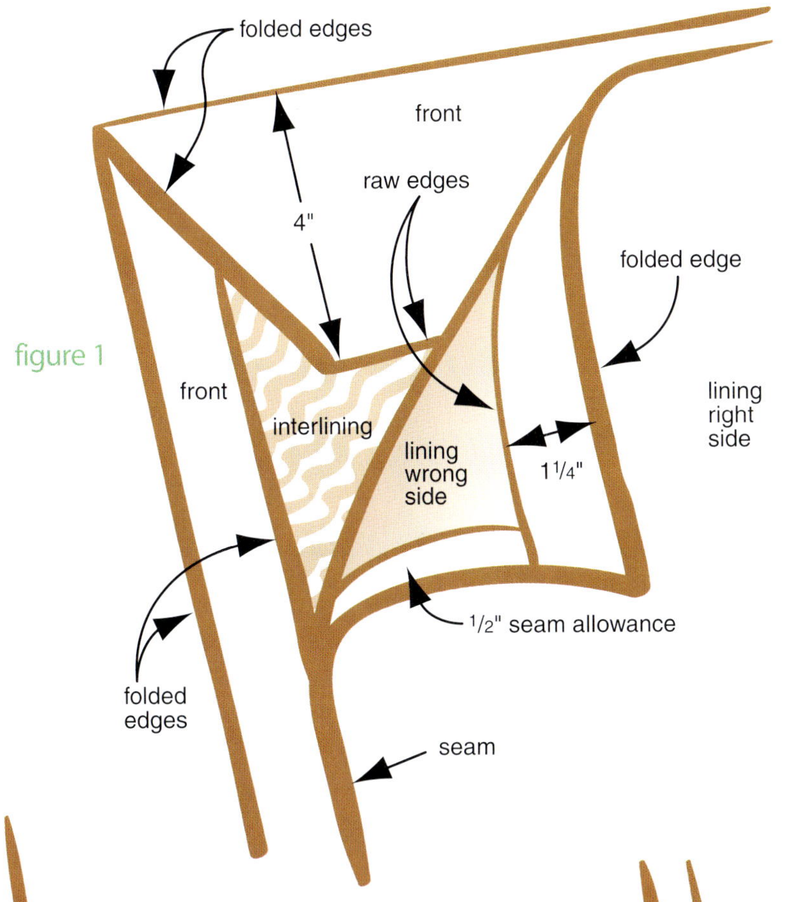

figure 1

6 Turn the top edge of the lining back away from the front panel and interlining. Turn the front panel under 4", folding the sides at angles (see Figure 1). Press. Turn under the top edge of the lining 1¼". At the sides, above the side seam, turn under the lining's unstitched edges ½". Press. Using needle and thread, stitch the lining to the curtain front along all folded edges. Also stitch the angled folds of the curtain fronts.

7 At the top corners of each curtain, catch the edge in curtain rings. Evenly space the remaining clips between the corners (9 clips per curtain). Pinch together 3" or 4" of fabric in each clip to make easy pleats. Insert the rod through the rings and hang the curtain.

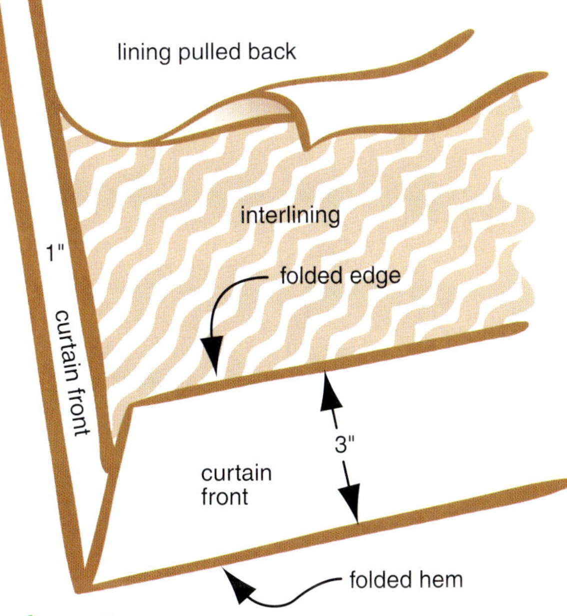

figure 2

8 Turn under the curtain front hem so that the edge meets the floor. Pin. Remove the curtains from the rod. Press the fold, then open it. If necessary, trim the interlining even with the fold. Measure the fabric for the hem on each curtain. Trim, if necessary, to make the hems even, leaving 6" for the hem. Keeping the lining edge free, turn the raw edge of the curtain front to meet the folded hem edge. Press. Refold the hem, making angle folds at the ends similar to those at the curtain top (see Figure 2). Hemstitch the folded edge.

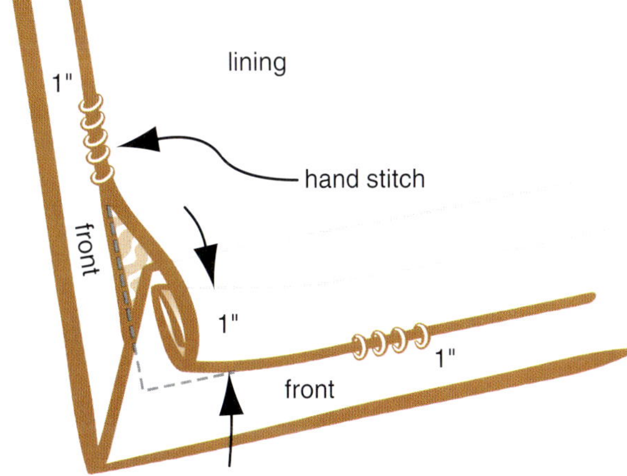

figure 3

9 Turn under the lining 1" shorter than the curtain front. Press. Measure 2" from the fold and trim the excess. Turn under the raw edge to meet the crease. Turn under the side edges ½". Working from the wrong side, edgestitch the lining hem close to the folded edge. Hand-stitch the lining and curtain together (see Figure 3).

For an easy yet lavish **romantic treatment** to frame the windows and soften the look of a room, try layered panels. Softly gather each panel with an ordinary drawstring and hang the panels from curtain rings. For privacy, combine the panels with a shade.

layered panels

You decorate your home with patterns, texture, color, and light. Why settle for only one fabric in the window treatment? Take the lead from a collection of pillows to combine fabric patterns and designs at the window.

The panels shown in the photograph opposite dress the window but do not cover it. Their purpose is to soften the architectural framework and to add pattern and subtle color to the room. For controlling light and creating privacy, a roller shade or wood blind hangs behind the curtains.

For the primary curtain, choose a fabric that coordinates with your bedding to create a unified look; the under curtain can be a sheer, a contrasting solid, or a contrasting print. To achieve a more evolved-over-time look, choose a fabric for the top curtain that is a shade darker or lighter than your bedding, but in the same color family.

making layered panels:

materials

54"-wide decorator fabric
54"-wide complementary decorator fabric
Wooden curtain rod and mounting hardware
Curtain pins
Curtain cord
Curtain rings with screw eyes

tools

Electric drill and drill bits
Screwdriver

sewing tools

Sewing machine
Iron and ironing board
Fabric marking pen or pencil
Pins
Needles
Large safety pin
Thread
Scissors
Tape measure
Liquid ravel preventer

skill level: beginner
time required: 1½ days

1 Install the curtain rod according to the manufacturer's directions. Measure from the top of the rod to the floor and add 12". For each pair of curtain panels, you will need fabric twice this length. The panels are unlined and cut from a full width of decorator fabric. Consider the length of the fabric repeat before you purchase fabric (see page 77 for information on measuring the fabric repeat).

2 Trim the selvages from the fabric. Cut 2 panels the measured length from the rod to the floor plus 10". Begin each piece at same point in the fabric repeat. From the complementary fabric, cut 2 more panels in the same manner.

3 On each long side edge of one panel, turn under 1½" twice. Press. Working on the wrong side, edgestitch the hems in place. Hem the side edges of the remaining panels in the same manner.

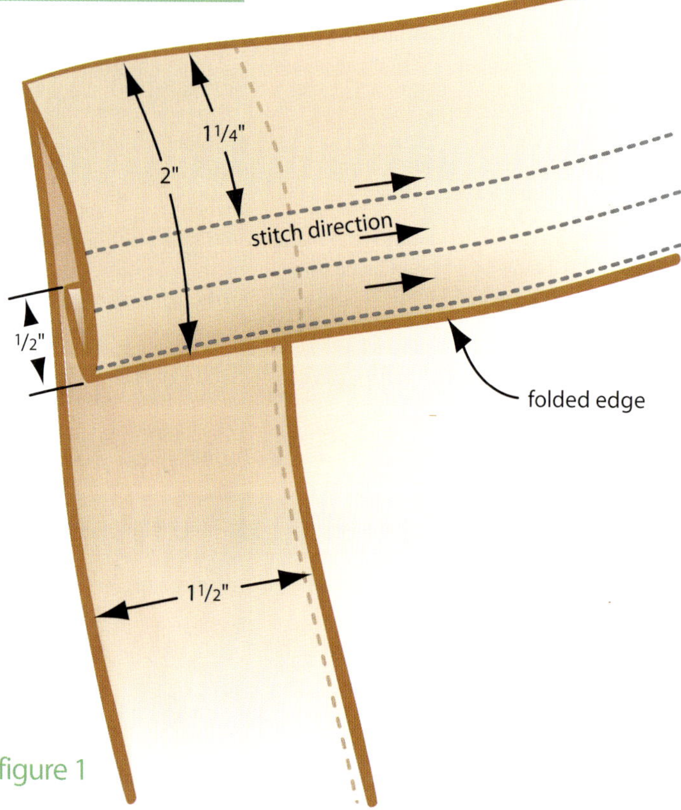

figure 1

4 To make the heading and casing, on the top edge of one panel, turn under ½" and press. Turn the edge under 2" again. Press and pin. On the wrong side of the panel, measure and mark a line 1¼" from the top folded edge. Stitch along the marked line (see Figure 1). Edgestitch the free edge of the heading close to the folded edge, stitching in the same direction as the first line of stitching. Make a third stitching line midway between the first and second lines of stitching, again working in the same direction. Repeat to make the heading and casing on each remaining panel.

5 Determine the arrangement of curtain panels on the window. Choose one edge on each panel to be the outside edge: From this outside edge, begin lacing cord through the casings. Using a safety pin, thread the cord from the outside edge of one panel to the leading edge through the bottom casing. Turn the cord and thread the safety pin back through the upper casing from the leading edge to the outside edge (see Figure 2). Smooth the panels flat. Knot the cord ends together close to the edge of the curtain. Lace the cord through the casings in the remaining panels in the same manner.

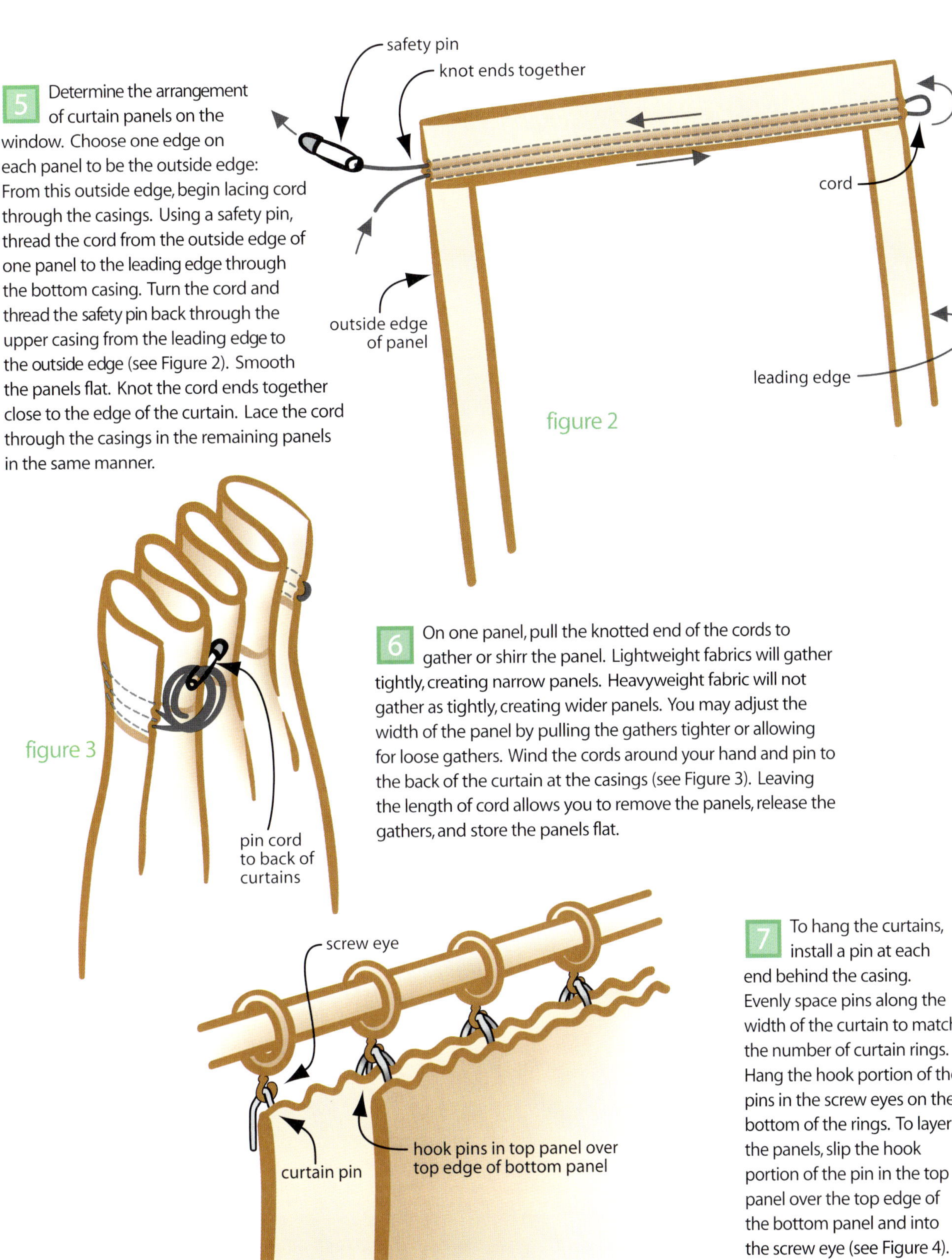

figure 2

figure 3

6 On one panel, pull the knotted end of the cords to gather or shirr the panel. Lightweight fabrics will gather tightly, creating narrow panels. Heavyweight fabric will not gather as tightly, creating wider panels. You may adjust the width of the panel by pulling the gathers tighter or allowing for loose gathers. Wind the cords around your hand and pin to the back of the curtain at the casings (see Figure 3). Leaving the length of cord allows you to remove the panels, release the gathers, and store the panels flat.

figure 4

7 To hang the curtains, install a pin at each end behind the casing. Evenly space pins along the width of the curtain to match the number of curtain rings. Hang the hook portion of the pins in the screw eyes on the bottom of the rings. To layer the panels, slip the hook portion of the pin in the top panel over the top edge of the bottom panel and into the screw eye (see Figure 4). When layering the panels, set the leading edge of the top panel back from the leading edge of the bottom panel by hooking the first pin in the second ring. Adjust the rings on the rod for balanced placement, since you will use one less pin on the top panel.

As a rule, curtains should be generous enough to cover the windows, even if you never draw them. However, there are always exceptions to the rule. If privacy isn't an issue but you want the architecture-softening effects of a window treatment, try these panels with swags. Bringing texture and dimension to the walls, they also dress the windows without blocking light or views.

panels & swags

Tailored lined panels and generous swags complement the direct, no-fuss style of a bold and sophisticated dining room. This window treatment is purely decorative because the panels are never drawn. Instead, the curtains and swags help soften the architecture of the room and make the window itself the focal point. To create a mood of restful calm and enlarge the sense of space, choose fabrics in the same color tones as the walls for a monochromatic color scheme. If you want to call more attention to the windows, choose fabric that contrasts with the walls but harmonizes with your upholstery fabric.

SEASONAL INSPIRATIONS

The weather changes. Shouldn't your home change with the seasons too?

- This dining room is dressed to chase a winter's chill. When summer temperatures soar, change the striped panels for crisp sheers. Cut a length of sheer fabric the length of your curtains plus 2" for hems. Trim off the selvages. Turn under 1/2" twice on each edge, press, and edgestitch the folded edge. With a needle and thread, loosely stitch the sheer panels to the curtain rings. Snip the threads with scissors when it's time to remove the sheers.

- Change the accessories with the seasons as well. Display large seashells or fill a bowl with treasures from your last beach trip to recall summers at the shore. Masses of candles capture the softer light of autumn. Baskets of fir and pinecones or twigs evoke winter's restrained beauty. For spring, force bulbs indoors to celebrate a season of awakenings.

materials

54"-wide decorator fabric
Lining fabric
Contrast fabric
Thread
18 curtain pins
Iron rod with mounting hardware
14 iron curtain rings

tools

Electric drill and drill bits

sewing tools

Sewing machine
Iron and ironing board
Scissors
Tape measure
Pins
Needle
Thread

skill level: intermediate
time required: 1½ days

making panels & swags:

1 Measure the width of the window frame from outside edge to outside edge. Mount the rod just outside the frame and place the curtain rings on the rod. Measure the window height from the bottom of the rings to the floor. Add 10" to the measured height to find the cut length of the panels for the curtains. Each panel is cut from a single fabric width. Purchase fabric and lining after taking measurements. For swags, purchase 2 yards of contrasting fabric. Consider the length of the fabric repeat.

2 Trim the selvages off the fabrics and lining. From the decorator fabric, cut 2 front panels the measured window length plus 10". Be sure each piece starts in the same point in the fabric repeat. From the lining, cut 2 panels the measured window length plus 4".

3 Lay each front panel right side up. Place the top edge of the lining 3" from the top edge of the panel. Smooth the lining down the length of the panel. If necessary, trim the lining so that it is 1" narrower on each side than the front panel. Slide the lining to one side edge. Measure and mark 8" from the top edge and 12" from the bottom edge. Using a ½" seam allowance, stitch the front and lining together between the marks. Slide the lining to the opposite side edge of the curtain front. Stitch the front and lining together in the same manner. Press the seams open.

4 Turn the curtain to the right side and lay the lining side up. Center the lining over the front so there is 1" of curtain fabric turned to the lining side on each side edge. Press the folds and seams.

5 Turn the top edge of the lining away from the curtain front. Turn the curtain front under 4", folding the sides at angles. Press. Turn under the top edge of the lining 1¼". Turn under ½" along the side edges of the lining's unstitched side edges (the top 8"). Press. Using a needle and thread, stitch the lining to the curtain front along all folded edges. Also stitch the angle folds of the curtain front. Repeat for the remaining panel.

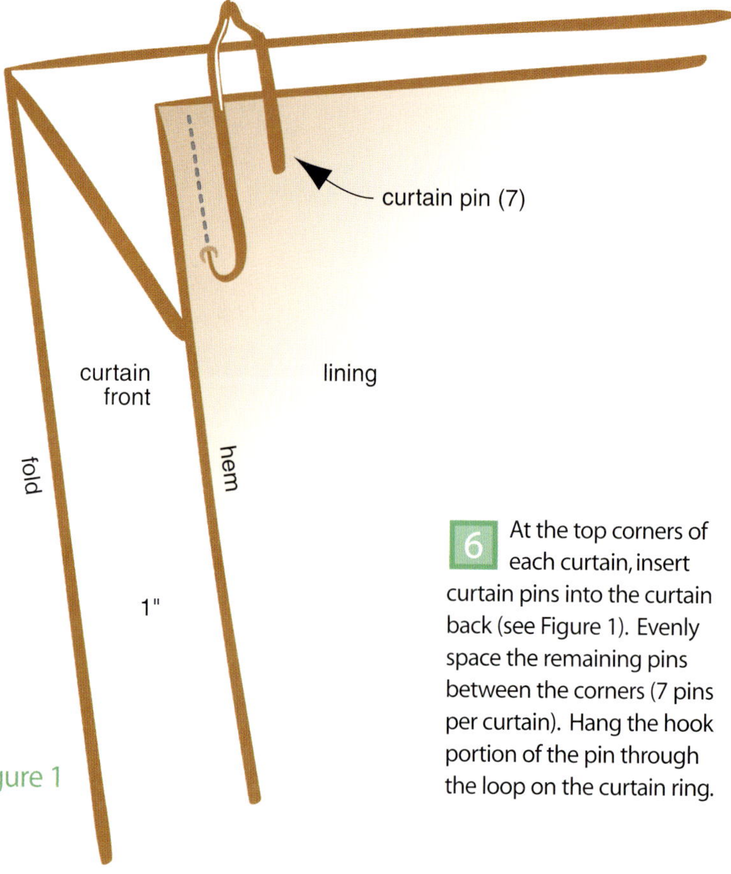

figure 1

6 At the top corners of each curtain, insert curtain pins into the curtain back (see Figure 1). Evenly space the remaining pins between the corners (7 pins per curtain). Hang the hook portion of the pin through the loop on the curtain ring.

7 Turn under the curtain front hem so the edge meets the floor. Pin. Remove the curtains from the rod. Press the fold. Open the fold. Measure 6" from the fold and trim the excess. Keeping the lining edge free, turn the raw edge of the curtain front to meet the folded hem edge. Press. Refold the hem, making angle folds at the ends similar to those at the curtain top. Hemstitch the folded edge.

8 Turn under the lining 1" shorter than the curtain front. Press. Measure 2" from the fold and trim the excess. Turn under the raw edge to meet the crease. Turn under the lining's lower, unstitched side edges ½". Press. Working from the wrong side, edgestitch the lining hem close to the folded edge. Using a needle and thread, stitch the lining and curtain together below the side seams by hand.

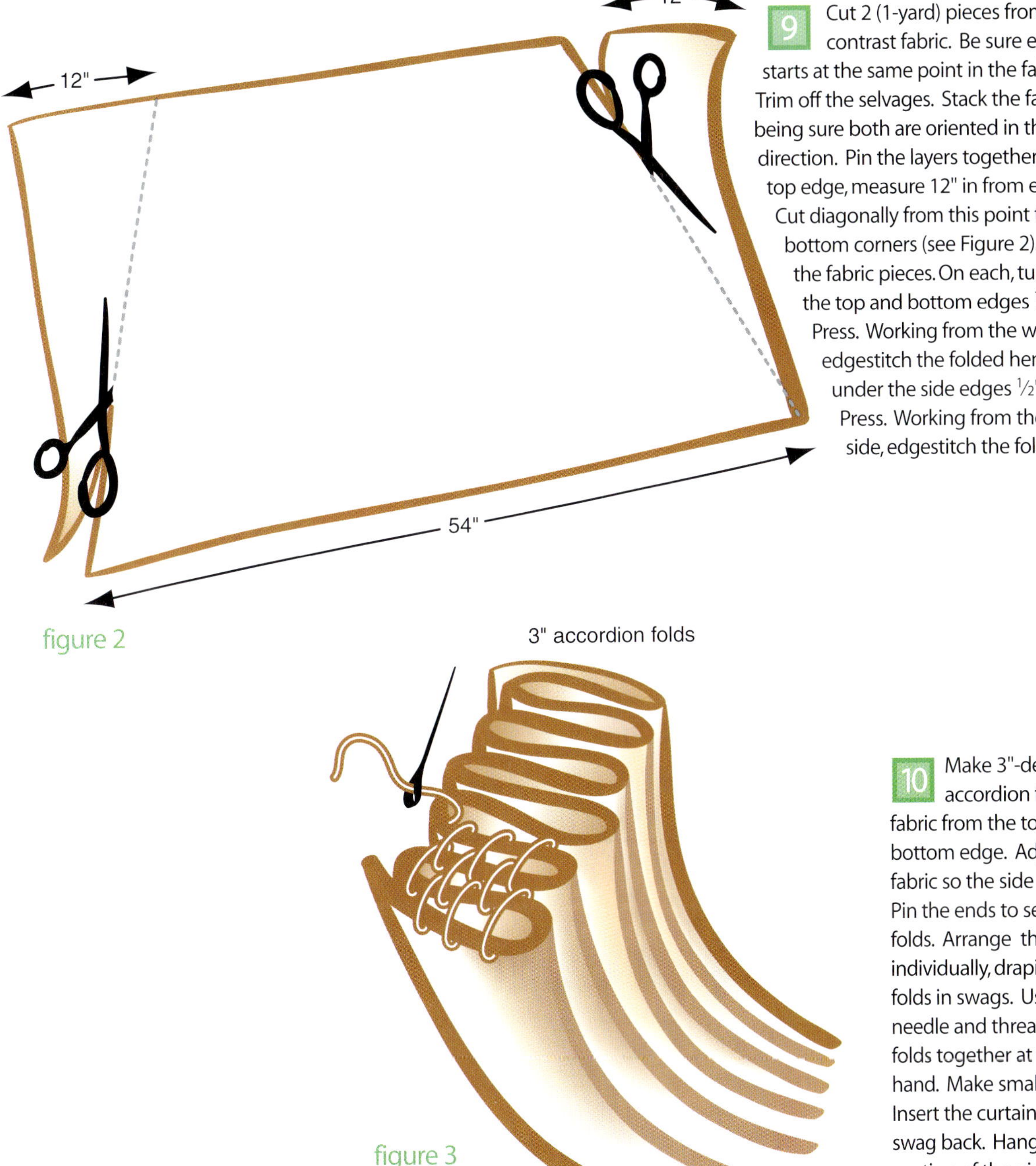

figure 2

9 Cut 2 (1-yard) pieces from the contrast fabric. Be sure each piece starts at the same point in the fabric repeat. Trim off the selvages. Stack the fabric pieces, being sure both are oriented in the same direction. Pin the layers together. On the top edge, measure 12" in from each corner. Cut diagonally from this point to the bottom corners (see Figure 2). Separate the fabric pieces. On each, turn under the top and bottom edges ½" twice. Press. Working from the wrong side, edgestitch the folded hem. Turn under the side edges ½" twice. Press. Working from the wrong side, edgestitch the folded edges.

figure 3

10 Make 3"-deep accordion folds in the fabric from the top to the bottom edge. Adjust the fabric so the side edges meet. Pin the ends to secure the folds. Arrange the pleats individually, draping the soft folds in swags. Using a needle and thread, stitch the folds together at the ends by hand. Make small stitches. Insert the curtain pin in the swag back. Hang the hook portion of the pin in the loop on the ring with the pin for the panel.

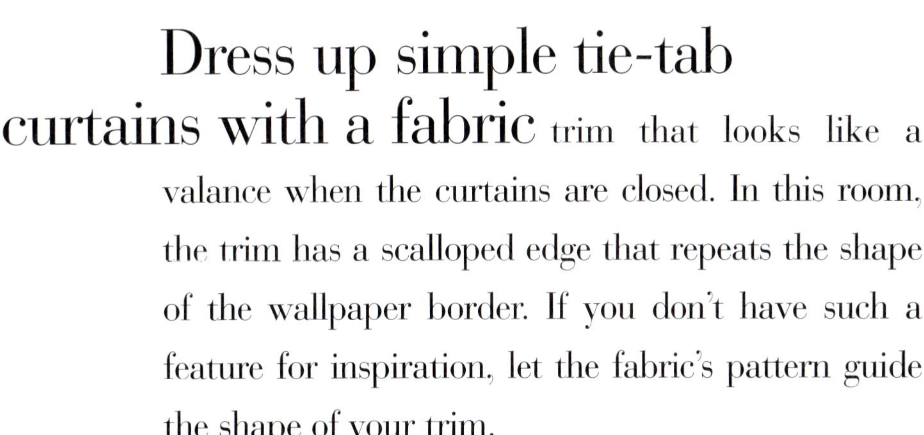

Dress up simple tie-tab curtains with a fabric trim that looks like a valance when the curtains are closed. In this room, the trim has a scalloped edge that repeats the shape of the wallpaper border. If you don't have such a feature for inspiration, let the fabric's pattern guide the shape of your trim.

tie tabs & fabric trim

A diamond pattern, for example, can suggest a sawtooth edge for the trim. You also can use a repeating motif on a novelty print, like the one on page 32, as a distinctive guideline for a shaped edge. The trim adds body to the tie tab heading, stabilizing it with additional layers of fabric.

Because the curtains open into the room on swing-arm rods, double-face the curtains or line them with a coordinating decorator fabric. That way, they'll present a finished look both open and closed.

Each panel is cut from a full width of decorator fabric (usually 54 to 60 inches wide). The heading trim is applied to both the front panels and the lining panels before sewing the front and lining together. The ties extend from between the front and lining panels.

Choose hardware to suit the style of your room. Here, the forged iron swing-arm rods evoke a historical style that suits a Victorian, farmhouse, or cottage setting. Swing-arm rods are also available in other metals and styles from home decorating catalogs. Rods found at antiques fairs and flea markets add character to windows. If you prefer, choose stationary iron rods or wooden poles for hanging the curtains.

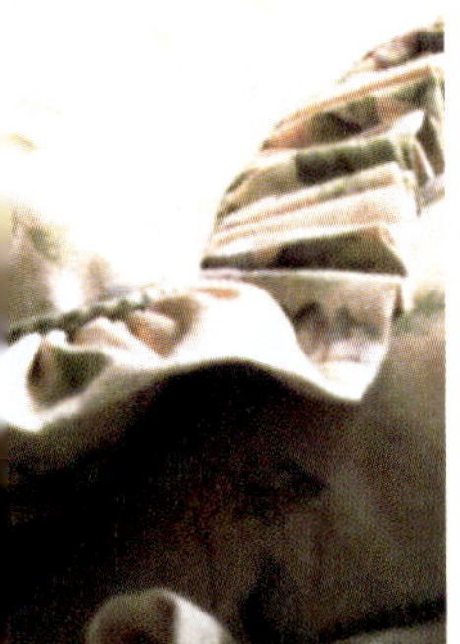

materials

Pair of swing-arm curtain rods with mounting hardware
54"-wide decorator fabric*
54"-wide complementary decorator fabric for lining and trim*
54"-wide accent decorator fabric*
1 yard (18"-wide) lightweight fusible interfacing

tools

Electric drill and drill bits
Screwdriver
Dinner plate

sewing tools

Sewing machine
Iron and ironing board
Fabric marking pen or pencil
Pins
Thread
Hand-sewing needle
Scissors
Tape measure
Liquid ravel preventer

*(Note: Yardage estimate does not allow for matching patterns. Compare cut size of panels to fabric design to find how much fabric you will need.)

skill level: intermediate
time required: 1½ days

making tie-tab curtains with fabric-trim heading:

1 Measure the window from side to side outside the frame. Select swing-arm rods that when paired will cover the window width. Install the rods outside the window moldings, level with the top of the frame.

2 To calculate fabric requirements for one curtain panel, measure the length of the swing-arm rod and multiply by 1½. This gives the width of one curtain front. To determine the length, measure the window from the rod to the windowsill; add 6" (for seam allowances and hem) plus the amount needed for a fabric repeat. Multiply by the number of curtain fronts required to obtain total yardage. Use the same figure for the lining. For the trim heading, you will need 1 yard of fabric. For the bias-cut ties and binding for the trim pieces, you will need 2 yards of accent fabric.

3 Trim the selvages from the fabric. Cut 2 curtain fronts the measured length from rod to windowsill plus 2". Cut the width of each panel to 1½ times the length of the rod plus 1". Cut 2 lining panels in the same manner. Begin each panel at the same point in the fabric repeat.

4 To determine the number of trim pieces needed, start with the width of each curtain panel. For small or narrow windows, divide the width of the panel into 4 sections. On wider windows, make more sections; to determine their width, take the measured width of the curtain panel, subtract 1", and divide by the desired number of sections. The resulting number is the width of each trim piece. Use a small plate or saucer of this diameter to draw off the trim pieces.

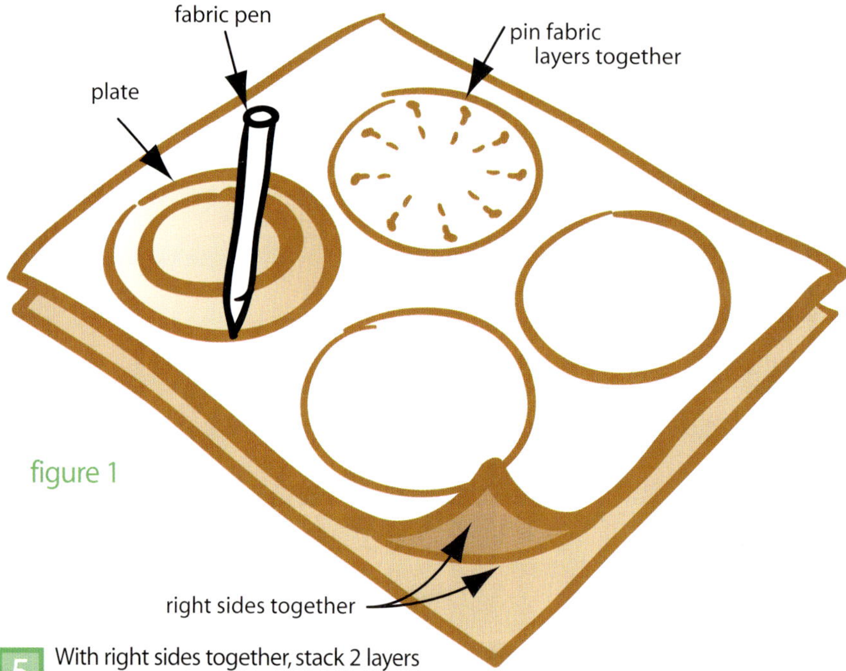

figure 1

5 With right sides together, stack 2 layers of the complementary fabric. Place the plate on the wrong side of the fabric and trace around it (see Figure 1). The traced line is the cutting line for 4 trim units. Mark the number of circles needed. (For the curtains in the photograph, page 60, 4 circles provide 16 half-circle trim units.) Pin the layers of fabric together inside the circles. Cut through both layers on the marked line. Remove the pins and separate the layers. Set aside the circles.

6 From the accent fabric, cut enough 2"-wide bias strips to make trim for each of the 8 cut circles. Set the remaining fabric aside. With wrong sides facing, fold each bias strip, matching the long edges. Press to crease the center fold. Open the fold. Turn under each long raw edge to meet the center fold. Press to crease.

swing-arm rods

Hinge-mounted curtain rods that open like shutters are called swing-arm rods or crane rods. The forged iron design shown on page 58 suggests an American country cottage look. Manufacturers also offer designs with high-tech brushed steel finishes or classic chrome rods.

Choose swing-arm rods to cover narrow windows. When closed, the rods should meet at the center of the window.

Swing-arm rods also solve the problem of how to curtain a functioning French door. Mount one on the outside edge of each door so they can swing back, allowing the door to be operated in a normal fashion.

You can use swing-arm rods to dress a window that's tucked into a corner, too. The arm can be opened halfway to meet the adjacent wall. The curtain fabric softens the abrupt architectural design and disguises the problem corner.

making tie-tab curtains with fabric-trim heading (continued)

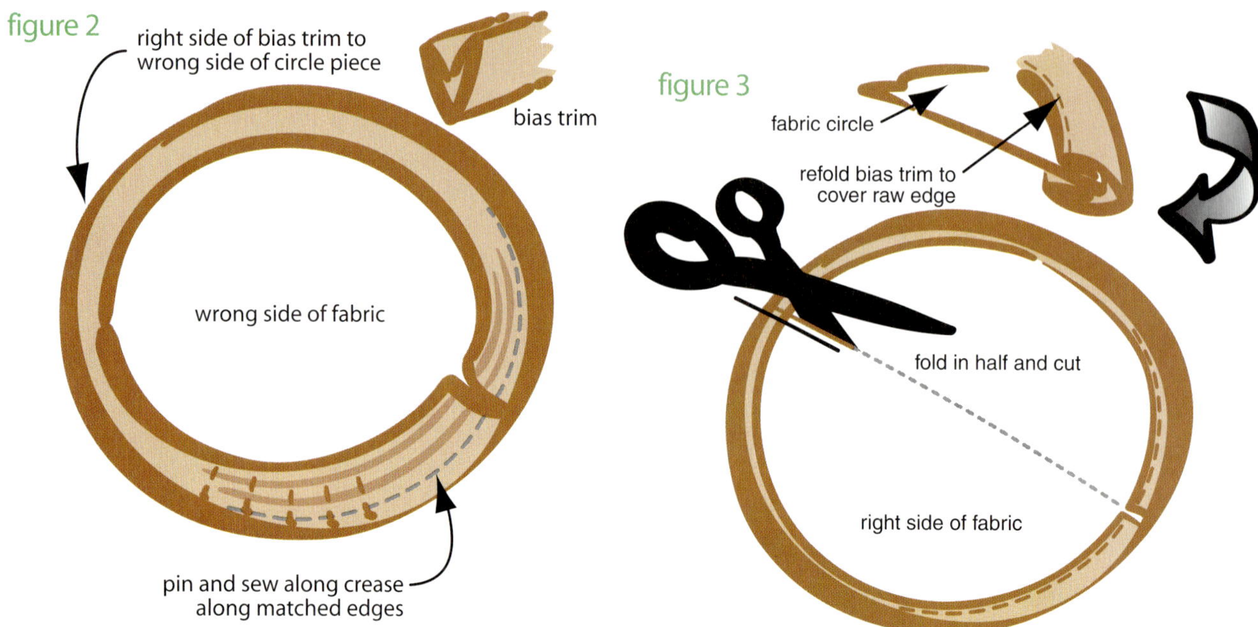

7 Open the folds in one piece of bias trim. With the right side of the bias tape to the wrong side of the circle piece and raw edges aligned, pin one piece of bias trim to one circle. Where the bias trim ends meet, cut off the excess trim. Stitch along the first crease in the bias trim (see Figure 2).

8 Refold the bias trim along the creases, covering the raw edges and turning the bias trim to the right side of the circle. Press flat. Pin the bias trim. Topstitch to the circle following the inside edge of the trim closely. Fold each circle in half, having the ends of the bias trim on the fold. Cut the circle in half on the fold (see Figure 3).

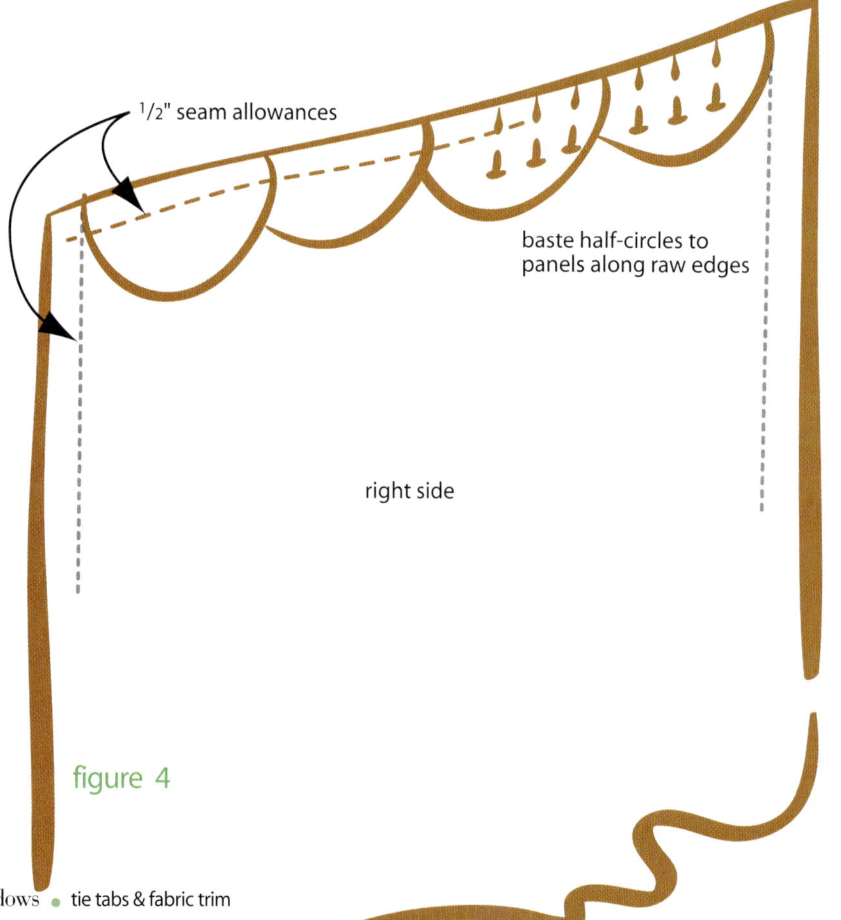

9 Lay the curtain and lining panels right sides up. Place 4 bias-trimmed semicircles with right sides faceup along the top edge of each curtain and lining panel. Allow ½" at each side of the curtain for side seams. If necessary, overlap the circles slightly to fit the edge. Align the raw edges of the half-circles with the top raw edges of the panels (see Figure 4). Pin in place. Using a long stitch length and ½" seam allowance, baste the half-circles to the panels along the raw edges.

10 Following the manufacturer's instructions, fuse interfacing to the wrong side of the remaining accent fabric for tie tabs. From the interfacing-backed fabric, cut 2"-wide bias strips. You will need 2 (12"-long) bias strips for each pair of ties. There are 5 pairs of ties on each curtain shown in the photograph. With wrong sides facing, fold each bias strip, matching the long edges. Press to crease the center fold. Open the fold. Turn under each long raw edge to meet the center fold. Press to crease. Edgestitch the folded edges of the ties together.

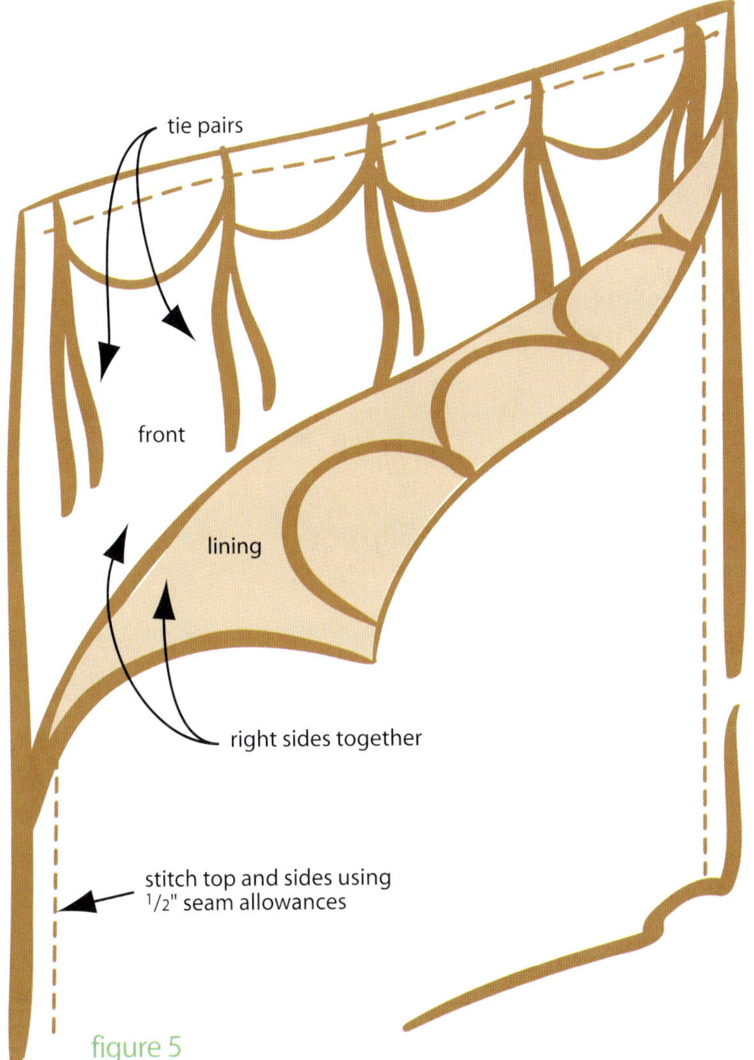

figure 5

11 Match the pairs of ties. Lay each curtain front right side up. Place one pair of ties at each side edge of the curtain front over the trim unit. (The ties will be attached to the curtain fronts only.) Place the remaining pairs of ties on the curtain front between the trim units in the same manner. Align the raw ends of the ties with the raw edges of the trim units and curtain front. Pin. Using a long stitch length, baste the ties to the curtain fronts following the previous basting (see Figure 5).

12 With right sides together and raw edges aligned, pin one curtain front to one curtain lining along the top and side edges, sandwiching trim and ties in between (see Figure 5). Leave the bottom edges of the curtain free. Using a 1/2" seam allowance, stitch the pinned edges together. Grade the seam allowances, but do not grade the tie seam allowances. Clip the corners and press the seams open. Turn to the right side. Place the seams on the edge and extend the ties and trim units from the seam at the top edge. Press the curtain flat. Turn the trim units down over the curtain tops and press.

making tie-tab curtains with fabric-trim heading (continued)

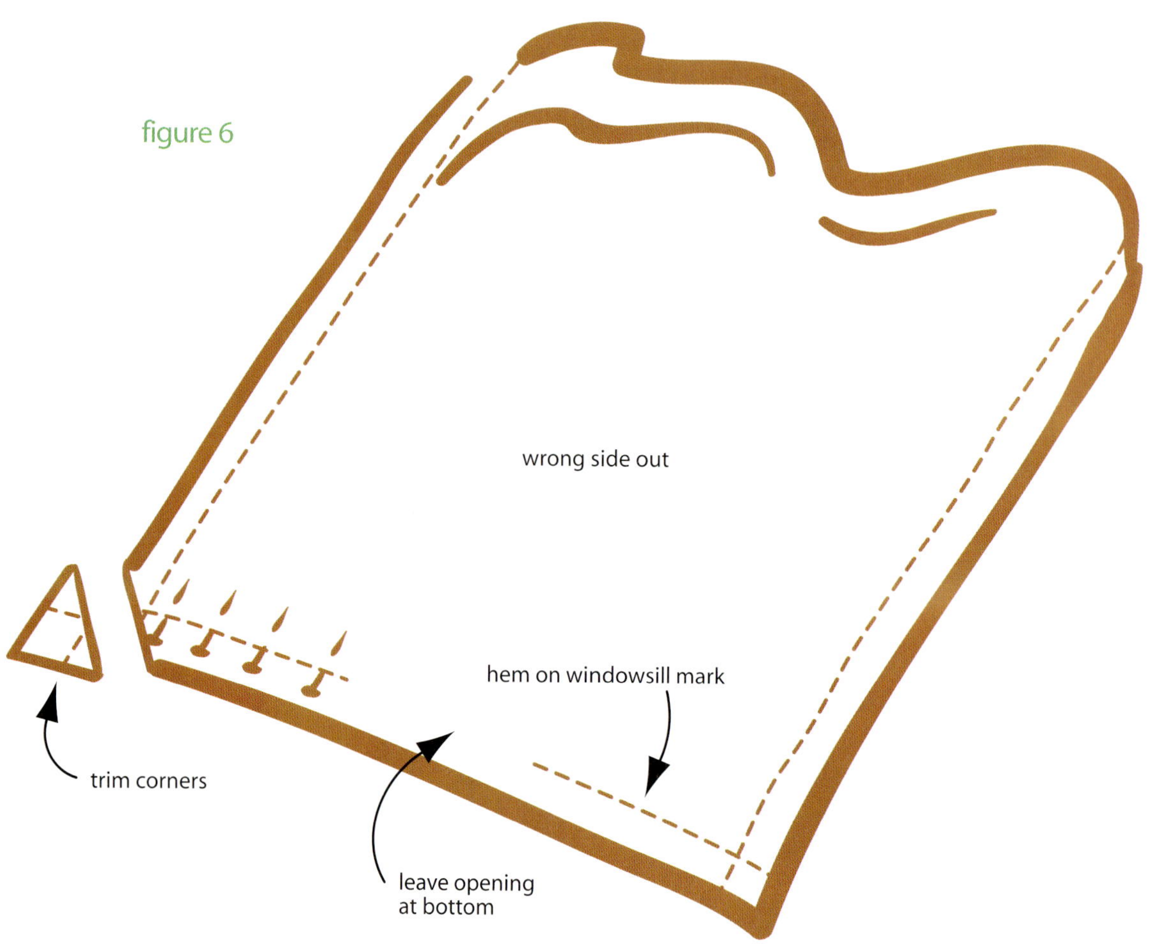

13 To mark the curtain hem, hang the curtains by knotting the pairs of ties around the rod. Mark the lower edge of the curtains at the windowsill, then remove the curtains from the rods. Turn each curtain to the wrong side. With right sides together and raw edges aligned, pin each curtain front to the lining on the hem edge and stitch along the windowsill marking, leaving a wide opening at the center of the seam for turning (see Figure 6). Grade the seam allowances and clip the corners. Turn to the right side through the opening. Place the seam on the edge and turn the raw edges to the inside along the opening. Press the curtains flat. Using a needle and thread, stitch the opening closed by hand. Hang the curtains. Trim the excess length from the tie ends if desired. Apply ravel preventer to cut the ends of the ties. Let dry.

making unlined panels

If you install an iron or wood rod instead of a swing-arm rod, you will not need to double-face the curtains. Just a few modifications make this design a simple unlined panel with a trimmed heading.

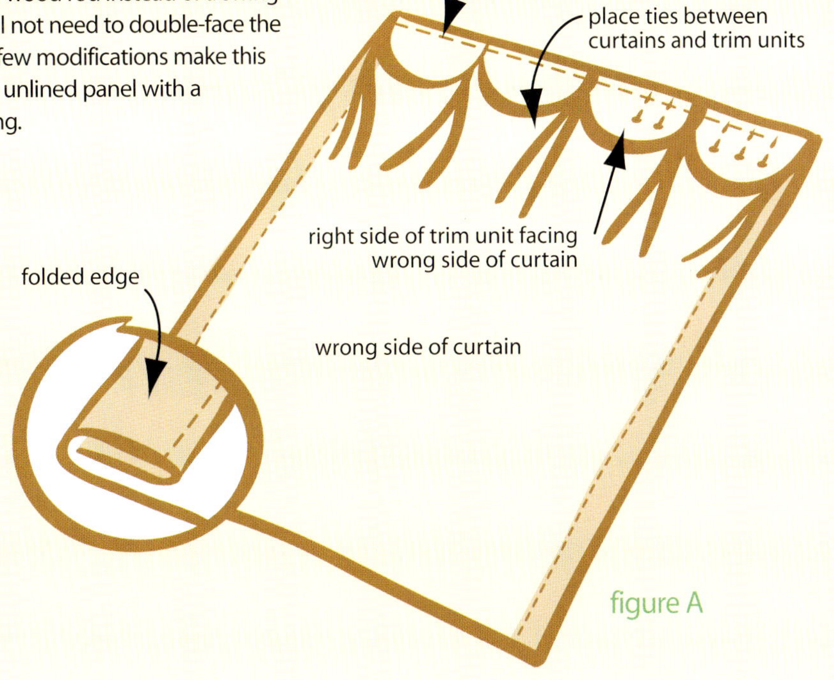

figure A

1 Measure the length of the curtain rod. Cut a fabric piece for each unlined panel as wide as the measured length of the rod. Cut each panel the measured length from the top of the rod to windowsill or floor plus 6". On the long side edges of each curtain, turn under 1½" twice. Press. Working on wrong side, edgestitch the hem in place.

2 Make the trim units and ties as for the double-faced curtains. On the wrong side of the curtain panel, arrange the trim units. Place each unit right side down, facing the wrong side of the curtain panel. Overlap the ends of the units as necessary to fit the curtain width. Align the raw edges of the units with the raw edge of the curtain. Match the pairs of ties. Insert the ends of the ties between the trim unit and the curtain panel (see Figure A). Pin. Using a ½" seam allowance, stitch the units and ties to the curtain panel. Grade the seam allowances. Finish the seam allowances.

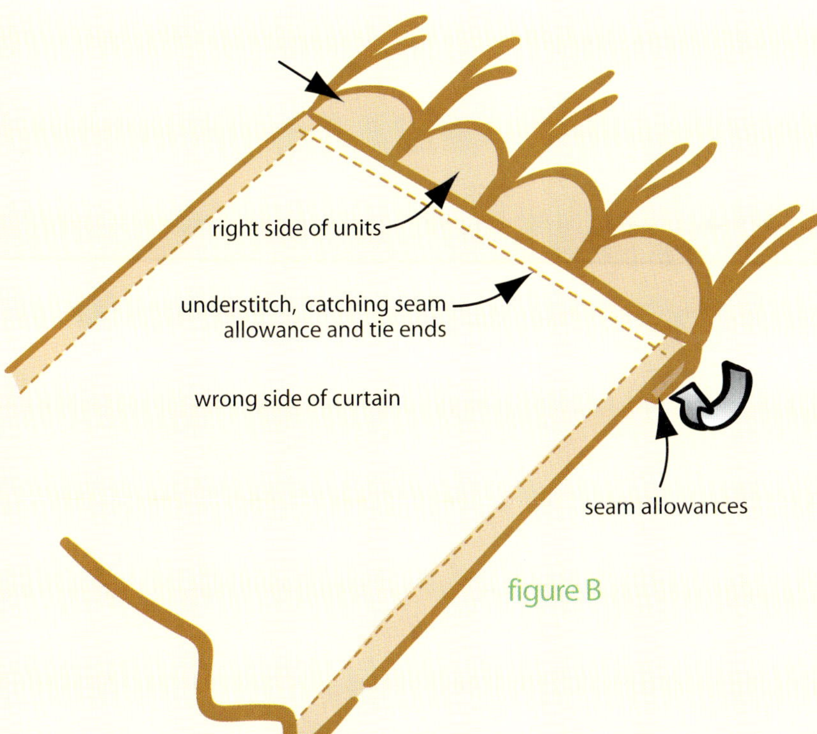

figure B

3 Press the seam allowance toward the curtain panel. Lay the trim seam allowances and the raw ends of the ties toward the curtain panel. Lay the loose tie ends toward the trim units (see Figure B). Working from the wrong side of the curtain panel, understitch the panel, catching the seam allowances of the trim units and the tie ends in stitching. Turn the trim units to the right side of the curtain panel. Place the seam on the edge with the ties extended straight up from the seam. Press flat.

4 Hang the curtains on the rod in the same manner as the double-faced curtains. Turn under the hem so the edge meets the windowsill or floor. Pin in place. Remove the curtains from the rod and press the fold. Turn under the raw edge to meet the crease. Press. Hemstitch the folded edge to finish the curtains.

Breezy cafe curtains are ideal for kitchens, breakfast nooks, or powder rooms, where you want to admit light but preserve some privacy. Installation couldn't be easier with tension rods that fit inside the window frame or with brackets that attach to the window frame or wall.

cafe curtains

Depending on your fabric choice, cafe curtains can have a retro look or evoke country cottage charm. You may omit the valance if you don't need to filter light. If you do include a valance, plan on having it cover from one-third to one-half of the upper part of the window. Shorter than that, the valance will look skimpy; longer, and it will appear top-heavy.

For the best results, choose crisp fabrics. If the hand of the fabric is somewhere between that of a dress shirt and a lightweight canvas, it's a perfect choice.

materials

54"-wide decorator fabric
Spring tension rod or cafe rod and mounting hardware
Cafe curtain rings

tools

Electric drill and drill bits
Screwdriver

sewing tools

Sewing machine
Thread
Iron and ironing board
Tape measure
Pins
Needle
Scissors

skill level: beginner
time required: ½ day

making cafe curtains:

1 Measure the window height and width inside the frame (see Figure 1). The valance and curtains hang on rings that slide along the tension rod, which is purchased to fit the window's inside width measurement. The finished valance width is twice the measured window width. You may need to seam together fabric widths to create adequate fullness in the valance. Each curtain panel equals the measured window width. In general, you need a length of fabric two times the measured height of the window for both the valance and curtains. Consider the length of the fabric repeat before you purchase fabric.

figure 1

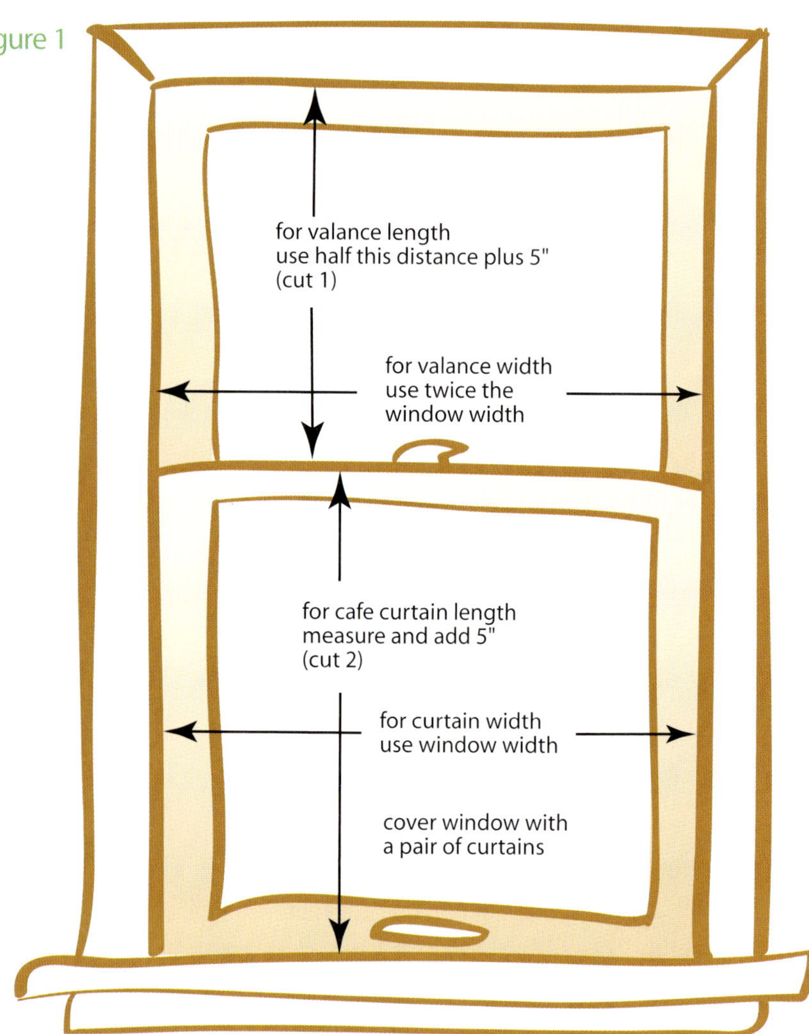

2 Trim the selvages off the fabric. For curtains, measure from the top of the window sash to the windowsill and add 5". Measure the window width. Cut 2 curtain panels this size. If you choose a floral or similarly patterned fabric, be sure each piece begins at the same point in the fabric repeat.

3 For the valance, measure from the top of the sash to the upper inside edge of the window frame. Divide this measurement in half and add 5". Measure the window width and double it. Cut one piece to this size. For wide windows, you may need to seam together fabric widths to achieve the desired fullness. Be sure each piece of a floral or patterned fabric begins at the same point in the repeat.

4 On the side edges of each curtain and the valance, turn 1½" under twice. Press. Working on the wrong side, edgestitch the hem in place. Using a wide stitch width and a short stitch length, zigzag the top raw edge of the curtain. Fold the top under 2" to make a facing. With a needle and thread, tack the facing to each side hem by hand.

5 Clip the cafe rings to the top edge of the curtains and valance. Place one ring at each corner, spacing the remaining rings along the edge, not more than 6" apart. Insert the tension rod through the rings. Fit the valance (or cafe) rod into the top of the window. Fit the curtain tension rod into the window at the sash. Mark the hems. Remove the curtains and valance from the window.

6 Turn under the hem along the marked line and press. Open the fold and turn under the raw edge to meet the crease. Press. Refold the hem and hemstitch the folded edge. Slip the curtains and valance on the rods, and return them to the window.

HARDWARE MADE EASY

tension rods are narrow, two-part, spring-loaded poles with rubber tips at each end. These rods hold their position inside the window frame by exerting an outward force at both ends. You'll find rods of different lengths to fit a variety of windows. They can be adjusted a few inches in length by twisting the two parts of the rod. In the kitchen on page 66, tension rods support the cafe curtains and valance. The white rods blend with the crisp white moldings. In general, tension rods are not intended to be a feature, but rather to serve a utilitarian function in window treatments. A similar but smaller, flatter rod, called a sash rod, is often used in pairs to hold shirred curtains in place close to the window glass.

mount

cable wire rods are the new generation of tension rods. These high-tech curtain rods consist of two anchors or mounts with a tight cable wire stretched between the two. Anchors are available in several styles to allow you to mount inside the frame or outside the frame.

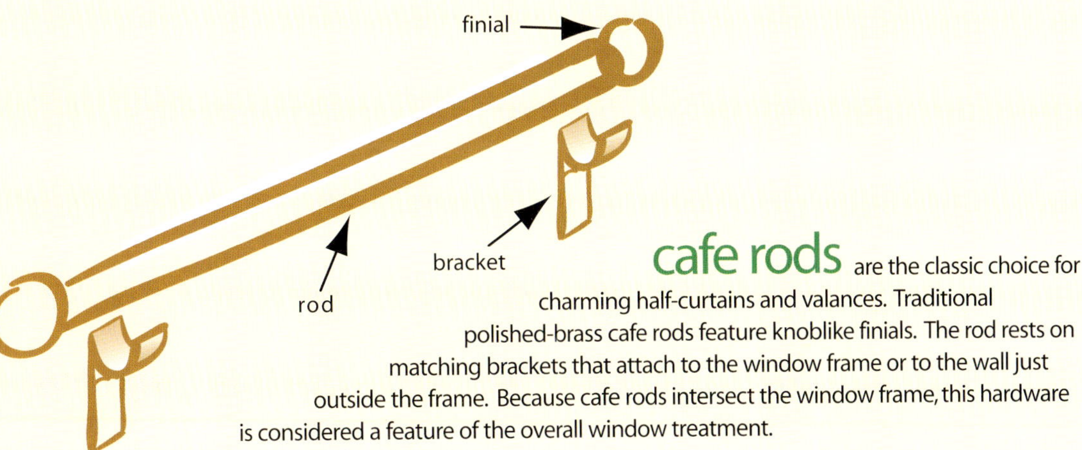

cafe rods are the classic choice for charming half-curtains and valances. Traditional polished-brass cafe rods feature knoblike finials. The rod rests on matching brackets that attach to the window frame or to the wall just outside the frame. Because cafe rods intersect the window frame, this hardware is considered a feature of the overall window treatment.

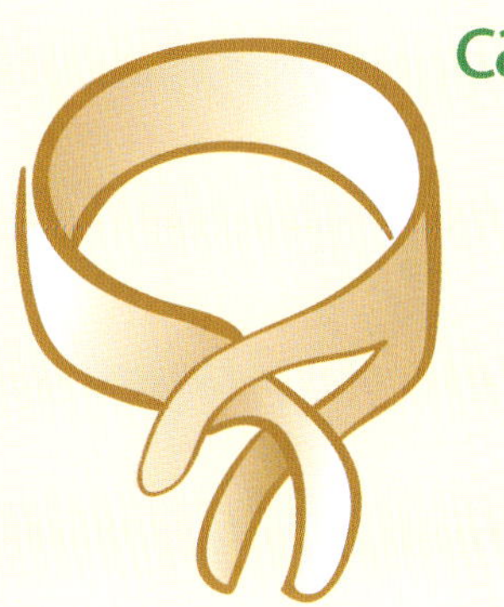

cafe rings clip onto fabric with a pinching action. They are removed easily on laundry day. Perhaps this is why the use of cafe curtains with cafe rings is so widespread in bistros around the world. When using rings with a rod other than that for which they were manufactured, such as with tension rods, be sure to check the fit. Cafe rings should slide freely along the rod.

A gathered valance with a gently arched lower edge makes a graceful topper for gathered panels. Use the same fabric for both curtains and valance to emphasize the window treatment as a single unit. If you prefer, choose a solid for the valance and a coordinating print for the curtains. Repeat the color of the solid elsewhere in the room, such as in pillows or on a chair.

rod pockets

Curtains that hang by rod pockets have three parts—the stand, the pocket, and the drop. The stand is the ruffle that extends above the curtain rod. The pocket acts as the casing into which you insert the rod for hanging. The drop is the length of the finished curtain, measured from the bottom of the curtain rod.

Stands can be either decorative or functional. A stand of about 2 inches makes a crisp stand-up ruffle, like the one on this valance. Narrow ¼-inch stands keep a curtain from twisting on the rod, giving a neater finished look to the treatment.

The type of curtain rod you choose determines the size—and therefore the decorative appearance—of the pocket. Here, the lined valance hangs on a wide curtain rod called a Continental rod, making a feature of the shirring. The unlined panels hang on a simple adjustable rod mounted behind the Continental rod. The pockets in the curtain panels are functional rather than decorative, so they are just large enough to receive the rod.

ADD PERSONALITY WITH BANDS

- Combine several bands of sheer and opaque fabrics in the curtain panels. Sheer fabrics feature opaque images that range from abstract swirls to floral motifs and flaunt saucy colors such as persimmon, sunflower, lime, and hot pink. Mix in a linen print or luxurious silk dupioni for rich texture.

- For flair and fun, stitch rows of bead fringe or charms along the seams. Or scatter silk flower heads randomly over the curtain panels for a romantic effect.

- As you plan the curtain, remember to add seam allowances to each band at every seam. If you forget to include the seam allowances, the finished curtain panel may be too short. Also, place the heaviest fabric at the bottom of the panel. This will weight the panel and improve the curtain's appearance.

materials

54"-wide decorator fabric
Lining
2½" Continental rod
Adjustable rod

tools

Electric drill and drill bits
Screwdriver

sewing tools

Sewing machine
Iron and ironing board
Tape measure
Pins
Thread
Scissors
Fabric marking pen
or pencil

skill level: intermediate
time required: 1 day

making rod pockets:

1 Measure the width of the window and purchase curtain rods for the required measurement. Install the adjustable rod just outside the window frame. Position the Continental rod just outside the adjustable rod, allowing ½" to 1" between the mounting hardware for each rod.

2 Measure the window length from the top of the adjustable rod. You will need a fabric piece for each panel that is as wide as the window measurement and as long as the measured length plus 12". For the valance, you will need a fabric piece and lining piece that are each twice as wide as the window measurement and 20" in length. Compare the 20" length of the side edges of the valance to your window; the valance should be one-fourth to one-third the window height. Adjust the valance length to fit your window. It may be necessary to stitch together fabric widths in order to achieve the desired fullness. Consider the length of the fabric repeat before you purchase fabric.

3 Trim the selvages off the fabric and lining. Cut 2 curtain fronts the measured length from rod to floor plus 8". Be sure each piece begins at the same point in the fabric repeat. If necessary to achieve the required width in the curtain panel, use flat-fell seams (page 74) to stitch together fabric lengths. On the long side edges of each curtain front, turn under 1½" twice and press (see Figure 1). Working on the wrong side, edgestitch the hem in place. Turn under the top edge ¼". Press. Turn the same edge under 1½". Press. Working from the wrong side, edgestitch close to the first fold, forming the bottom of the rod pocket. Topstitch ¼" from the second fold, forming the top of the rod pocket.

4 Insert the adjustable rod into each pocket. Hang the curtain panels. Turn under the hem so that the edge meets the floor. Pin. Remove the curtain from the rod. Press the fold. Turn under the raw edge to meet the crease. Press. Hemstitch the folded edge to finish the curtain. Hang the curtains.

5 The valance consists of a 2" stand, 3" rod pocket, and 14" drop at the outside edges. From fabric and lining, cut pieces twice as wide as the window width and 20" long.

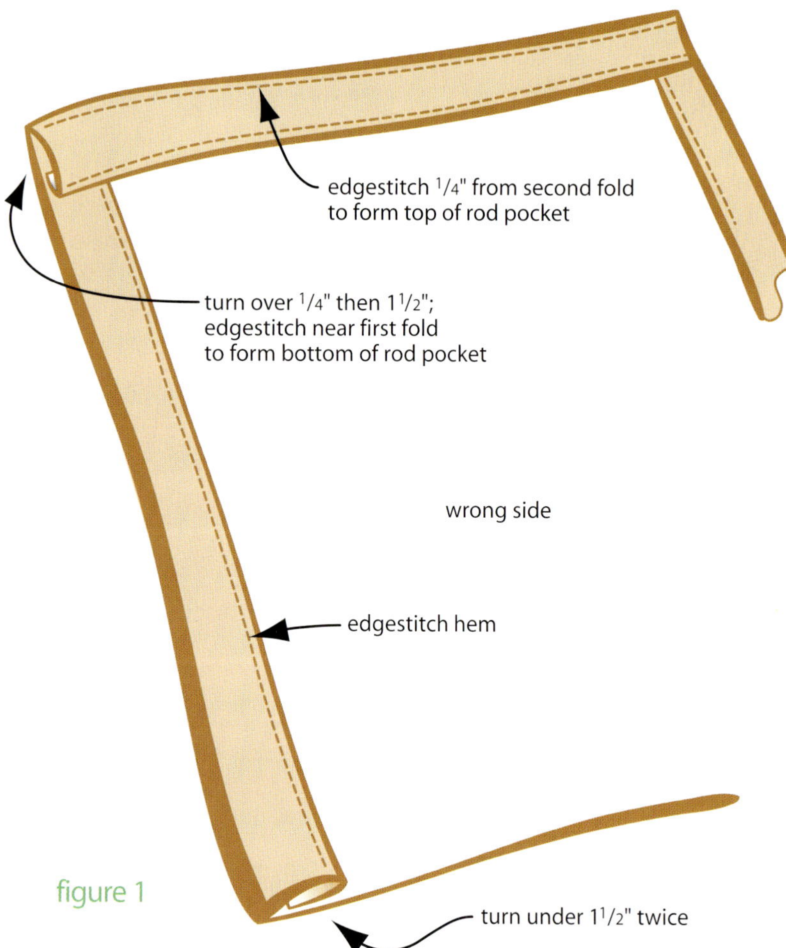

figure 1

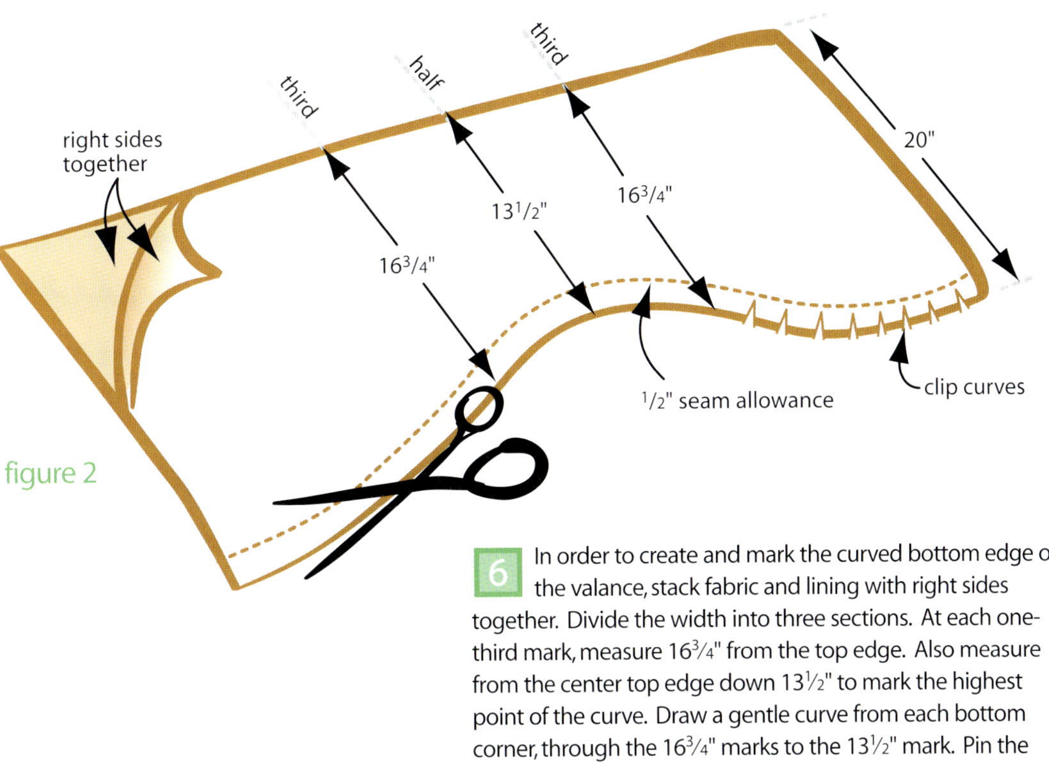

figure 2

6 In order to create and mark the curved bottom edge of the valance, stack fabric and lining with right sides together. Divide the width into three sections. At each one-third mark, measure 16¾" from the top edge. Also measure from the center top edge down 13½" to mark the highest point of the curve. Draw a gentle curve from each bottom corner, through the 16¾" marks to the 13½" mark. Pin the fabric layers together along this line. Stitch along the marked line. Trim the seam allowance to ½". Clip into the seam allowance along the curve. Using a ½" seam allowance, stitch the top edges of the valance together. Press each seam open (see Figure 2).

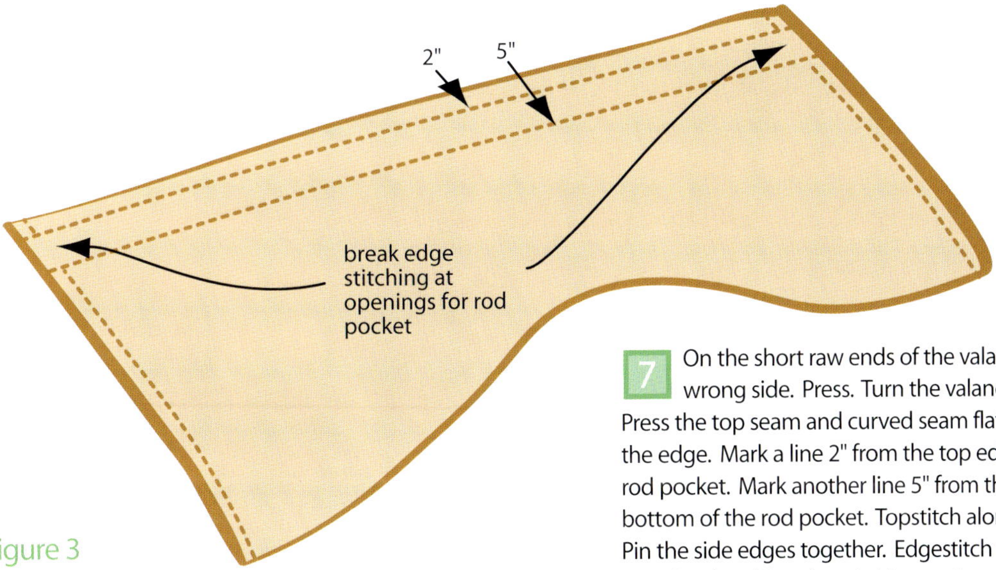

2"
5"
break edge stitching at openings for rod pocket

figure 3

7 On the short raw ends of the valance, turn ½" to the wrong side. Press. Turn the valance to the right side. Press the top seam and curved seam flat, placing each seam on the edge. Mark a line 2" from the top edge for the top of the rod pocket. Mark another line 5" from the top edge for the bottom of the rod pocket. Topstitch along the marked lines. Pin the side edges together. Edgestitch the fabric and lining together, breaking the stitching at the opening for the rod pocket (see Figure 3).

8 Insert the Continental rod into the pocket. Hang the valance. Adjust gathers by hand to make pleatlike folds in the curtain drop.

right sides together

start with 1/2" seam allowance

trim one seam allowance to 1/4"

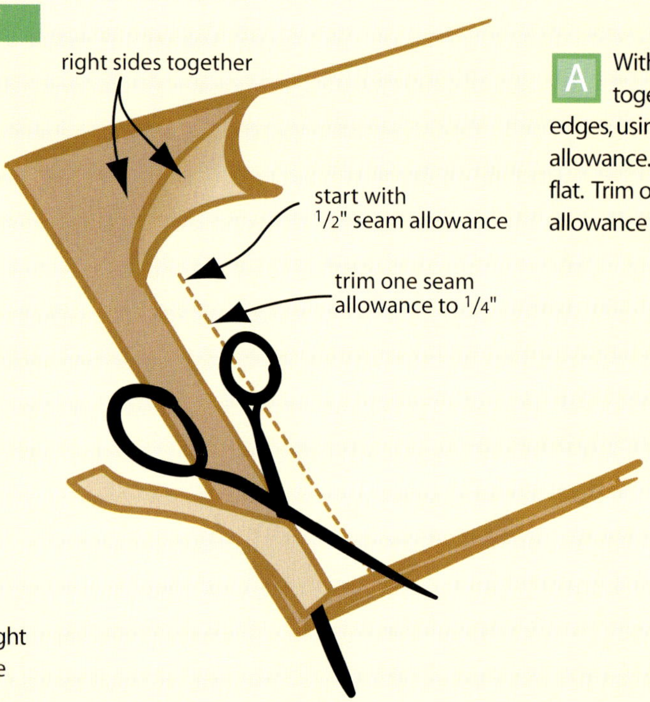

A With right sides together, stitch the edges, using a ½" seam allowance. Press the seam flat. Trim one seam allowance to ¼".

flat-fell seams

encase the raw edges of a seam allowance for a tailored, finished appearance. Whether seen from the right side or the wrong side, the finished seam looks like a conventional seam with a line of stitching parallel to it. Use this technique whenever you must join two lengths of fabric and you won't be covering the wrong side (and the seam allowance) with a lining or other backing.

fold longer seam allowance over shorter one

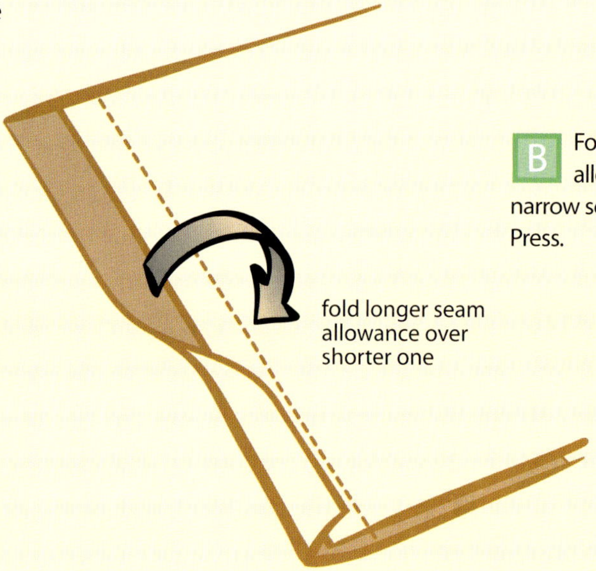

B Fold the longer seam allowance over the narrow seam allowance. Press.

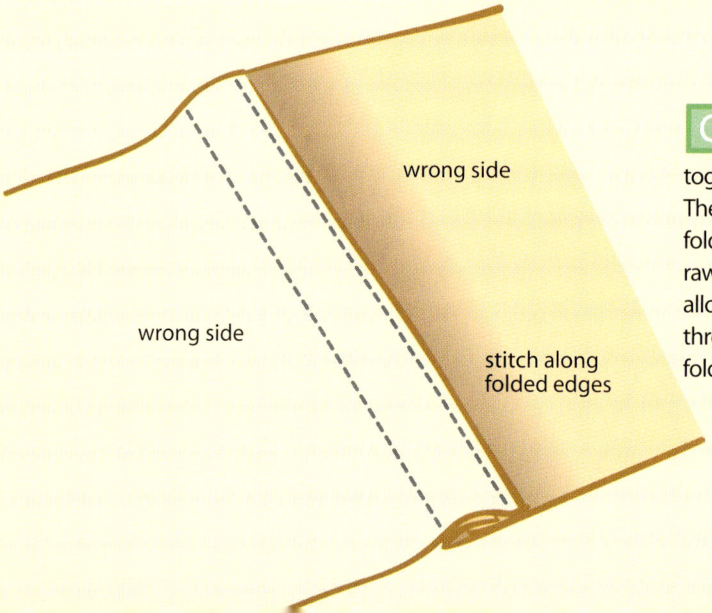

wrong side

wrong side

stitch along folded edges

C Open fabric. Turn both seam allowances together to the narrow side. The allowance with the folded edge will cover the raw edge of the trimmed allowance. Edgestitch through all layers along the folded edge.

HARDWARE MADE EASY

adjustable rods are the workhorses of window decoration, easy to find and install and easy on the pocketbook. Adjustable rods, however, are not pleasing to look at. They are best covered either with the shirred fabric of the rod pocket or by a valance that completely conceals the rod. Pay attention to the depth of the rod, or how far the rod projects from the wall, particularly if you are going to hang a valance over curtain panels as shown on page 70.

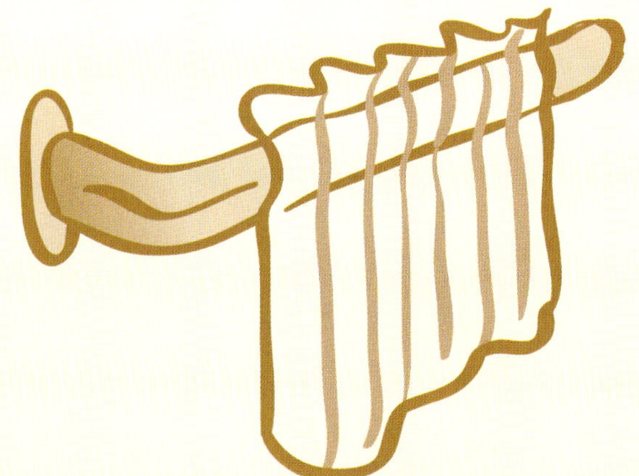

Continental rods create a richly shirred effect on valances and drapes constructed with rod pockets. Like adjustable rods, they are easy to find and install. Rods are available in two widths, 2½" and 4". Make sure the width of the rod is in proportion to the size of the window you are decorating and the ceiling height of the room. (A taller ceiling or larger window calls for the wider rod.)

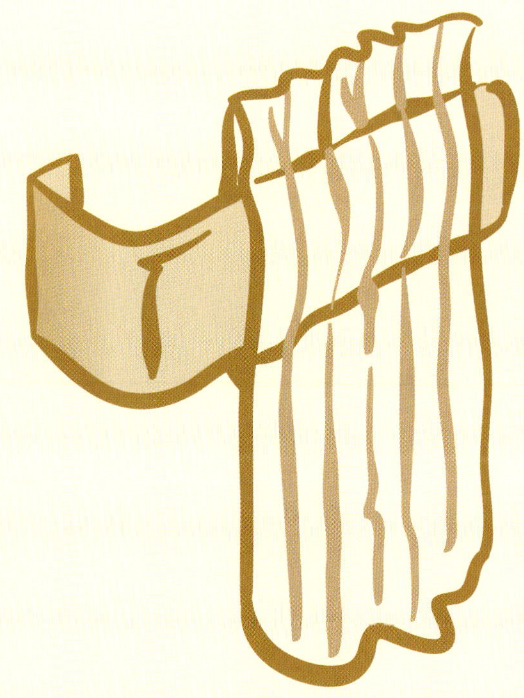

Staples of traditional window dressings, handmade pleats work comfortably in both formal and informal rooms. Hang the draperies on weighty curtain rings slipped onto overscaled rods for an updated look that suits casual settings. For more conservative formality, pair pleated draperies with hard or soft cornices (see pages 82 and 98).

handmade pleats

For a window treatment that is elegant but not too formal, opt for shapely handmade pleats. Choose a sturdy medium-weight fabric and trim the long sides of each panel with tassel fringe for a custom-finished look. Always remember that a pair of curtains should be wide enough to cover the window when drawn, even if you never intend to close them. Hang the draperies from boldly scaled rods and curtain rings to give the treatment importance. In the room shown opposite, the fluted wood rod mounts outside and above window moldings. This placement fills the narrow wall space between the window frame and the wide crown moldings.

MATCHING FABRIC REPEATS

1 When you need to join fabric lengths to make up a required width, first measure the fabric repeat. To make this easy, look at the selvage for the registration marks. The length between two marks is the fabric repeat.

2 Consider how the length of the fabric repeat will affect the amount of fabric needed for each panel. When cutting more than one fabric length for a window treatment, be sure that each piece starts at the same point in the repeat. This may result in a short length of fabric left over between the two cuts; discard it or use it to make pillows.

3 The registration marks on the left and right selvages match. Use these marks to match the pattern across seam lines. With right sides together, align the marks and pin the fabric sections together. Trim the selvages and stitch the lengths together.

materials

54"-wide decorator fabric
Lining fabric
Tassel fringe
2 drapery tiebacks with tassel ends
12 curtain pins
Wood rods with mounting hardware
12 wood curtain rings
Heavy paper

tools

Electric drill and drill bits

sewing tools

Sewing machine
Iron and ironing board
Scissors
Tape measure
Pins
Thread

skill level: intermediate
time required: 2 days

making handmade pleats:

1 Measure the width of the window frame from the outside edges. Mount the rod and place the curtain rings on the rod. Measure the distance from the bottom of the rings to the floor (this is the window length). Add 10" to this measurement to find the cut length of the panels. Each curtain panel is as wide as the measured window width before making the pleats. Consider the length of the fabric repeat when making calculations; purchase fabrics after making calculations.

2 Trim the selvages from the fabric and lining. From the fabric, cut 2 front panels the measured window length plus 10". Be sure each piece starts at the same point in the fabric repeat. From the lining, cut 2 panels the measured window length plus 4".

3 Lay each front panel right side up. Place the top edge of the lining 3" from the top edge of the panel. Smooth the lining down the length of the panel. If necessary, trim the lining so that it is 2" narrower than the front panel. Slide the lining to one side edge. Measure and mark 8" from the top edge and 12" from the bottom edge. Using ½" seam allowance, stitch the front and lining together between the marks. Slide the lining to the opposite side edge of the curtain front. Stitch the front and lining together in the same manner. Press the seams open.

4 Turn the curtain to the right side. Lay the curtain lining side up. Center the lining over the curtain front so there is 1" of curtain fabric turned to the lining side on each side. Press the folds and seams.

5 Turn the top edge of the lining back away from each curtain front. Turn the curtain front under 4", folding the sides at angles. Press. Turn under the top edge of the lining 1¼". Turn under the lining's unstitched side edges (the top 8") ½". Press. Using a needle and thread, stitch the linings to the curtain fronts along all folded edges. Also, stitch the angle folds of the curtain fronts.

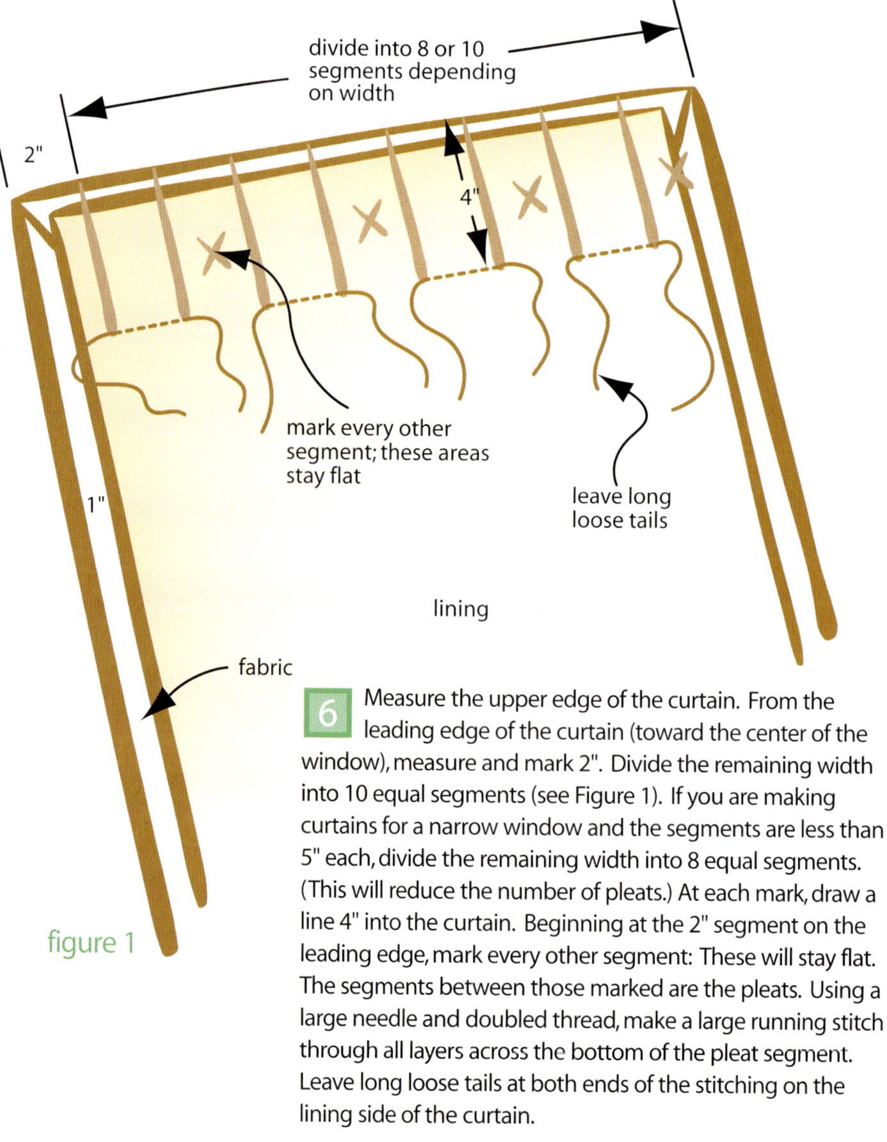

figure 1

6 Measure the upper edge of the curtain. From the leading edge of the curtain (toward the center of the window), measure and mark 2". Divide the remaining width into 10 equal segments (see Figure 1). If you are making curtains for a narrow window and the segments are less than 5" each, divide the remaining width into 8 equal segments. (This will reduce the number of pleats.) At each mark, draw a line 4" into the curtain. Beginning at the 2" segment on the leading edge, mark every other segment: These will stay flat. The segments between those marked are the pleats. Using a large needle and doubled thread, make a large running stitch through all layers across the bottom of the pleat segment. Leave long loose tails at both ends of the stitching on the lining side of the curtain.

7 Fold each pleat, lining sides together, matching the marked lines. Topstitch through all layers at the lines. Working on the lining side, center each pleat behind the seam. Press flat. Pull both tails of the running stitches to gather the lower edge of the pleat. Knot the thread ends together. Fingerpress each pleat to resemble the bowl of a water goblet.

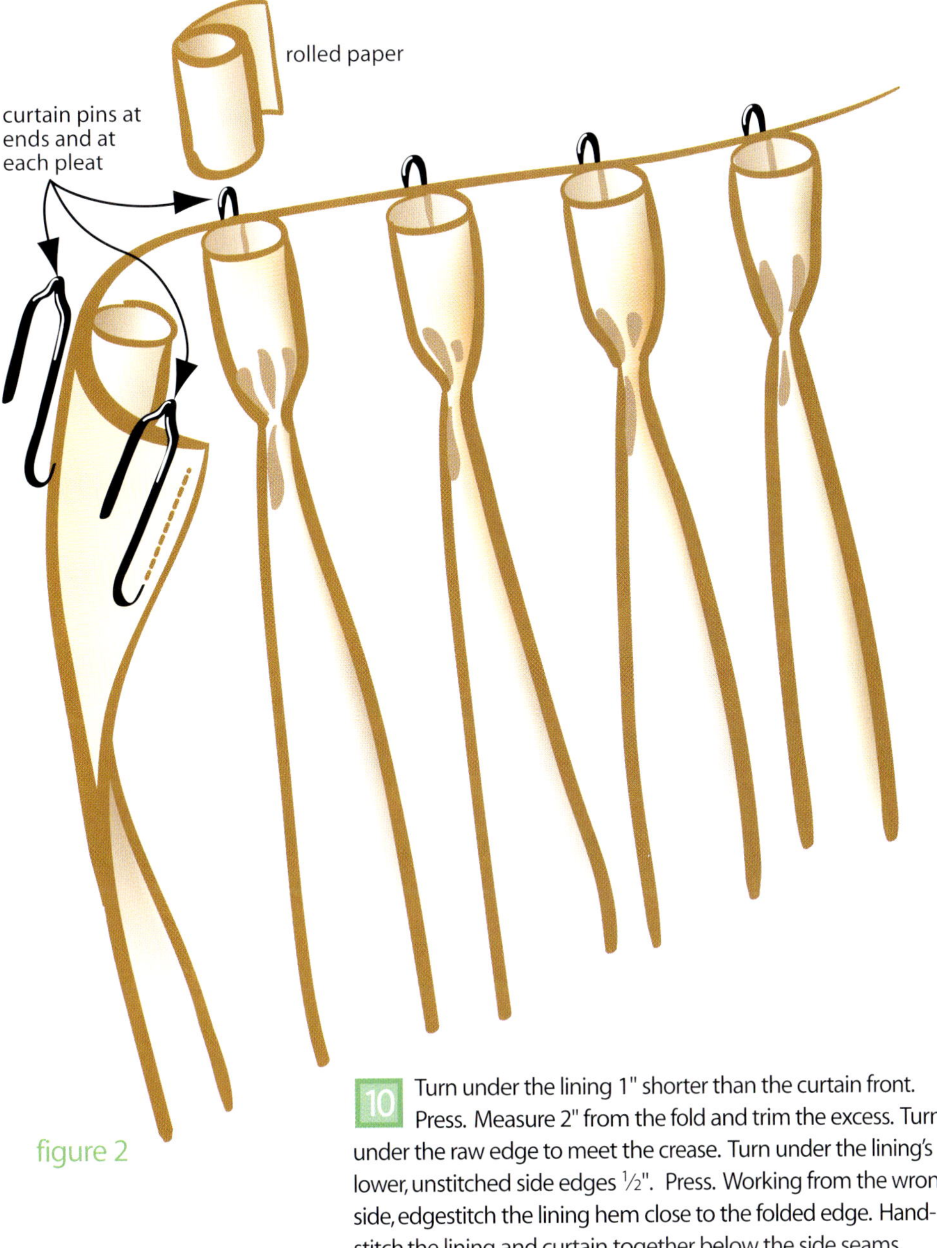

figure 2

8 Insert curtain pins into the back of each pleat and at the top corners of each curtain (see Figure 2). Hang the curtain hooks in the screw eyes on the wooden rings. To keep well-formed pleats, slip a rolled strip of stiff paper (such as a file folder) into each pleat.

9 Turn under the curtain hem so that the edge meets the floor. Pin. Remove the curtains from the rod. Press the fold. Open the fold. Keep the lining edge free. Measure 6" from the fold and trim the excess. Turn the raw edge of the curtain front to meet the folded hem edge. Press. Refold the hem, making angle folds at the ends similar to those at the curtain top. Hemstitch the folded edge.

10 Turn under the lining 1" shorter than the curtain front. Press. Measure 2" from the fold and trim the excess. Turn under the raw edge to meet the crease. Turn under the lining's lower, unstitched side edges ½". Press. Working from the wrong side, edgestitch the lining hem close to the folded edge. Hand-stitch the lining and curtain together below the side seams.

11 Remove the curtains from the window. Measure the fringe against the leading edge and outside edge of each curtain. Add 1" at each end. Apply ravel preventer to the braid portion of the fringe. Let dry. Cut through the braid at the ravel preventer. Apply more ravel preventer to the cut ends. Let dry. Place the braided edge of the fringe on the curtain. Turn under the ends 1". Using a long stitch length, topstitch the fringe in place along each edge of the braid. Hang the curtains.

HARDWARE MADE EASY

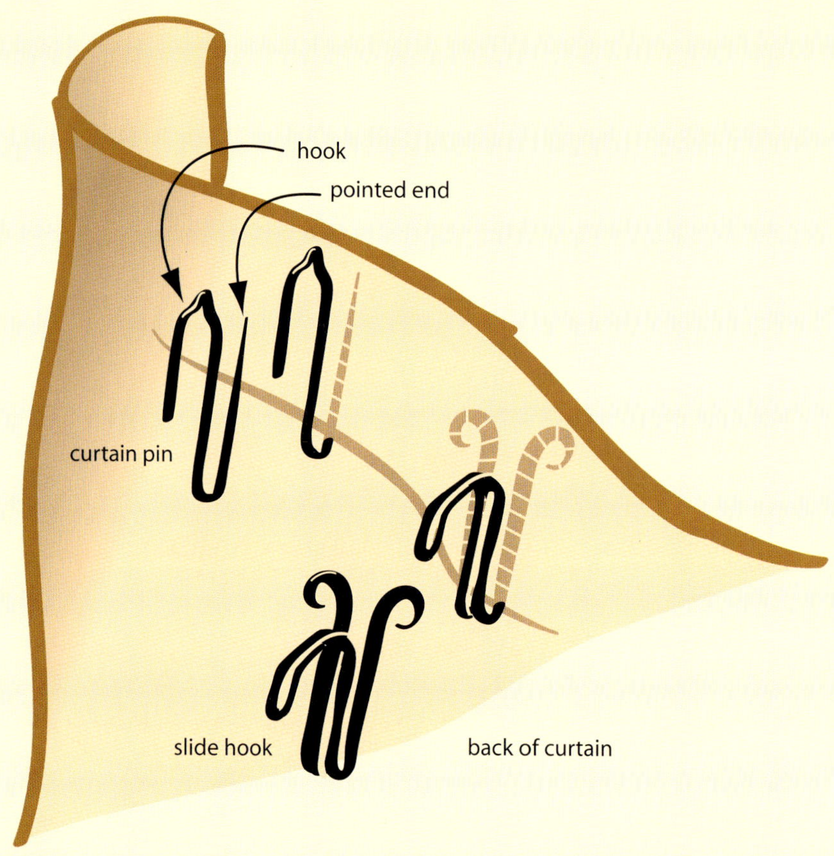

curtain pins almost invisibly attach curtains to the curtain rings. To use the pins successfully, the curtain should have a closed heading. The sharp pin portion of the device is inserted into the back or lining side of the curtain. One pin is inserted ½" to 1" from each end and the rest are evenly spaced along the width between. For a pleated heading, insert one pin into the back of each pleat. Place the pin so that the tallest portion extends ¼" above the curtain front. Place all pins at the same level. Just one pin out of line can cause the curtain to hang crooked.

slide hooks are used in the same manner as curtain pins, but they are intended for curtains with an open or folded heading. Fold under the curtain heading the same depth as the back portion of the slide hook. Slip the back portion of the hook into the heading as you would a paper clip. The slide hook is totally hidden behind the curtain because the top of the hook is not as high as the back portion of the hook.

wood poles easily fit into almost any decorating scheme. Painted white, they have country charm. Stained dark, they offer traditional elegance. Finials, the decorative knobs that finish the ends of the pole, come in styles from plain to ornate. The poles themselves may be smooth or fluted. Most poles rest on brackets mounted on the window frame or on the wall surrounding the window. The brackets usually come with the screws needed to fasten the bracket to solid wood, such as the window frame or a wall stud. If you choose to mount the bracket in a location where no stud exists, use wall anchors to secure the brackets. For help in choosing the appropriate hardware for mounting in special circumstances, visit the "fasteners" aisle of your local hardware store.

CHOOSING LININGS

Asking for lining at the fabric store can elicit a number of questions from the sales associate, the most important being what type of lining you need: basic, thermal, or blackout. Here are some fast facts to help you answer those questions.

basic lining, a tightly woven cotton or cotton-blend fabric, adds body to the draperies and provides some protection against sun damage. It is available in white or off-white.

thermal lining is basic lining with a synthetic coating applied to the wrong side. The coating makes the fabric less air permeable, increasing the warming values of closed draperies. Take care in pressing to avoid marring the coated surface. It is easy to find in white. Off-white thermal lining may be more difficult to find.

blackout lining is also basic lining with a synthetic coating applied to the wrong side. The coating is thick and often gray in color and is used to block sunlight. In windows with a western or southern exposure where harsh light is a factor, blackout lining can preserve the beauty of the curtain fabric. Care should be taken when pressing to avoid marring the coated surface. It is easy to find in white. Off-white blackout lining may be more difficult to obtain.

interlining is not a lining, but a thin flannel-like fabric used between the curtain front and the lining. It adds fullness to the curtain fabric, helps to absorb sound, and provides some insulating benefits. It is ivory in color.

Both practical and decorative, a cornice conceals the curtain hardware and adds architectural importance to the window. Use a cornice whenever you want to make the window look taller or grander. To give the cornice a custom-designed look, create a shaped lower edge inspired by an element in the room—the curves of a Chippendale chair, for example—or the curtain fabric itself.

hard cornice

A cornice box mounts above the window frame and should extend at least 8 inches down over the window. As a general rule, cornices should measure one-third the window height, but if you have floor-length draperies, the box may need to be taller to balance the draperies visually.

Cornices are made from plywood and usually consist of a front or face board, a top or dust board, and two sides (for instructions to make one, see page 87). Once assembled, they may be painted, stenciled, or covered with fabric or wallpaper. To give the cornice a custom-designed look, create a shaped edge—draw inspiration from objects or motifs in the room or use the drapery fabric as your starting point. The crisp harlequin fabric in the curtains opposite sparked the idea for this pennant-shape edge. Heavy cording and companion tassels with yellow, green, and red threads repeat the colors found in the rug, curtains, and walls, unifying the room's design.

materials

3/8" plywood
2×4 pine board
11 (1") No. 6 wood screws
3 (3") No. 8 wood screws
2 (2") No. 8 wood screws
Spray adhesive
Clear-drying fabric glue
54"-wide decorator fabric
Lining fabric
Cord
Tassels
Adjustable rod
14 curtain pins

tools

Electric drill and drill bits
Electric saw
Screwdrivers

sewing tools

Sewing machine
Iron and ironing board
Tape measure
Upholstery or tapestry needle
Pins
Fabric marking pen or pencil

skill level: advanced
time required: 2 days

covering the hard cornice:

1. Install the 2×4 pine board and the adjustable rod and drill pilot holes through the top of the cornice box into the 2×4 as directed in Steps 4 and 5 on page 87. Remove the cornice box from the window.

figure 1

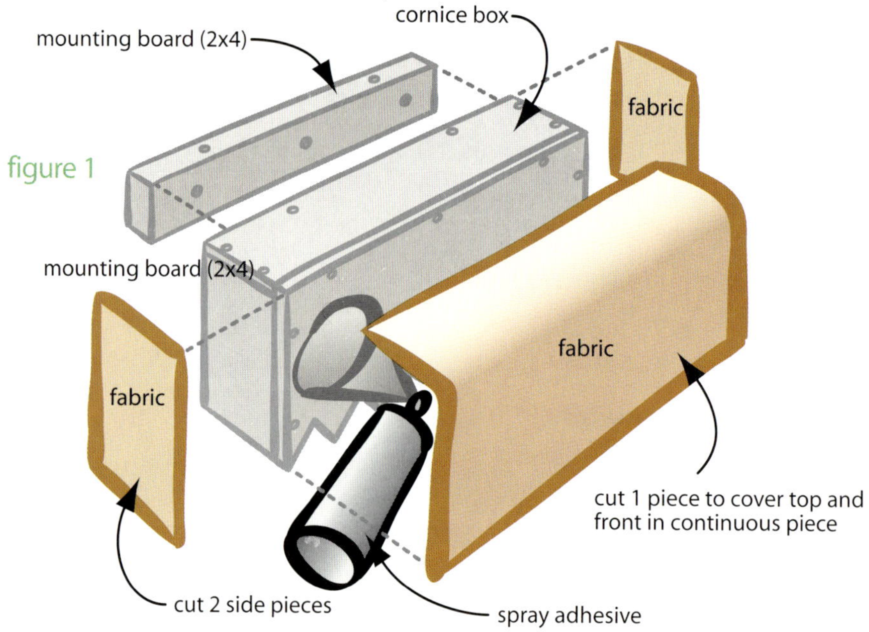

2. From the fabric cut 2 side pieces to fit the cornice box sides. Also, cut a piece to fit the cornice box top and front in one continuous piece. Do not cut the lower edge of the fabric to match the edge of the box front at this time. Following the manufacturer's instructions, apply spray adhesive to the box front. Place the fabric so the pattern matches the custom cuts on the lower edge of the box front. Smooth the fabric onto the box and wrap it over the box top (see Figure 1). Apply spray adhesive to one end of the box. Matching the pattern at the corners, smooth the fabric onto the box end. Repeat for the opposite end. Punch small holes through the fabric into the pilot holes on the box top.

3. Let the adhesive dry thoroughly. Trim the fabric at the bottom edge of the front to match the custom-cut box edge (see Figure 2).

4. Using fabric glue, attach cording to the custom edge of the box, covering the raw edge of the fabric. With an upholstery needle, stitch one tassel to the cord at each point in the custom edge.

5. Measure the window length from the top of the adjustable rod. Trim the selvages off the fabric and the lining. From the fabric cut 2 front panels the measured window length plus 10". Be sure each piece starts at the same point in the fabric repeat. From the lining, cut 2 panels the measured window length plus 4". If necessary to make up required width, cut additional fabric and lining lengths and seam panels together.

figure 2

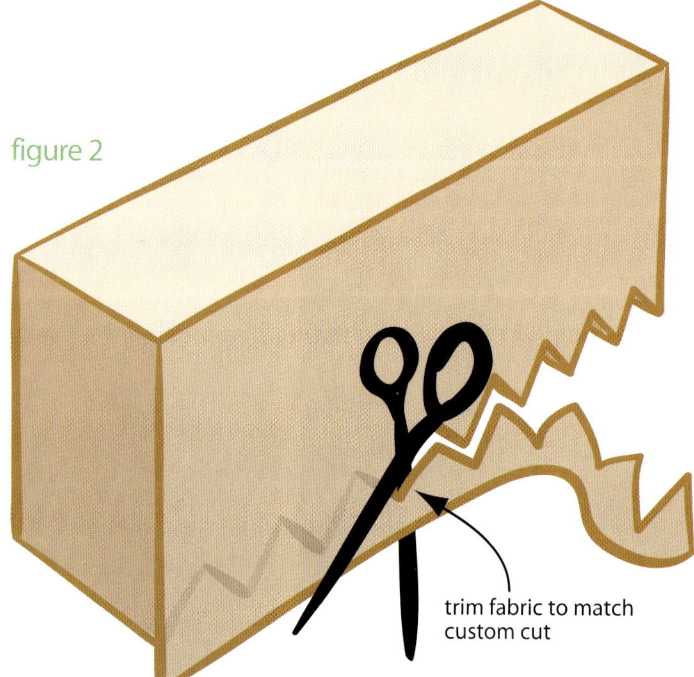

6 Lay each front panel right side up. Place the top edge of the lining 3" from the top edge of the panel. If necessary, trim the lining so it is 1" narrower on each side than the front panel (see Figure 3). Slide the lining to one edge. Measure and mark 8" from the top edge and 12" from the bottom edge. Using a 1/2" seam allowance, stitch the front and lining together between the marks. Slide the lining to the opposite side of the curtain front. Stitch the front and lining together in the same manner. Press the seams open.

7 Turn the curtain to the right side. Lay the curtain with the lining side up and center lining so there is 1" of curtain fabric turned to lining side on each side. Press the folds and seams.

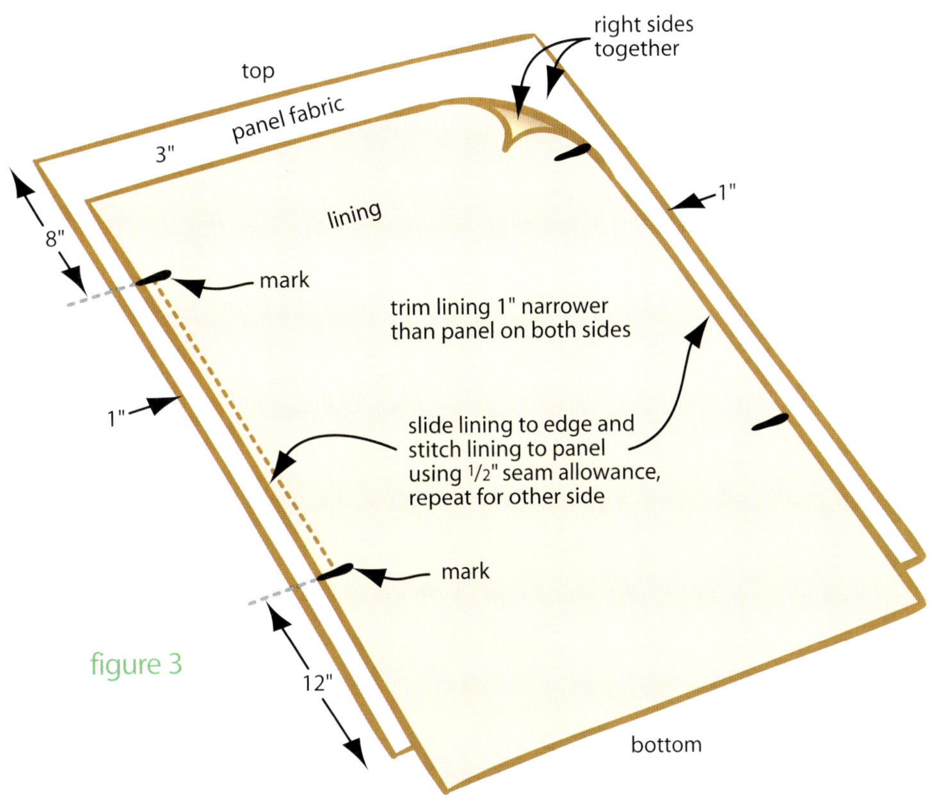

figure 3

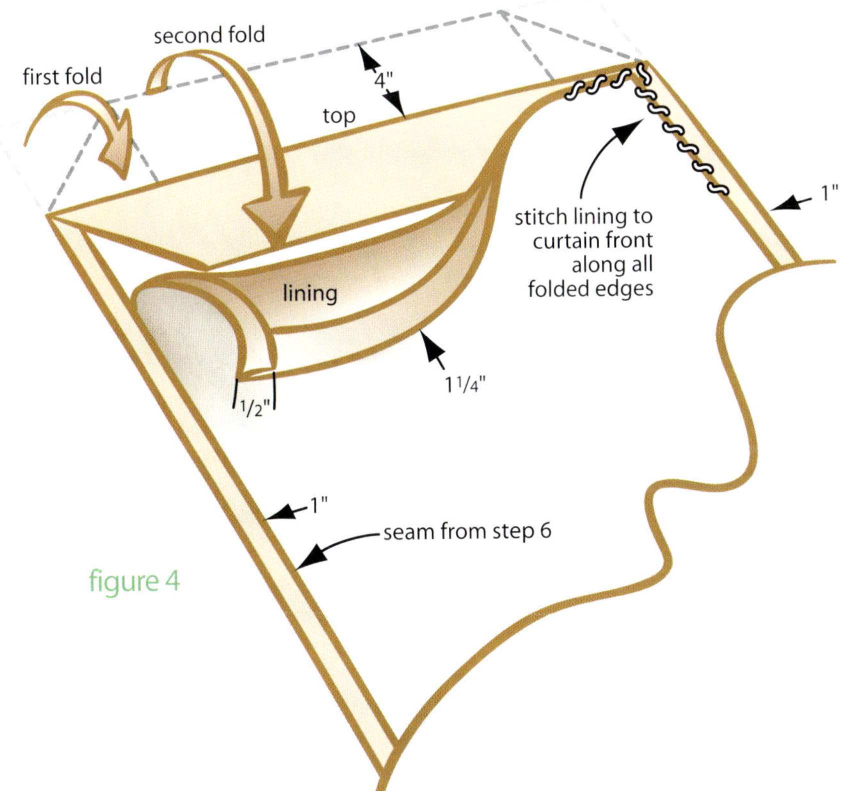

figure 4

8 Turn the top edge of the lining back away from each curtain front. Turn under the curtain front 4", folding the sides at angles. Press. Turn under the top edges of the lining 1 1/4" and the side edges 1/2". Press. Using a needle and thread, stitch the lining to the curtain front along all folded edges and the angle folds of the curtain fronts (see Figure 4).

9 At the top corners of each curtain, insert curtain pins into the curtain back. Evenly space the remaining pins between the corners (7 pins per curtain). Hang the hook portion of the pins on the rod.

making the curtain panels:

10 Turn under a hem for each curtain front so the edge just meets the floor. Pin. Remove the curtains from the rod. Keeping the lining edge free, press the hem fold. Open the fold. Measure 6" from the fold and trim the excess. Turn under the raw edge of the curtain front to meet the crease for the hem. Press, then refold the hem, making angle folds at the ends similar to those at the curtain top. Using a needle and thread, hemstitch the folded edge.

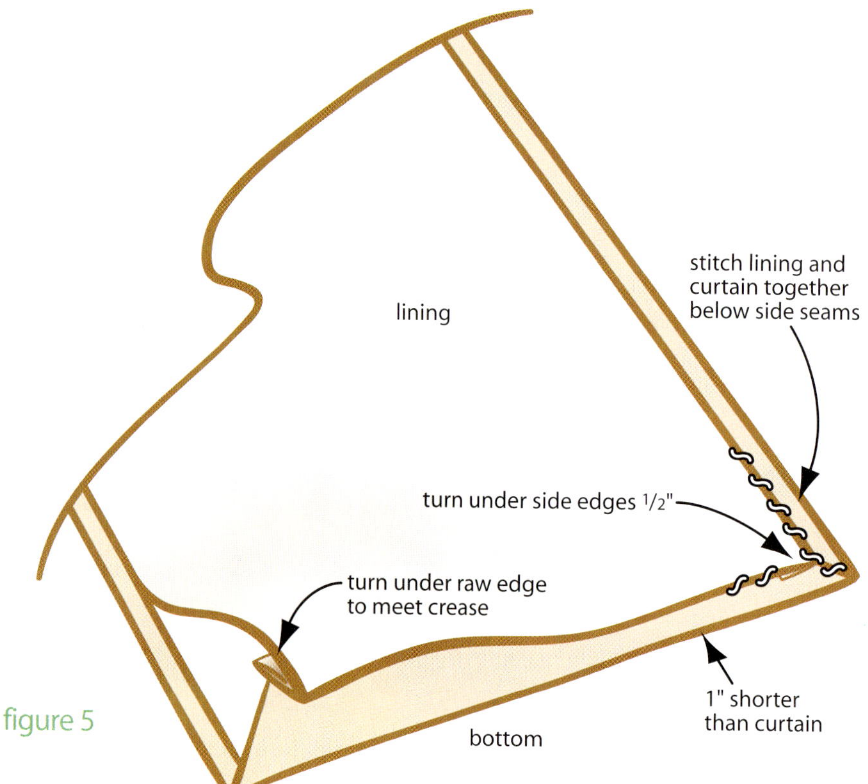

figure 5

11 Turn under the lining 1" shorter than the curtain front. Press. Measure 2" from the fold and trim the excess. Turn under the raw edge to meet the crease. Turn under the side edges 1/2". Press. Working from the wrong side, edgestitch the hem close to the folded edge (see Figure 5). Using a needle and thread, stitch the lining and curtain together below the side seams. Replace the curtains on the rod.

12 Place the cornice box on the mounting board and install with 2" wood screws through the pilot holes.

MAKING AND MOUNTING A CORNICE BOX

Cornice boxes are fabric- or wallpaper-covered boxes that serve as a valance treatment for windows. For easy installation, fasten a 2×4 above the window as a mounting board for any hard cornice box. The weight of the box is then distributed over a wider area than if it were mounted on inside corner braces. It is also much easier to install the final screws from above the box than from inside and below.

1 Measure the width of the window frame. Cut the 2×4 to the window width less 1". Determine where you want the top of the cornice to be. Measure from that point to the floor and divide by 4: This is the finished height of the box. For pleasing proportions, the box should be at least 8" tall.

2 From plywood cut the following pieces: the cornice front (the window width by the height of the box), the cornice top (the window width by 5"), and 2 cornice sides (5" by the height of the box less 3/8"). For the lower edge of the cornice front, make a pattern. Trace the fabric design on paper; transfer the design to one long edge of the cornice front. Your local hardware store may cut the plywood into these pieces for you for a moderate charge.

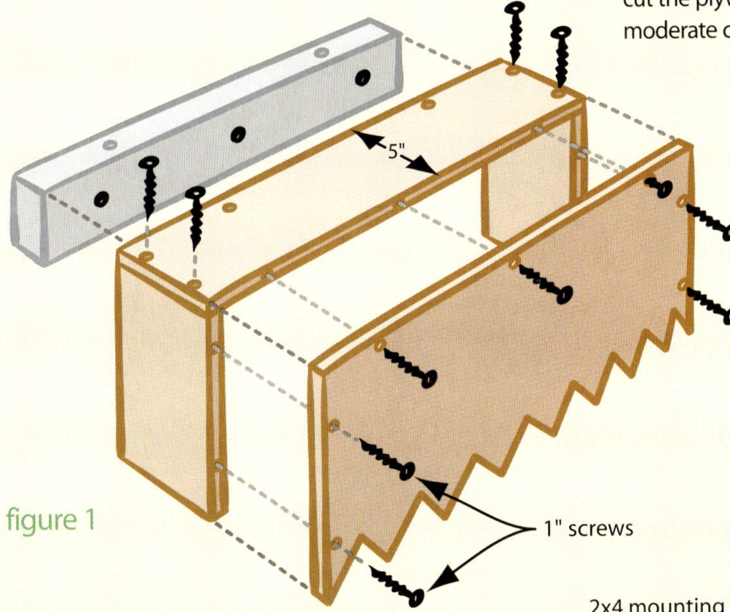

figure 1

3 Place the cornice top on the edge of each cornice side. Make sure the corners are flush and square. Drill pilot holes and attach the pieces with 1" screws. Place the cornice front on the front edge of the sides and top. Make sure the edges are flush and square. Drill pilot holes and attach with 1" screws (see Figure 1). Paint the inside of the box and all edges in a color to match the curtain fabric. Also paint the 2×4.

4 Hold the cornice board above the window to find the desired placement. Lightly mark the top edge on the wall. Center the 2×4 over the window 1/2" below the mark, having the wide side of the board against the wall. Drill pilot holes and install with 3" screws (see Figure 2). Install the adjustable rod just outside the window frame.

5 Set the cornice box on top of the board. Drill pilot holes through the top of the box into the 2×4. Remove the box from the window and cover with fabric as directed on page 84.

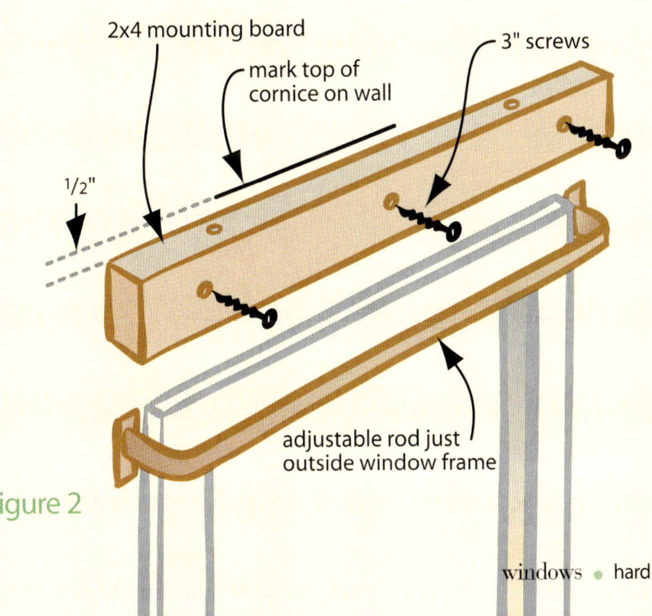

figure 2

Making your own cornice lets you be creative and design a window topper that's uniquely suited to your room. Keep in mind the type of shade or curtain it will be combined with—here the scalloped edge of the cornice repeats in the softly gathered edge of the shade for a harmonious effect.

hard cornice & soft shade

Large windows flood rooms with light. In a bathroom, however, large windows raise questions of privacy. One beautiful solution is to team a cornice box with a soft shade for light control. The balloon-like shade can be lifted or lowered as needed. Constructed in a manner similar to a Roman shade, this treatment gathers loosely along two columns of rings. The result is a loosely draped pouf with a soft, unstructured look.

To keep the window treatment uncluttered, cover the cornice box with the same paper as the surrounding walls. In this room, the pale colors and simple design help expand the space. The shade mounts inside the top of the box, which conceals the the shade mechanics. The box mounts on the wall on a 2×4 pine board.

materials

- ⅜" plywood
- 2×4 pine board
- 12 (1") No. 6 wood screws
- 3 (1¼") No. 8 wood screws
- 3 (3") No. 8 wood screws
- 5 (2") No. 8 wood screws
- Clear-drying fabric glue
- Wallpaper
- Bobble fringe trim
- 54"-wide decorator fabric*
- 54"-wide decorator lining fabric*
- Shade-and-blind tape or plastic O-rings
- Shade-and-blind cord
- 4 curtain weights
- 1×2 pine board
- Cleat with fasteners
- 3 screw eyes

tools

- Electric drill and drill bits
- Electric saw
- Screwdrivers
- Wallpaper hanging tools, such as knife, brush, and water tray

sewing tools

- Sewing machine
- Iron and ironing board
- Fabric marking pen or pencil
- Pins
- Needles
- Thread
- Scissors
- Tape measure
- Liquid ravel preventer

(*Note: Yardage estimate does not allow for matching patterns. Compare cut size of panels to fabric design to find how much fabric you will need.)

skill level: advanced
time required: 2 days

making the hard cornice & soft shade:

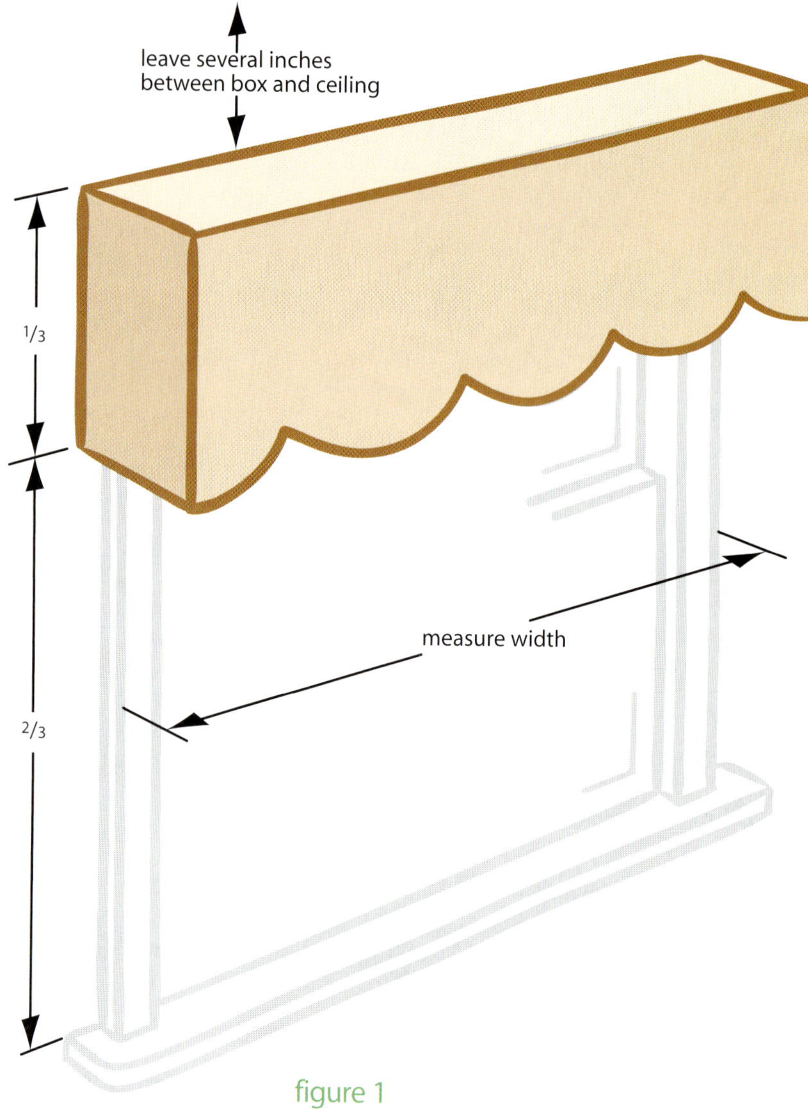

figure 1

1 The cornice box attaches to a mounting board that you install above the window. To determine the measurements of the box, measure the width of the window frame, then decide where you want the top of the cornice to be (allow at least several inches between the box and the ceiling). Measure from that point to the windowsill and divide by 3: This is the finished height of the box (see Figure 1).

2 From plywood cut the following pieces: the cornice front (window width plus 5" by the height of the box), the cornice top (window width plus 5" by 5"), and 2 cornice sides (5" by the height of the box less ⅜"). For the lower edge of the cornice front, trace the edge of a dinner plate to draw a scalloped edge. Using a jigsaw, cut along the marked line. Your local hardware store may cut the plywood into these pieces for you for a moderate charge.

3 Place the cornice top on the edge of each side piece, making sure the corners are flush and square. Drill pilot holes through the top into the sides and attach with 1" screws. Place the cornice front on the front edge of the sides and top, aligning edges. Drill pilot holes through the front into the sides and top and attach with 1" screws. Paint the inside of the box and all edges in a color to match the background of the wallpaper. Cut a 2×4 to equal the window width less 1". Paint it to match the wallpaper as well.

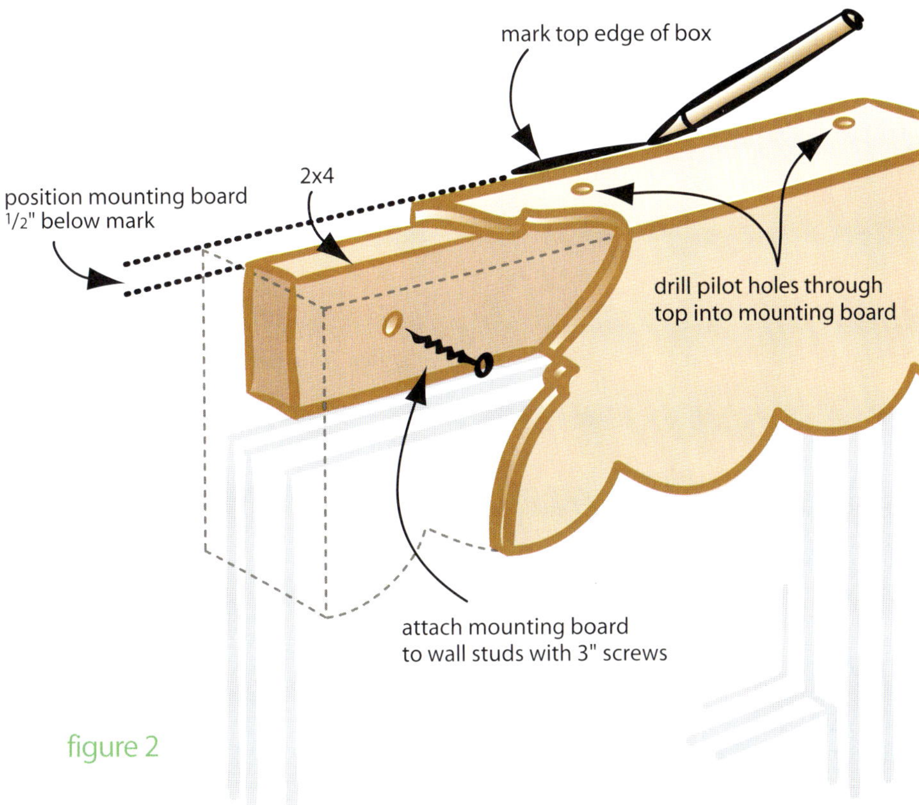

figure 2

4 Hold the cornice board above the window to find the desired placement. Lightly mark the top edge on the wall. Center the 2×4 over the window 1/2" below the mark, with the wide side of the board against the wall. Drill pilot holes through the 2×4 into the wall at the wall studs and install the mounting board with 3" screws. Center the cornice box on top of the mounting board, making sure the box is flush with the wall. Drill several pilot holes through the top of the box into the mounting board (see Figure 2). Remove the box.

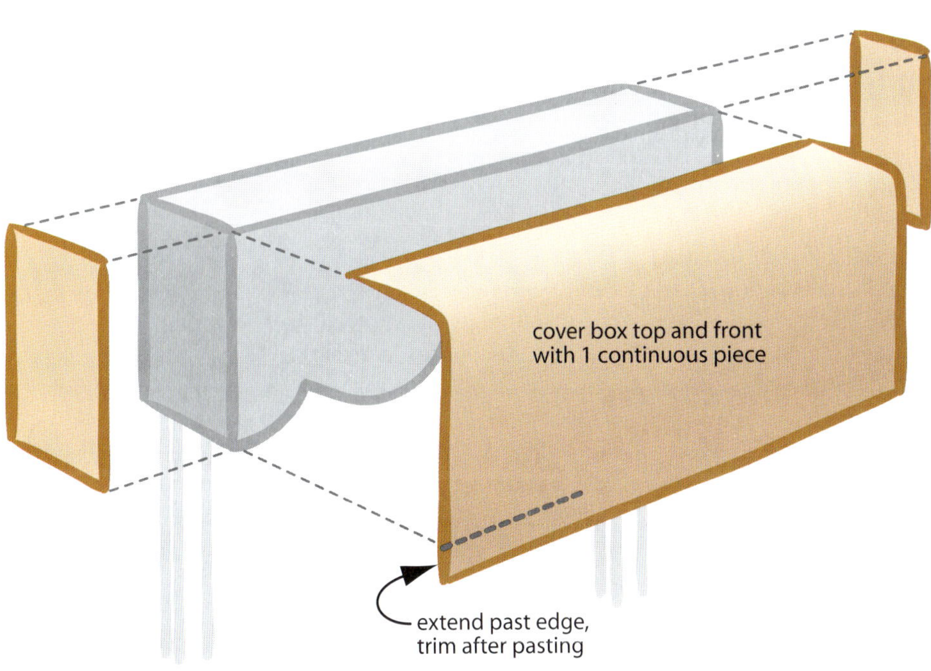

figure 3

5 Plan the wallpaper layout on the box. Arrange lengths of wallpaper to cover the box, wrapping the paper from the bottom front edge, up and across the top to the back edge in one continuous piece (see Figure 3). Do not cut the wallpaper to match the shaped lower edge of the box at this time. Match the pattern at the corners. Following the manufacturer's instructions, apply the paper to the box. Let the adhesive dry.

6 Trim the lower edge of the paper along the shaped edge of the box. Punch small holes through the paper at the pilo[illegible] on the box top. [illegible] braided edge of [illegible] trim to the shaped [illegible] covering the raw edg[illegible] the wallpaper.

making the hard cornice & soft shade (continued)

7 Cut the 1×2 to equal the measured window width. Center the board in the top of the cornice box with the wide edge against the box top (see Figure 4). Allow 2" at the back edge of the box. Measure 4" from each end of the 1×2 board. Drill pilot holes through the board into the box top, then remove the board from the cornice box. Divide the length of the board into 4 equal sections. Mark one point at the first and third dividers for screw eyes and drill one shallow pilot hole at each mark. Drill an additional pilot hole for a third screw eye 1" from the right end of the board. Set the board aside.

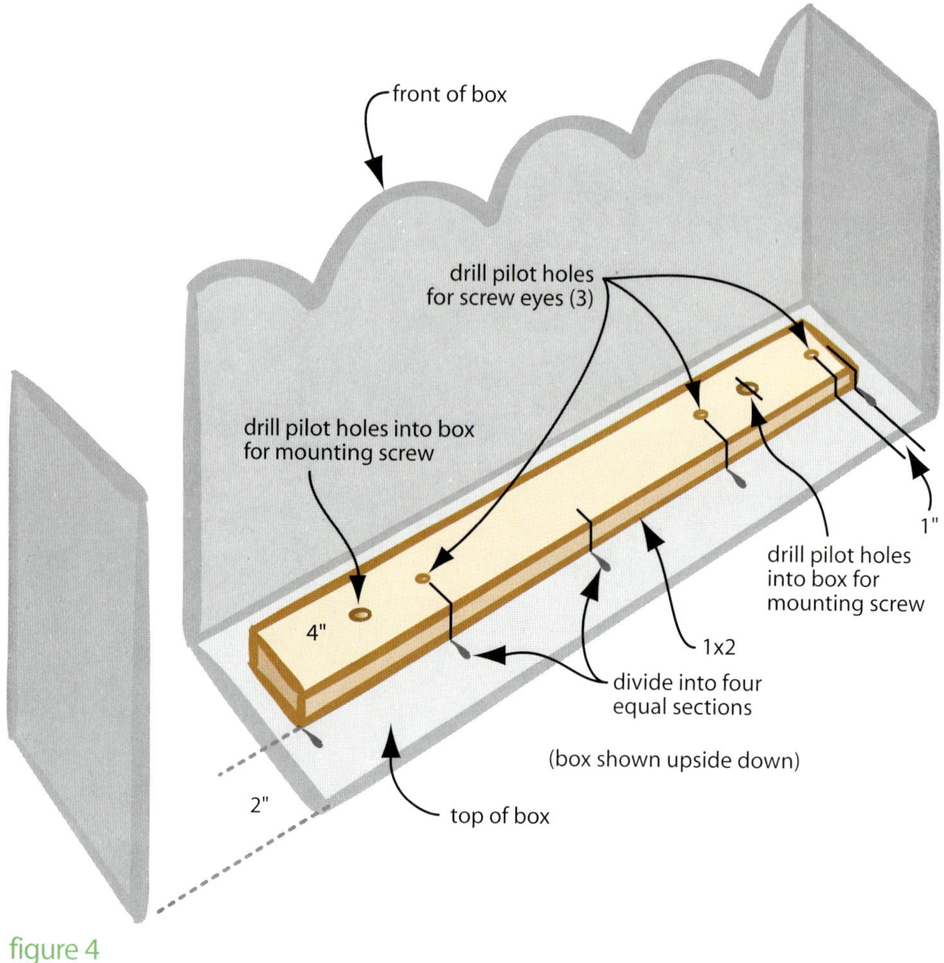

figure 4

8 Place the cleat on the right side of the window frame about midway between the top and bottom. The cleat holds the cords taut. If you have small children in your home, place the cleat closer to the top of the frame, lowering the risk of possible entanglement. Drill pilot holes in the frame. Mount the cleat with fasteners according to the manufacturer's instructions.

9 Measure the window length from the top of the 2×4 cornice mounting board to the windowsill and add 5". Measure the window frame from side to side and add 3". Trim the selvages off the fabric and lining. From the fabric, cut one front panel to this size. If necessary, stitch together fabric pieces to make one front panel to the required size. Be sure each piece starts at the same point in the fabric repeat.

10 For the lining panel, measure the window length from the top of the 2×4 mounting board to the windowsill and add 3". Measure the window frame from side to side. Trim the selvages off the lining. From the lining, cut one front panel to this size. If necessary, stitch together fabric pieces to make one front panel to the required size.

11 Lay the front panel right side up. Place the top edge of the lining 3" from the top edge of the front panel. Smooth the lining down the length of the panel. The lower edges will not align. Slide the lining to one side edge. Pin the edges together. Using a 1/2" seam allowance, stitch the front and the lining together on the pinned edge. Slide the lining to the opposite side edge of the front. Stitch the front and lining together in the same manner. Press the seams open.

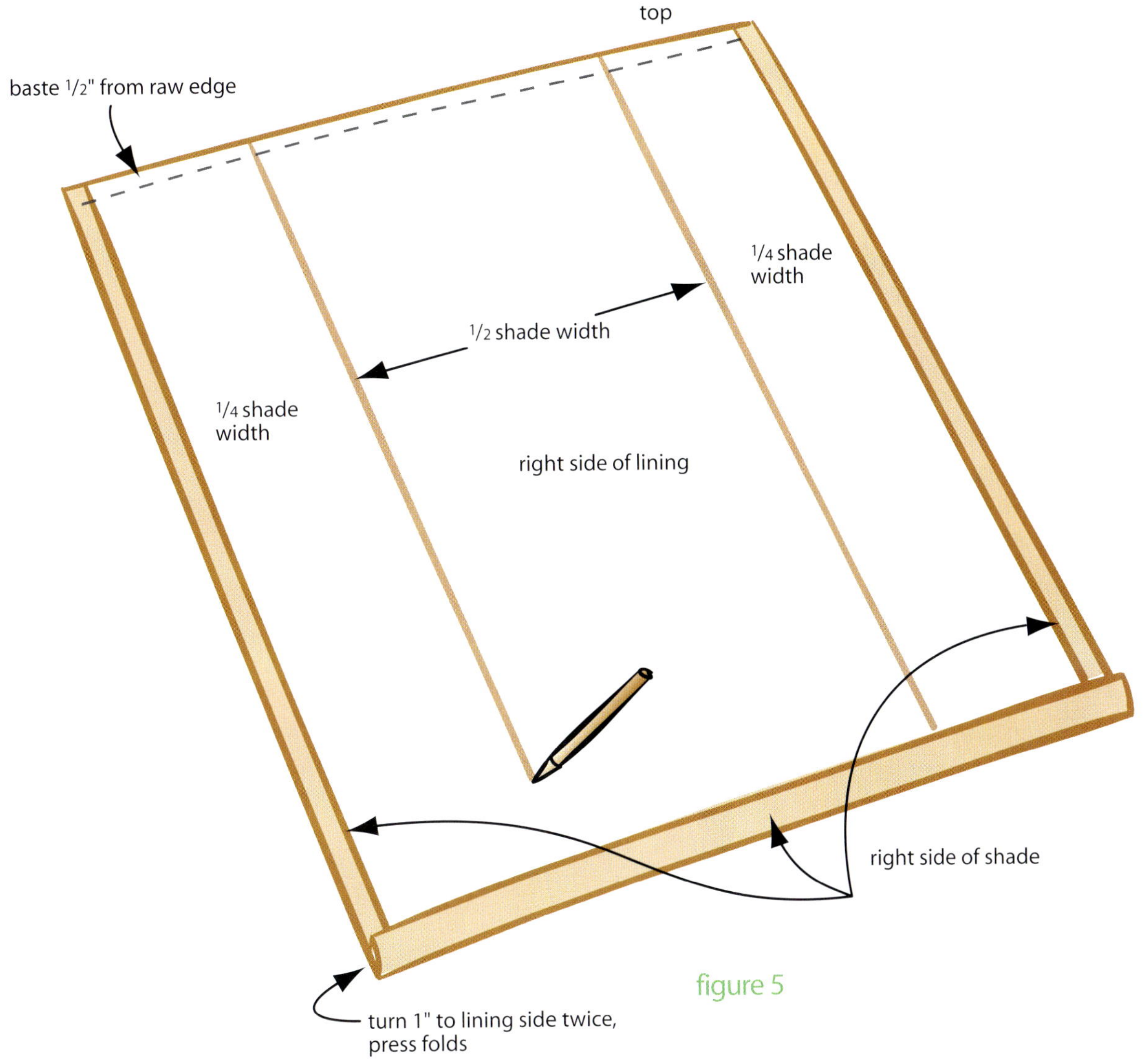

figure 5

12 Turn the panels to the right side. Lay the panel with the lining side up. Center the lining so there is 1" of shade fabric turned to the lining side on each side of the panel. Press the folds and seams. On the bottom edge, turn 1" to the lining side twice to make the hem. The raw edges of the front and lining will be enclosed in the hem. Press the folds. On the top edge, with wrong sides together and raw edges aligned, baste 1/2" from the raw edge to hold the layers together. On the lining side, measure and mark a line one-fourth the width of the shade from each side edge (see Figure 5).

making the hard cornice & soft shade (continued)

figure 6

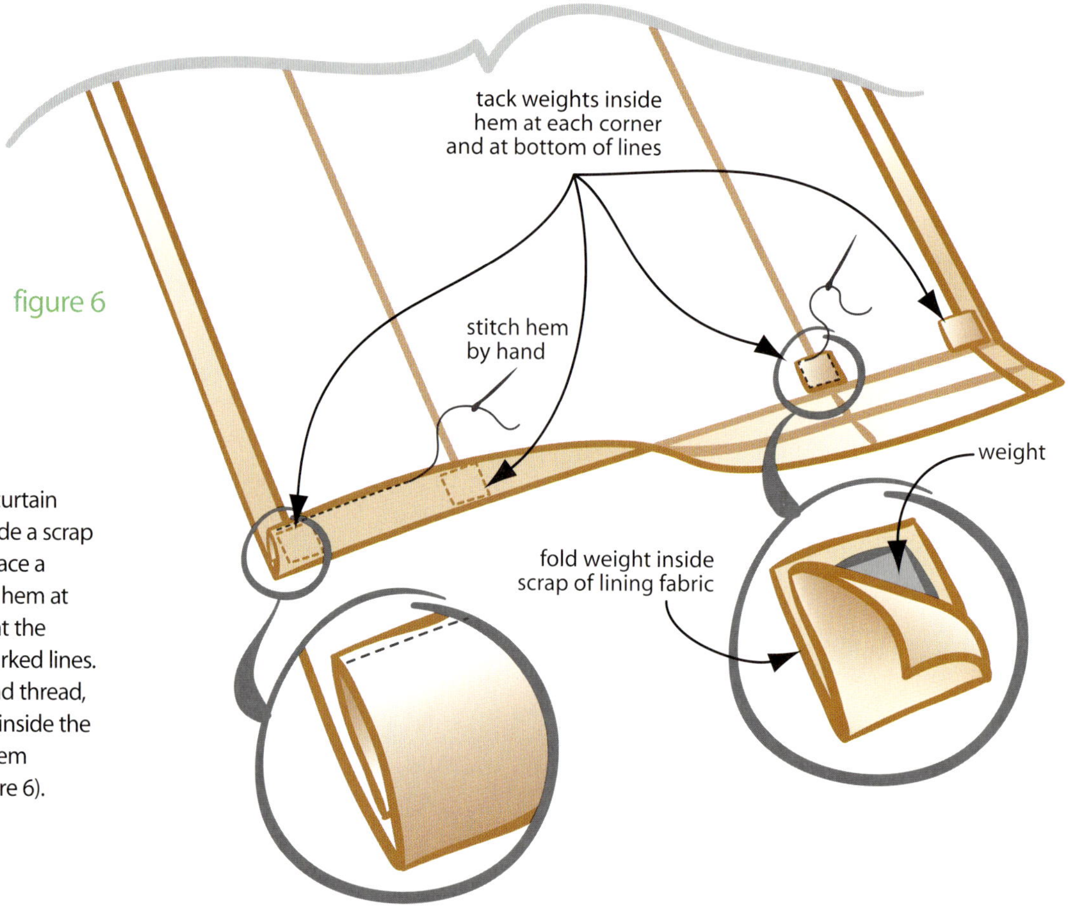

13 Fold each curtain weight inside a scrap of lining fabric. Place a weight inside the hem at each corner and at the bottom of the marked lines. Using a needle and thread, tack each weight inside the hem. Stitch the hem by hand (see Figure 6).

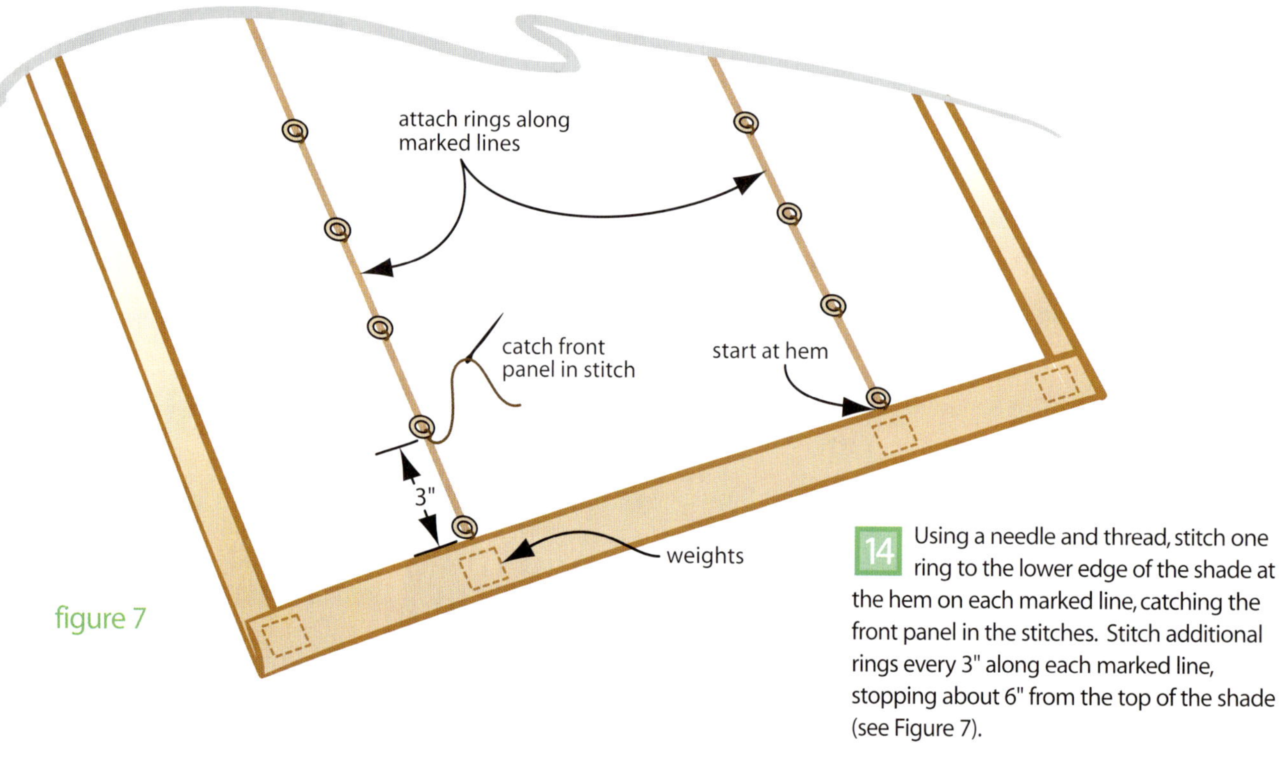

figure 7

14 Using a needle and thread, stitch one ring to the lower edge of the shade at the hem on each marked line, catching the front panel in the stitches. Stitch additional rings every 3" along each marked line, stopping about 6" from the top of the shade (see Figure 7).

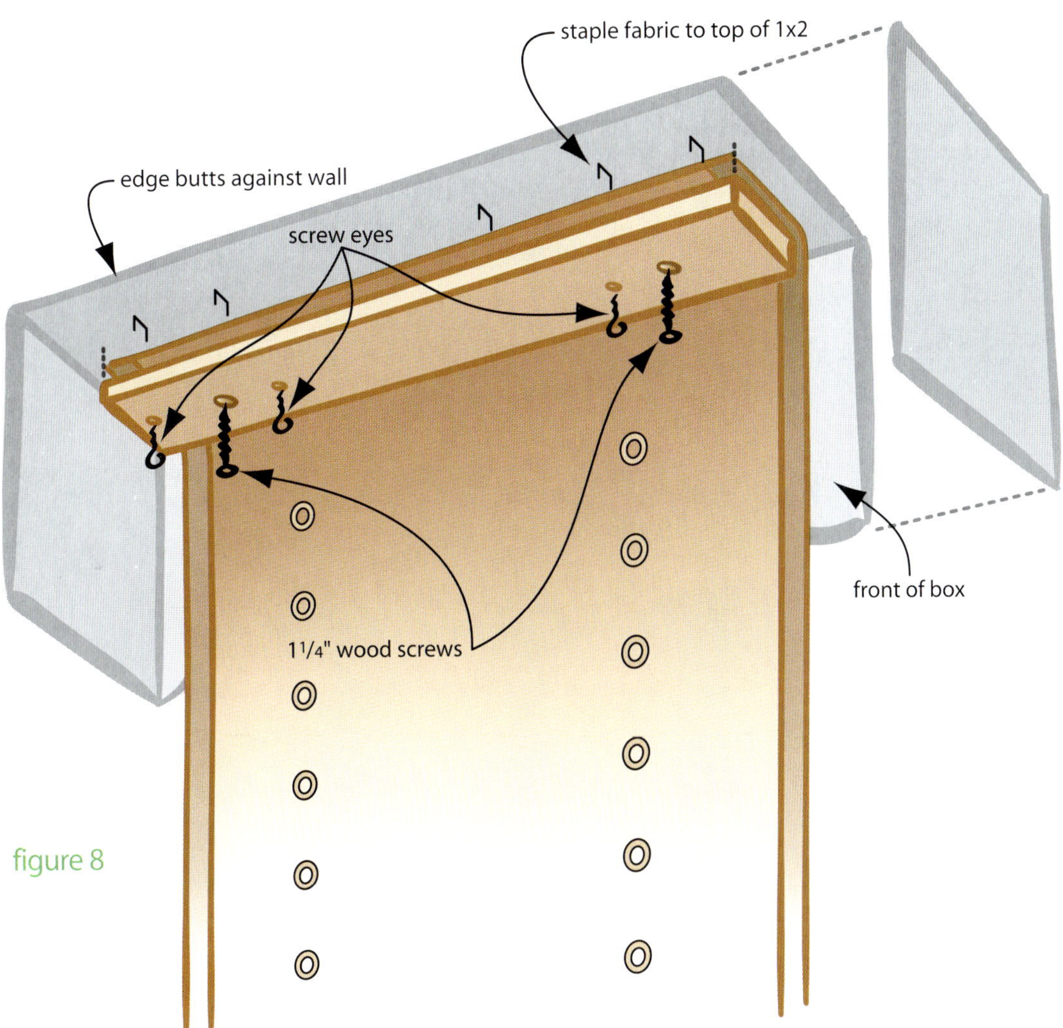

figure 8

15 Center the top edge of the shade, wrong side down, on the wide, top edge of the board with pilot holes. Staple the fabric to the board. Drop the fabric smoothly over the front edge of the board. Install the board inside the cornice box with 1 1/4" wood screws in the pilot holes. Install screw eyes in the remaining pilot holes (see Figure 8).

making the hard cornice & soft shade (continued)

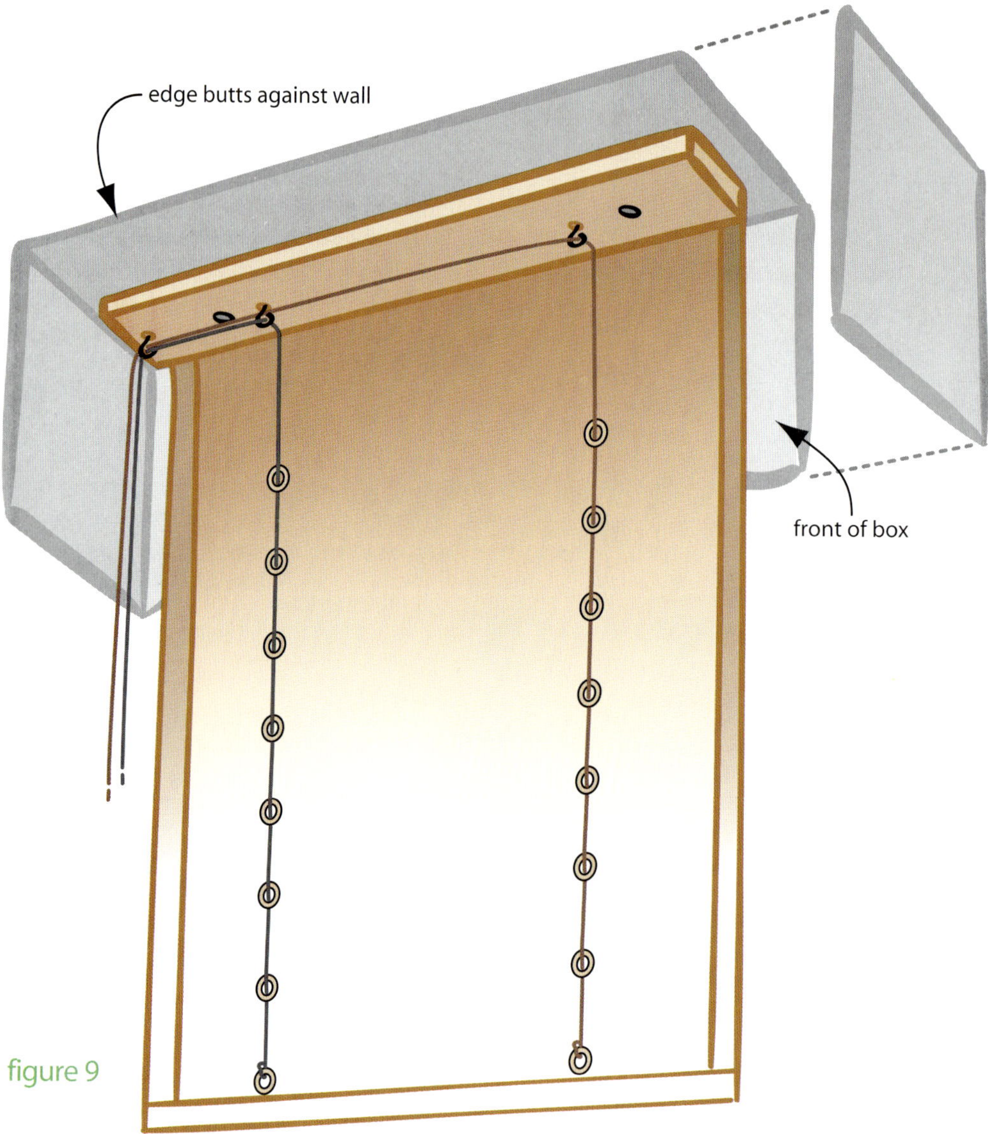

figure 9

16 Working from the back of the shade as shown in Figure 9, for the right cord, cut a length 2 times the measured shade length plus the measured width. Tie one end of the cord to the lowest ring on the right side of the shade. For the left cord, tie one end of the remaining length of cord to the lowest ring on the left side of the shade. Thread the cords through the column of rings and through the screw eye in the mounting board at the top of the column. Thread all cords through the extreme left screw eye (see Figure 9).

17 Place the cornice box on the mounting board. Install with 2" wood screws in the pilot holes. Pull the cords individually to take up slack. Trim the cord ends even. To raise the shade, gently pull the cords together, causing the fabric to gather. At the desired height, secure the cords to the cleat with a figure-eight motion. To dress the gathers, raise the shade to its highest position. Secure the cords and arrange the gathers by hand. After several weeks, the pleats will develop "memory" and will no longer need to be dressed by hand. If the outside edges of the shade need additional weight for a more defined drop, open the hem and insert additional curtain weights. Release the cords to raise and lower the shade as needed.

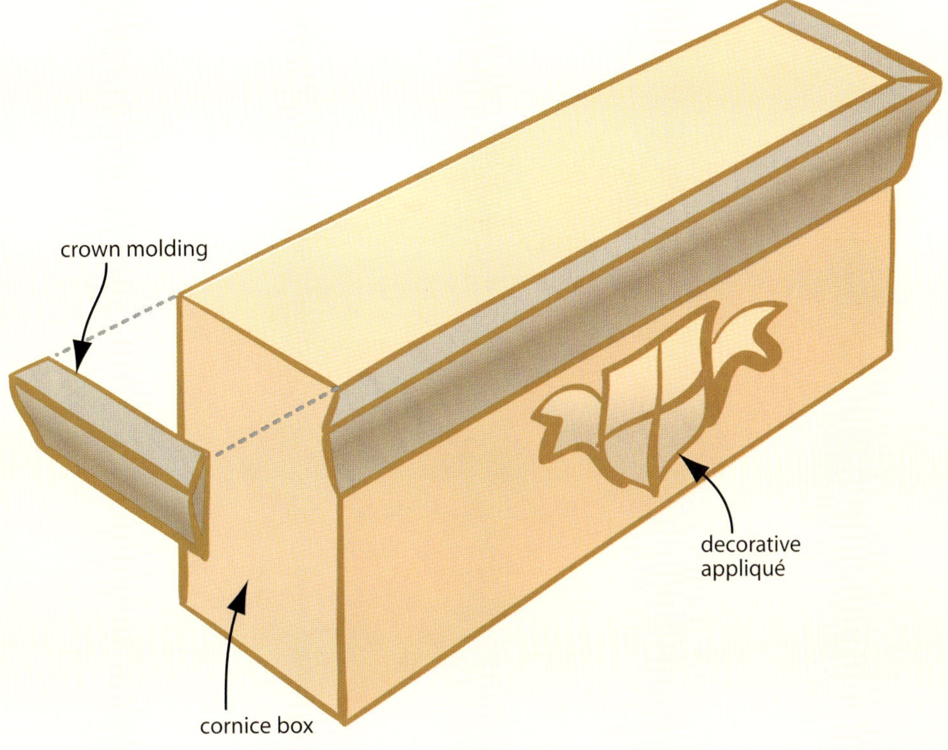

ARCHITECTURAL ACCENTS

Create architectural interest in your rooms with easy embellishments on a cornice box. In the bathroom on page 88, the cornice box was decorated to blend into the wall treatment to enhance the sense of space. You may also use a cornice box to punctuate the window and to underscore its importance in your room design.

■ To make the box a strong architectural accent, paint or stain it to match the existing moldings or trim in a room. This treatment instantly brings character to a newly constructed house or a boxy, blank apartment or condominium.

■ Choose 3/8" AA, AB, or AC interior plywood to build your box. The letter A identifies the plywood as having one face that is free of blemishes and appropriate for a stained or painted finish. The designation B or C tells you the opposite side of the plywood is of a lesser grade and contains some blemishes. Grade AA plywood is more expensive than AB or AC. If you plan to cover the wood with fabric or wallpaper, you can choose the most economical grade because the wood surface won't show. If your budget allows, shop for plywood made of wood other than pine, such as oak or birch.

■ Construct a plain box and add crown molding to the top edge. Use a miter box and backsaw to cut the crown molding on a 45-degree angle at the corners. Tack the molding to the box with 1" finishing nails. Cover the nail heads with latex caulk if you're going to paint the box. Fill the nail holes and gaps with wood filler, following the manufacturer's instructions, if you plan to use a stain.

■ To create even more architectural interest, glue decorative wood-like appliqués to the box. In a traditional room, accent the box with a wreath of laurel leaves, for example. These decorative cast-resin pieces are sold at crafts stores and hardware stores.

EL GRECO

In a formal living room, floor-length draperies topped by a deep, gathered valance offer a romantic variation on a traditional window treatment. The valance, hung from a shelf, functions like a cornice to hide the curtain's hardware and so might be considered a "soft cornice."

soft cornice

soft cornice

The fabric cornice is gathered at the corners for a look that's dressy but not fussy. This treatment softens the architecture and plays an important role in the room's palette of color and pattern. To let your draperies make the major pattern statement in the room, choose a large-scale floral, but make sure the repeat is small enough to fit the depth of the cornice. To blend the window treatment into the background, choose a mid-size floral, a small check, or a plain woven fabric.

SOFT CORNICE VARIATION

■ If gathers are not your style, consider pleats for a more tailored look. Make a newspaper pattern to help you work out the placement of the pleats. Cut out the fabric and lining, adding a ½" seam allowance all around. Add interlining or interfacing to the wrong side of the fabric (see page 81 for more information). Stitch the edges together. Turn the cornice to the right side and close the ends. Fold the pleats and tack them in place. Apply the loop half of hook-and-loop fastening tape to the lining side at the top edge and mount as directed on pages 100–103.

materials

54"-wide decorator fabric
Lining fabric
Pencil-style pleating tape
⅞"-wide hook-and-loop tape
1×4 pine board
Newspaper
2 (4") inside corner braces
4 (2") No. 8 wood screws
4 (3/4") No. 8 wood screws
Adjustable rod with mounting brackets and hardware

tools

Small plate or bowl
Jigsaw
Electric drill and drill bits
Pushpins

sewing tools

Sewing machine
Iron and ironing board
Tape measure
Pins
Scissors

skill level: advanced
time required: 2 days

making the soft cornice:

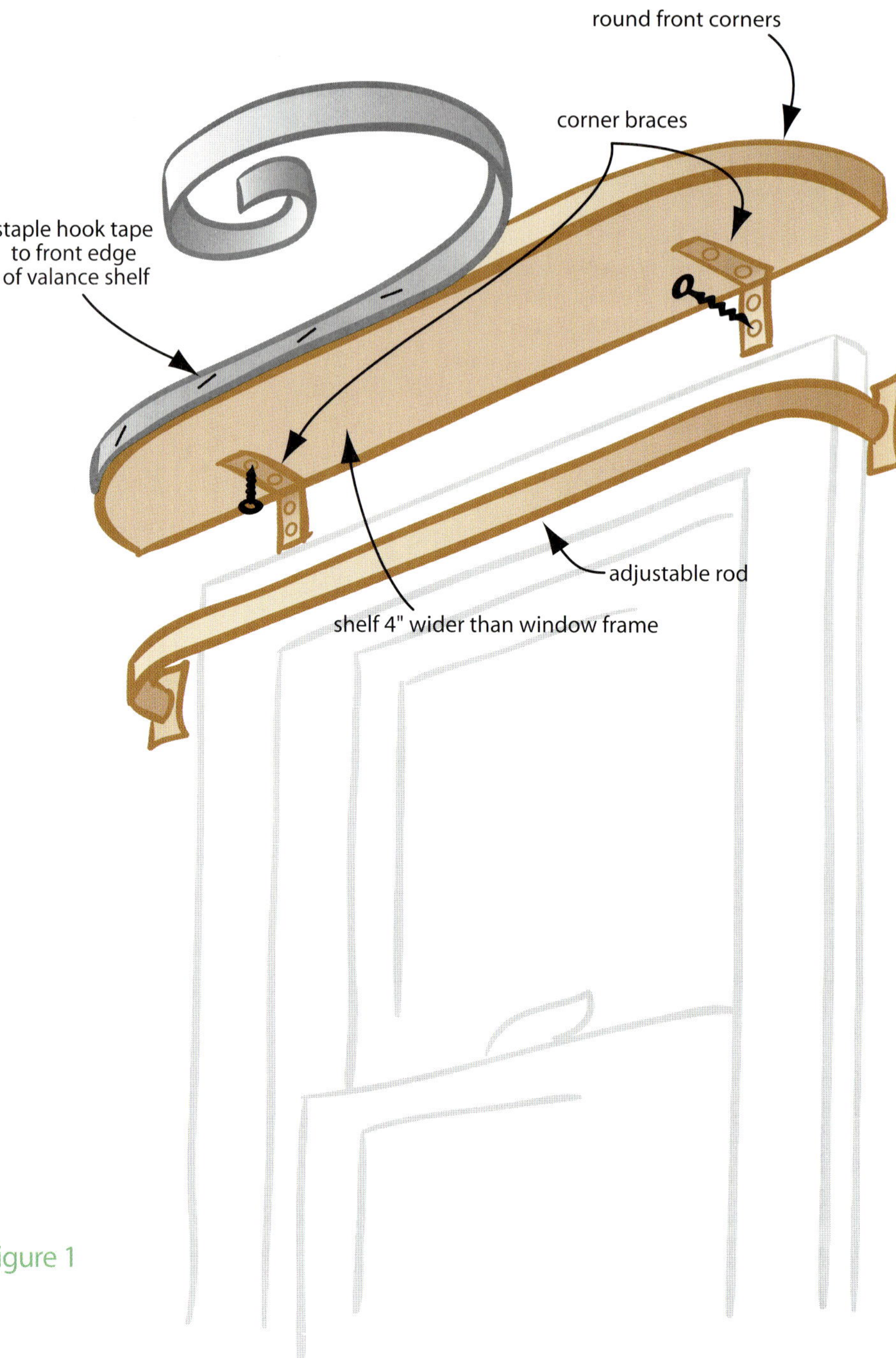

figure 1

1 Measure the window width outside the frame. Install the corner braces above the window into a stud using long screws. Cut the 1×4 to the measured width plus 4". Using a small plate or bowl as a template, draw round corners on one long side. Cut on the marked line with a jigsaw. Center the board on top of the braces (see Figure 1). Drill pilot holes in the board to attach it to the braces, and secure it with short screws. Measure the front edge of the shelf from wall to wall and cut the hook side of the fastener tape to this length. Staple the hook tape to the front edge of the shelf. Install the adjustable rod below the shelf and outside the window frame. Measure the length of the loop side of the fastener tape against the front edge of the shelf. Cut it to this length and set it aside.

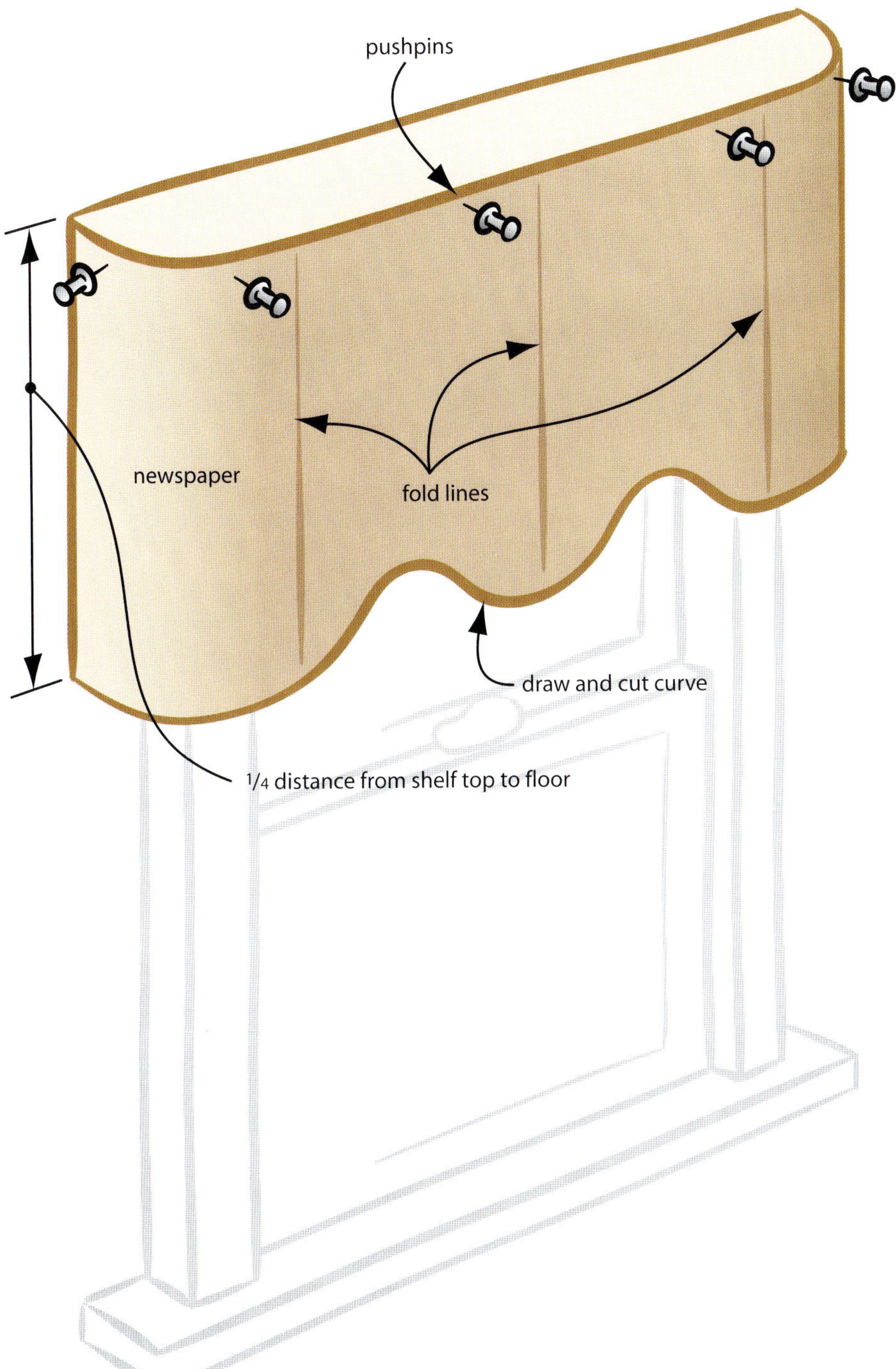

figure 2

2 Measure from the top of the valance shelf to the floor and divide by 4. Cut a piece of newspaper to this depth and as wide as the front edge of the valance shelf measures from wall to wall. Fold the paper in half, matching the short ends, then fold in half again in the same direction. Open the second fold. With scissors, cut a curve from the center of the paper to the second fold. Open the paper. Use pushpins to tack the newspaper pattern to the front edge of the valance shelf (see Figure 2). Step back to view the shape. Adjust and cut a new pattern if desired.

3 Trim the selvages from the fabric and lining. Measure the depth of the final newspaper pattern and add 1" for the cut length of the soft cornice. Multiply the measurement of the front edge of shelf by $2^1/_2$ for the cut width of the cornice. From the fabric and lining, cut enough lengths to make up the required width. Be sure each piece starts at same point in the fabric repeat. Use the full fabric width for the center panel. Seam half-widths of fabric to each side of the center, matching pattern repeats.

making the soft cornice (continued)

figure 3

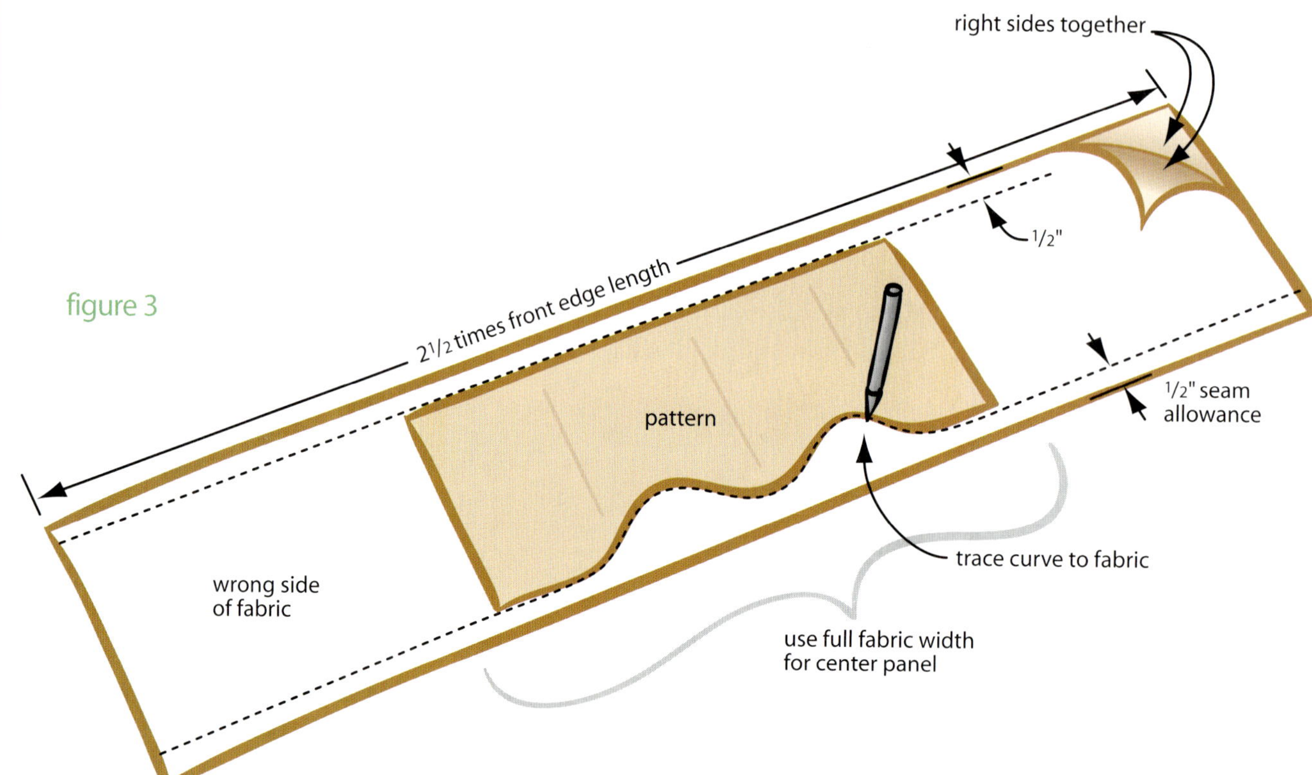

4 With right sides together, stack the fabric and lining with the fabric on top. Find the center and place the newspaper pattern on the fabric, aligning the center fold in the paper with the center of the fabric width and leaving $^1/_2$" at the top and bottom edges. Trace the curved edge onto the fabric (see Figure 3). Beginning at one edge, stitch the fabric and lining together along the lower edge, using a $^1/_2$" seam allowance. When the seam line meets the marked curve, stitch along the marked curve. Return to a $^1/_2$" seam allowance at the end of the curve. Trim the seam allowance along the curve to $^1/_2$". Clip the seam allowance to the stitching in the curves. Use a $^1/_2$" seam allowance to stitch the top edges together. Press both seams open.

5 Turn the cornice to the right side. Place the seams on the edge and press flat. On each open end, turn under the lining and fabric $^1/_2$". Press. Edgestitch through all layers, closing the cornice.

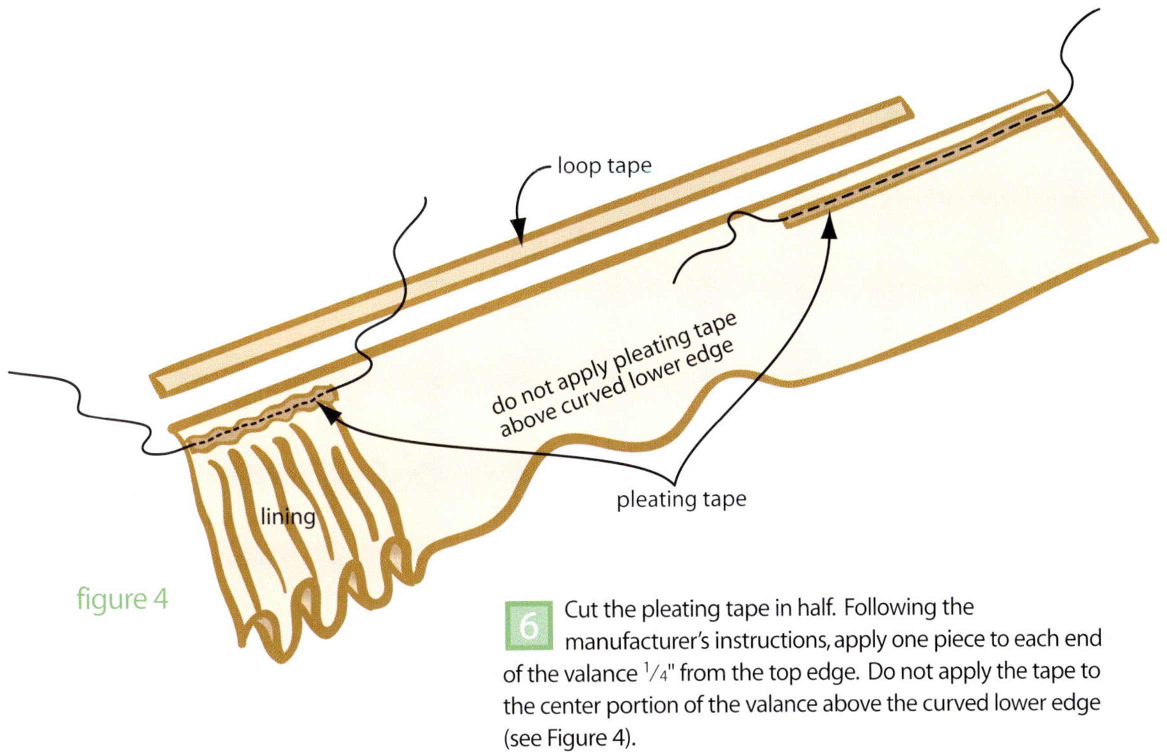

figure 4

6 Cut the pleating tape in half. Following the manufacturer's instructions, apply one piece to each end of the valance 1/4" from the top edge. Do not apply the tape to the center portion of the valance above the curved lower edge (see Figure 4).

7 Matching the center of the loop tape with the center top of the valance, pin the loop tape to the top of the cornice 1/4" from the edge. Pull up the cords in each side to fit the fabric to the loop tape. Tie off the cords. Using a needle and thread, stitch the loop tape to the cornice on each long edge. To install the soft cornice, press the hook-and-loop tapes together.

8 For the curtains, cut 2 front panels from fabric for each window; each panel should equal the window's measured height plus 10" by the measured width plus 3". Be sure each piece starts at same point in the fabric repeat. From the lining fabric, cut 2 panels for each window that are the measured height plus 4" by the measured width. If necessary, seam together fabric lengths and lining lengths to make up the required width.

9 Lay each front panel right side up. Place the lining right side down with the top edge of the lining 3" from the top edge of the panel. Smooth the lining down the length of the panel. If necessary, trim the lining 2" narrower than the front panel. Slide the lining to one side edge. Measure and mark 8" from the top edge and 12" from the bottom edge. Using a 1/2" seam allowance, stitch the front and lining together between the marks. Slide the lining to the opposite edge of the curtain front and repeat. Press the seams open.

10 Turn the curtain to the right side and lay the curtain lining side up. Center the lining so there is 1" of curtain fabric turned to the lining side on each side of lining. Press the folds and seams.

11 Turn the top edge of the lining back away from the curtain front. Turn the front under 4", folding the sides at angles. Press. Turn under the side edges of the lining 1/2" (above the top 8" of the stitching). Turn under the top edge of the lining 1 1/4". Press. Using a needle and thread, stitch the lining to the curtain front along all folded edges by hand. Also stitch the angle folds.

12 At the top corners of each curtain panel, insert curtain pins into the heading. Evenly space the remaining pins along the width of the curtain. Hang the hook portion of the pins on the rod.

13 Turn under the curtain hem so the edge meets the floor. Pin. Remove the curtains from the rod. Press the fold, then open it. Keeping the lining edge free, measure 6" from the fold and trim the excess from the curtain front. Turn under the raw edge of the curtain front to meet the fold. Press. Refold the hem, making angle folds at the ends like those at the curtain top. Hemstitch the folded edge.

14 Turn under the lining so it is 1" shorter than the curtain front. Press. Measure 2" from the fold and trim the excess. Turn under the raw edge to meet the crease. Turn under the lining's lower, unstitched side edges 1/2". Press. Working from the wrong side, edgestitch the hem close to the folded edge. Using a needle and thread, stitch the lining and curtain together below the side seams. Replace the curtains on the rod.

B Z

Bay windows add light, character, and a sense of spaciousness to a room, but they also can pose a decorating challenge. What is the best way to make the most of the panoramic view by day and create a cocoon at night? For traditional settings, curtains with a valance provide an elegant solution.

bay window

Framing each window with its own pair of curtains creates intimacy and softens the room by day. A shirred valance on a continuous valance shelf unifies the treatment and accents the architecture. Tassel fringe and cord emphasize the details of the valance, which conceals the curtains' traverse rods.

Choose a companion fabric to line the valance. Here, the flirty curved edge reveals a bit of the valance lining at each pleat. For lining or backing the panels, stay with traditional white or ivory curtain lining—from the outside, it will tend to disappear, so it won't detract from your home's curb appeal.

dressing a bay window:

materials

54"-wide decorator fabric
54"-wide contrast fabric
54"-wide lining fabric
Tassel fringe
Cord
1×4 pine boards
6 (4") inside corner braces
12 (2") No. 8 wood screws
12 (3/4") No. 8 wood screws
Finishing nails (dark color)
3 two-way traverse rods

tools

Electric drill and drill bits
Handsaw
Push pins
Staple gun and 1/4" staples

sewing tools

Sewing machine
Iron and ironing board
Pins
Tape measure
Fabric marking pen or pencil
Needle
Thread

skill level: advanced
time required: 2 1/2 days

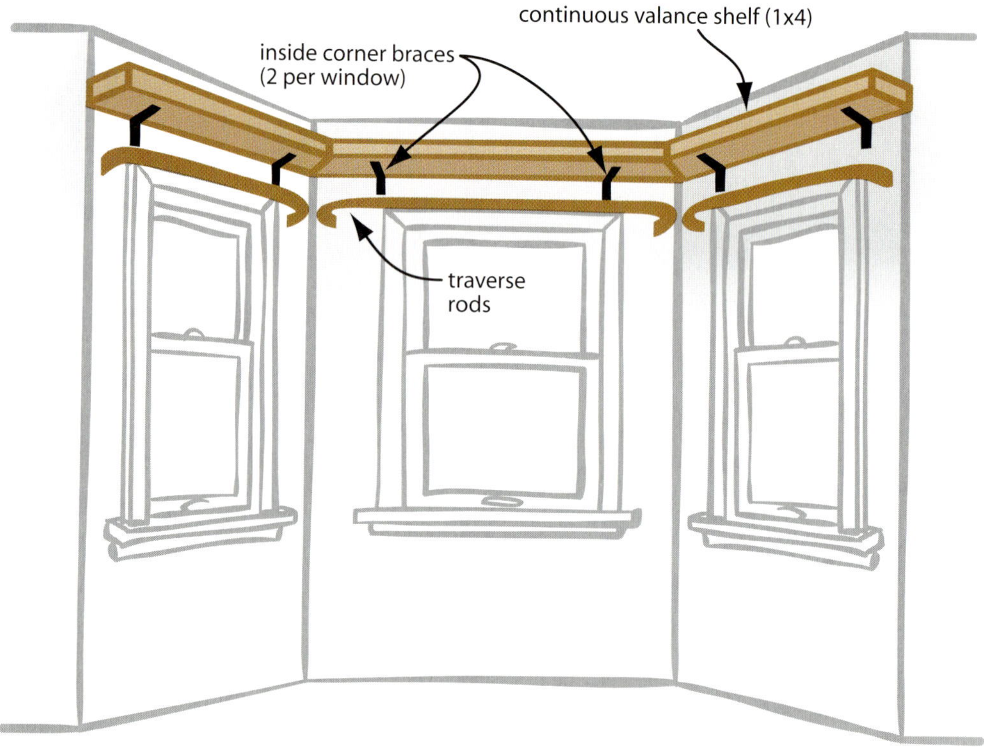

figure 1

1 Plan for the 1×4 boards to span the windows and the sections of wall between the windows as a continuous valance shelf. The boards will meet in the corners of the bay. Install 2 inside corner braces above each window with 2" screws. Place the 1×4 boards on top of the corner braces; the ends of the boards should just meet (see Figure 1). Mark and cut the ends if necessary. Drill pilot holes through the corner braces into the boards and attach with 3/4" screws. For the traverse rods, measure the width of each window, including the wall sections that are part of the bay. Mount the traverse rods outside the window frames. Position the rods end to end so the panels in the corners of the bay will appear as one.

2 Measure the width of the bay by measuring the front edge of the valance shelf, including the return. If working with solid or miniprint fabrics, multiply the measurement by 2 for the required width of the valance panel. Measure from the top of the valance shelf to the floor. Divide the measurement by 4 to find the finished length of the valance. The valance must be at least 8". Trim the selvages off the fabric and contrast fabric. Cut enough fabric lengths to make the required fullness. Be sure each piece starts at the same point in the fabric repeat. Using a 1/2" seam allowance, stitch the lengths together, matching the pattern repeat. To create a special effect with the placement of a motif or stripe in the fabric as was done in this valance, purchase enough fabric to cut 1 or 2 additional lengths to add to the valance width if needed.

3 The valance has 1 pleat at the center of each window and at each inside corner and outside corner of the bay. Divide the valance shelf into 8 sections (see Figure 2). Sections A and H are the return sections. Sections B, C, D, E, F, and G begin and end at the center of a pleat. Measure the length of each section.

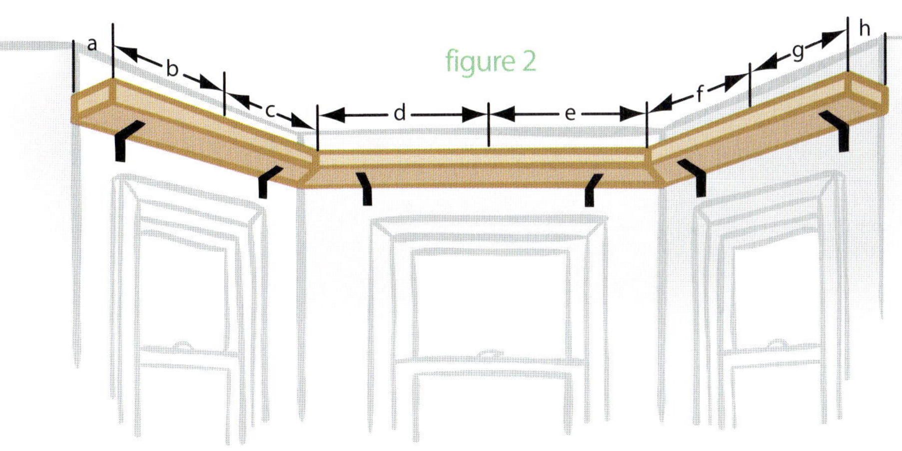

figure 2

mark center of each pleat

valance

match pattern motif to center of pleat

lining

2a 2b 2c 2d 2e 2f 2g 2h

measure 2 times the length of each section

figure 3

4 Stack the lining and valance front, right sides together, with the valance front on top. Note the upper edge of the valance. On the wrong side of the valance front, measure 2 times the length of each section. Mark the center of each pleat (see Figure 3). To emphasize a motif or stripe in the fabric by placing the motif at the center of the pleat, shift the entire pattern. It may be necessary to cut and seam additional valance lengths to each end in order to achieve the desired placement of motifs.

a b c d e f g h

6" from lower edge

trim lower edge of valance and lining along curve

figure 4

5 Draw a line from the marks for the centers of the pleats to the lower edge of the valance. At each mark, measure 6" into the valance from the lower edge. Draw a curve from the raw edge to the 6" mark and back to the raw edge (see Figure 4). This curve makes a scallop-like wave in the lower edge at each pleat. Make all curves uniform. Trim the lower edge of the valance and lining along the marked curves.

6 With the right sides together and using a ½" seam allowance, stitch the lower edges of the valance and lining together. Clip the curves. Stitch the upper edges together and press the seams open. Turn the valance to the right side. Place the seams on the edge. Press flat. On each end, turn under the valance and lining ½". Press. Edgestitch through all layers, closing the valance.

7 Measure the tassel fringe against the lower edge of the valance and add 2". Apply ravel preventer to the braid portion of the fringe. Let dry. Cut the fringe through the ravel preventer. Apply more ravel preventer to the cut ends. Turn under 1" at each end. Topstitch the fringe to the lower edge of the valance. Be sure to stitch both edges of the braid in the same direction.

8 On the sewing machine, loosen the upper thread tension and set a long stitch length. On a scrap of fabric and lining, stacked together, test gathering stitches and pull the bobbin thread to gather. Measure 1" from the top edge of the valance. Beginning and ending at the marked center of the pleats, stitch a line of gathering stitches. Leave long tails of thread when starting and stopping. Stitch a second line of gathering stitches in the same manner ⅜" from the top edge that is parallel to the first line. Pull the bobbin threads in both lines of stitching together to draw up the fabric.

dressing a bay window (continued)

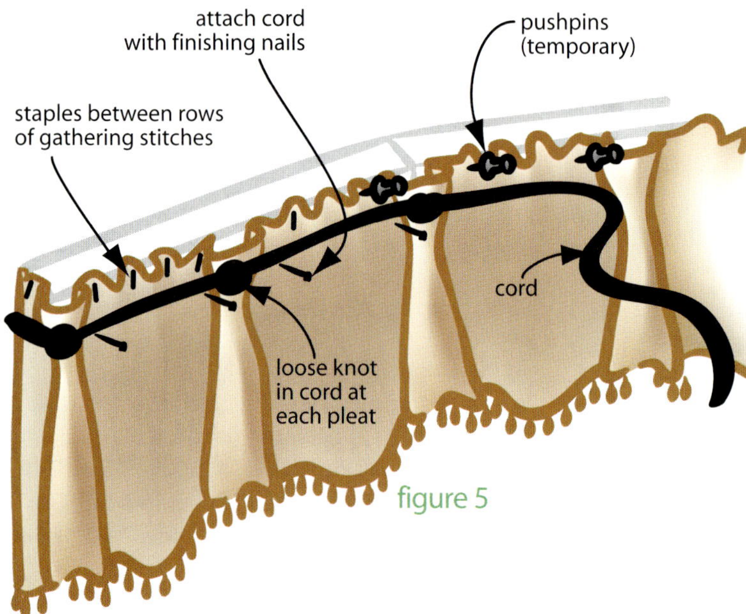

figure 5

9 Adjust the gathers and shape the inverted pleats by hand. Fit the valance to the shelf. Temporarily hold the valance in place with pushpins on the front edge of the shelf as you work. Staple the valance to the shelf between rows of gathering stitches. Apply ravel preventer to the ends of the cord. Use finishing nails to tack the cord to the valance over the gathers and staples. Make loose knots in cord at each pleat (see Figure 5).

10 For the curtains, measure the window height from the top of the rod to the floor. Add 10" to the measured height to find the cut length of the front panels. Measure the width of each individual window against the traverse rod, including the return at each end of the rod. From the fabric, cut 2 front panels for each window that are the measured height plus 10" and as wide as the measured width plus 3". Be sure each piece starts at same point in the fabric repeat. From the lining, cut 2 panels for each window that are the measured height plus 4" and as wide as the measured width. If necessary, seam together fabric lengths and lining lengths to make up the required width.

11 Lay each front panel right side up. Place the top edge of the lining 3" from the top edge of the panel. Smooth the lining down the length of the panel. If necessary, trim the lining so it is 1" narrower on both sides than the front panel. Slide the lining to one side edge. Measure and mark 8" from the top edge and 12" from the bottom edge. Using a ½" seam allowance, stitch the front and lining together between the marks. Slide the lining to the opposite edge of the curtain front. Stitch the front and lining together in the same manner. Press the seams open.

12 Turn the curtain to the right side. Lay the curtain lining side up. Center the lining over the curtain front so there is 1" of curtain fabric turned to the lining side. Press the folds and seams.

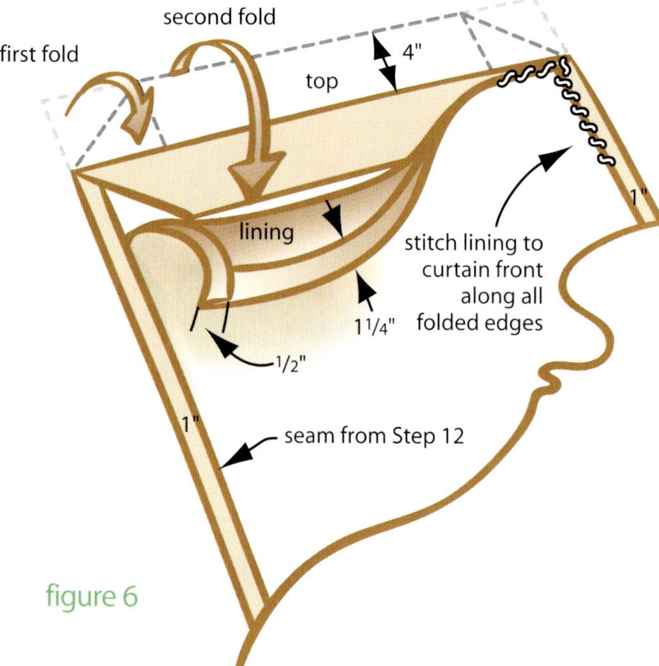

figure 6

13 Turn the top edge of the lining back away from each curtain front. Turn the curtain fronts under 4", folding the sides at angles. Press. Turn under the side edges of the lining ½". Turn under the top edges of the lining 1¼". Press. Using a needle and thread, stitch the lining to the curtain fronts along all folded edges (see Figure 6). Also stitch the angle folds of the curtain fronts.

14 Measure the upper edge of the curtain. From the leading edge of the curtain, measure and mark 2". Divide the remaining width into 10 equal segments. If you are making curtains for a narrow window and segments are less than 5" each, divide the remaining width into 8 equal segments. (This will reduce the number of pleats.) At each mark, draw a line 4" into the curtain. Beginning at the 2" segment on the leading edge, mark every other segment: These will stay flat. The segments between those marked are cartridge pleats (see Figure 7).

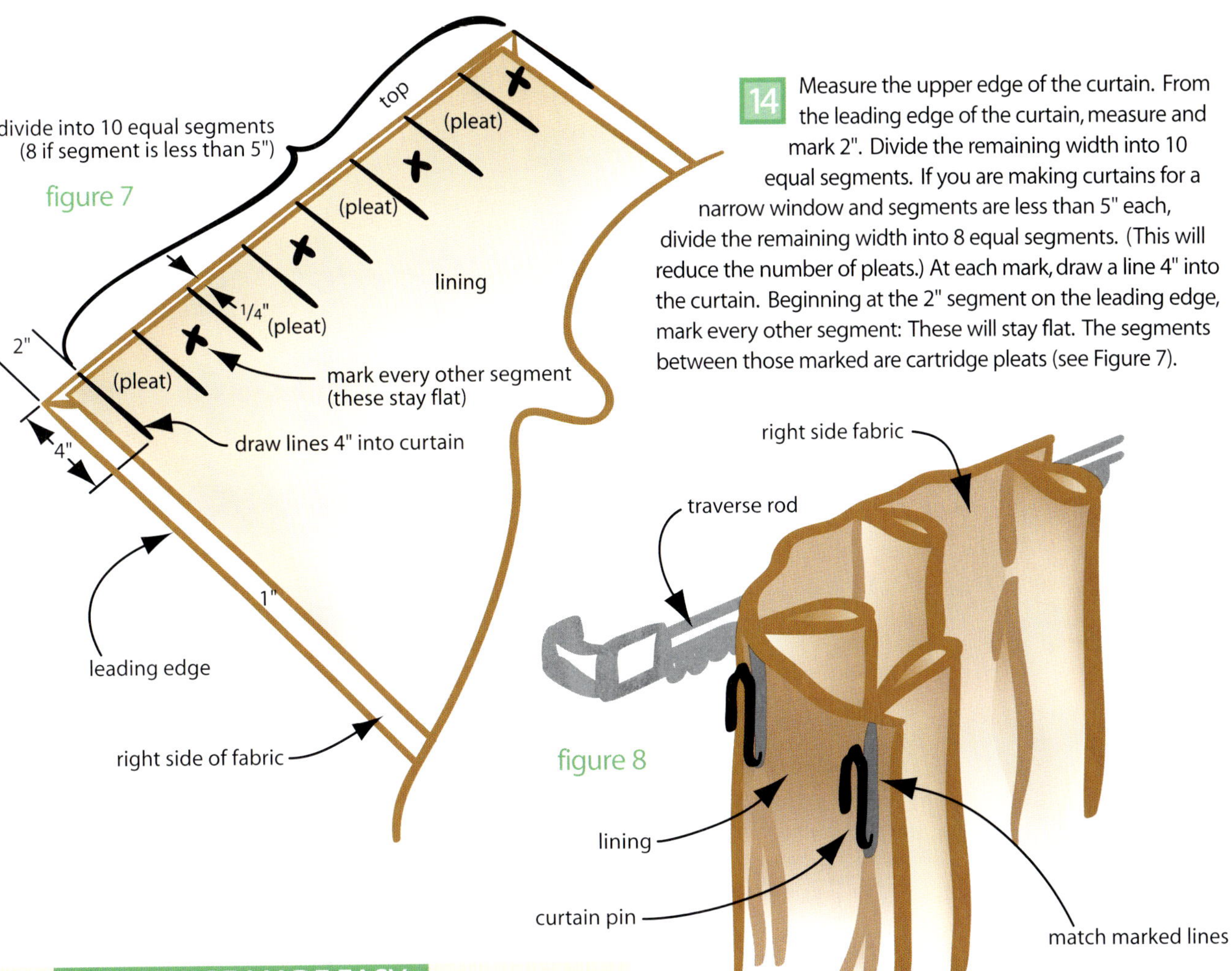

figure 7

figure 8

HARDWARE MADE EASY

decorative traverse rod

pull mechanism hidden behind decorative front

traverse rods move curtains by a pull mechanism across the window. Two-way draw traverse rods split a pair of curtains at the window center to move to each side. One-way draw rods pull a single panel to one side of the window. Follow the instructions provided by the manufacturer for easy installation of these rods.

Originally, traverse rods looked utilitarian, like adjustable rods. Decorative traverse rods are now on the market. Some look like brass cafe rods with rings; others resemble wood poles and rings. The pull mechanisms are hidden on the backside of a decorative front.

15 Fold each pleat, matching the marked lines. Topstitch through all layers at the lines (see Figure 8). Insert curtain pins into the back of each pleat and at the top corners of each curtain. Adjust the placement of the curtain pins so the top edge of the curtain will conceal the traverse rod. Hang the hook portion of the pins through the carriers on the rod.

16 Turn under the curtain front hem so the edge meets the floor. Pin. Remove the curtains from the rod. Keep the lining edge free. Press the fold, then open it. Measure 6" from the fold and trim the excess. Turn under the raw edge of the curtain front to meet the crease for the hem. Press. Refold the hem, making angle folds at the ends similar to those at the curtain top. Hemstitch the folded edge.

17 Turn under the lining to be 1" shorter than the curtain front. Press. Measure 2" from the fold and trim the excess. Turn under the raw edge to meet the crease. Turn under the side edges ½". Press. Working from the wrong side, edgestitch the hem close to the folded edge. Using a needle and thread, stitch the lining and curtain together below the side seams. Replace the curtains on the rod.

18 Follow the manufacturer's instructions to set up the cords on the traverse rods. To open and close the curtains, pull the cords.

If you think elegant jabots and graceful swag valances are more than you and your sewing machine can accomplish, think again. You can create this lavish, formal window treatment by breaking the project down into three easy components. The swags consist of three panels, and fanlike flags conceal the joinings. Self-pleating tapes ensure perfect curtain headings.

swag & jabot valance

The swag and jabot valance is actually a series of smaller pleated sections. Three panels make up the front or swag portion of the valance. The fanlike jabots and jabot tails are separate sections edged with welting made from the same fabric as the jabots themselves.

The curtains are made using self-pleating tape. This is a lightweight, sheer tape with several rows of draw cords. Sew the tape to the back side of your lined panel, and then pull up the cords. Tie off the cord ends to hold the pleats in place.

To adapt this arrangement of valance and curtains to your window, first make the curtains. Their finished look will help you scale the valance to the window properly. Next, work with large sheets of tissue paper to create a full-size paper valance. This way, you can adjust the proportions of the valance without the expense of working with fabric. For the best effect, choose a crisp polished cotton, chintz, or other smooth-finish decorator fabric for this project.

In the bedroom opposite, floor-length curtains with the swagged valance impart a feeling of grandeur. It's an equally good treatment for a living room or dining room.

materials

54"-wide decorator fabric
54"-wide lining fabric
54"-wide interlining
Pleating tape
Curtain pins
Adjustable rod with mounting hardware

tools

Electric drill and drill bits

sewing tools

Sewing machine
Iron and ironing board
Scissors
Tape measure
Pins
Thread
Liquid ravel preventer

skill level: advanced
time required: 1 1/2 days

making curtains with pleating tape:

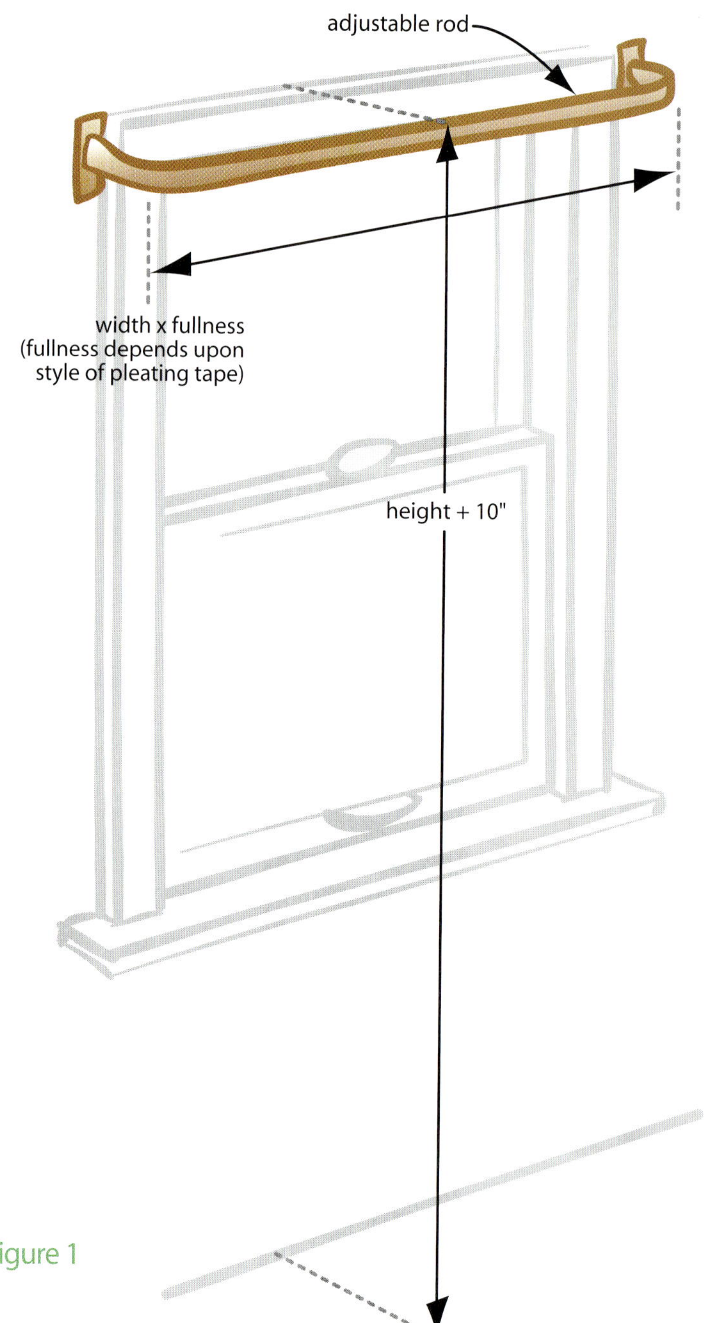

figure 1

1 Measure the width of the window frame from the outside edges. Mount the rod just outside the window frame, then measure the window height from the top of the rod to the floor (see Figure 1). Add 10" to the measured height to find the cut length of the front panels. To determine the width, first choose the style of pleating tape to be used: Each has different requirements regarding the width of the curtain panel (see page 115 for more information). It may be necessary to seam together fabric lengths to achieve the required fullness. Also consider the length of the fabric repeat in calculating yardage requirements.

2 Trim the selvages from the fabric, interlining, and lining. For each pair of curtains, cut 2 front panels from the curtain fabric the measured window length plus 10". Begin each piece at the same point in the fabric repeat. From the interlining, cut 2 panels the measured window length. From the lining, cut 2 panels the measured window length plus 4". If covering a wide window, cut additional panels of each fabric to seam together for the required width.

3 Lay each front panel flat, wrong side up. Place the top edge of one interlining panel 3" from the top edge of the front panel. Smooth the interlining down the length of the panel. If necessary, trim the width of the interlining so that it is 1½" narrower on each side than the front panel (see Figure 2). Using a needle and thread, tack the interlining to the curtain front. Take tiny stitches that are barely visible on the right side of the fabric and space the stitches 4" to 6" apart. Do not tack the last 12" of interlining to the curtain front.

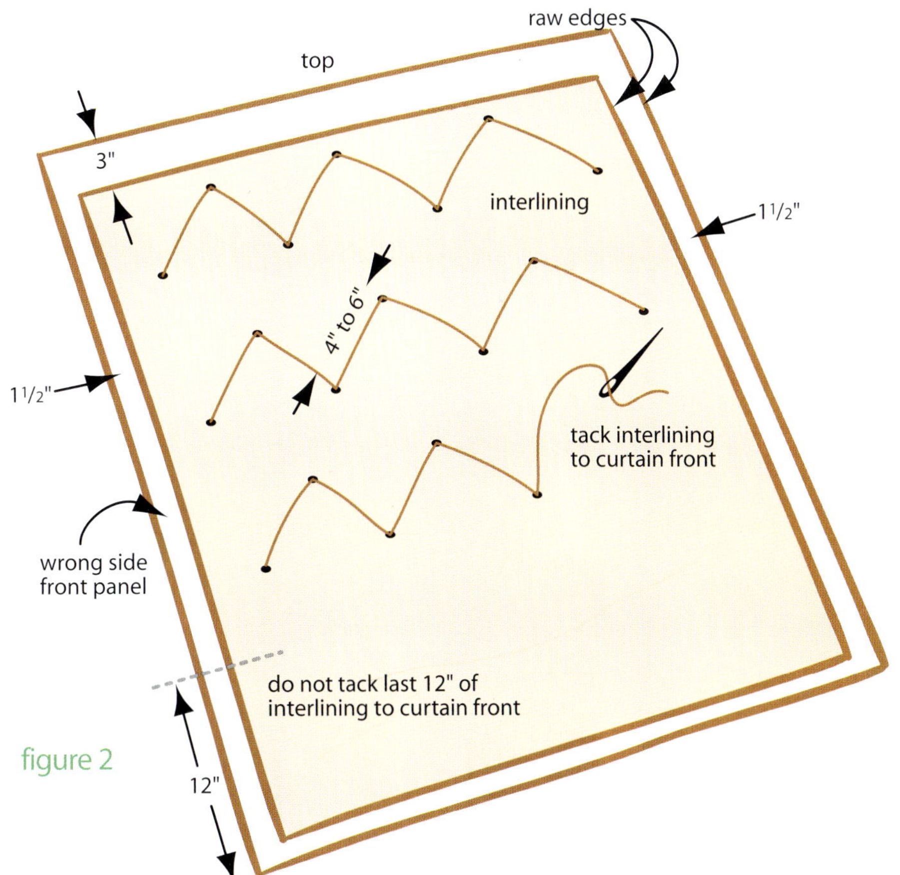

figure 2

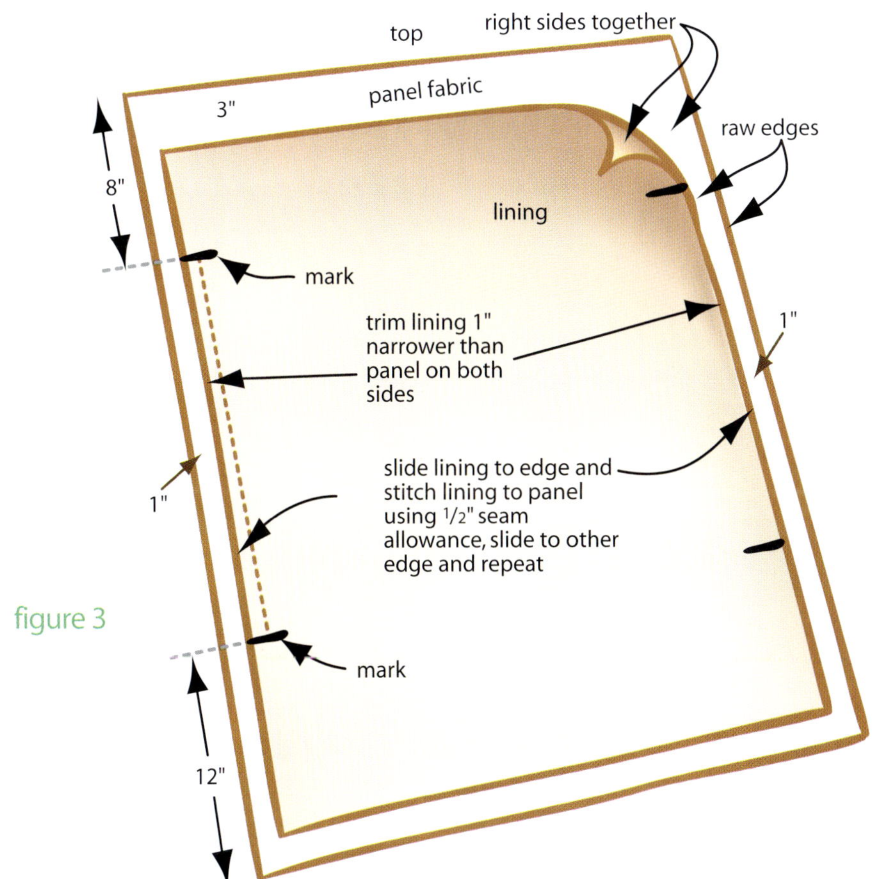

figure 3

4 Lay each front panel right side up. Place the top edge of the lining 3" from the top edge of the panel. Smooth the lining down the length of the panel. If necessary, trim the lining so it is 1" narrower on each side than the front panel. Slide the lining to one side edge. Measure and mark 8" from the top edge and 12" from the bottom edge. Using a ½" seam allowance, stitch the front and lining together between the marks (see Figure 3). Slide the lining to the opposite side edge and stitch the front and lining together in the same manner. Press the seams open.

making curtains with pleating tape (continued)

5 Turn the curtain to the right side and lay it with the lining side up. Center the lining over the curtain front so there is 1" of curtain fabric turned to the lining side on each side. Press the folds and seams. On the top raw edge of the front panel, turn under 3", covering the raw edge of the lining and interlining. Follow the manufacturer's instructions to pin pleating tape to the top edge of the curtain, covering the raw edge of the front panel (see Figure 4). Using a long stitch length, topstitch the tape to the curtains according to the manufacturer's instructions. Pull all cords in the tape together to make the pleats, then knot the cord ends together to hold them. Pin the cord ends to the back of the heading to allow the option of releasing the pleats later. At the top corners of each curtain, insert curtain pins into the back. Place the remaining pins behind each pleat. Hang the hook portion of the pins on the rod.

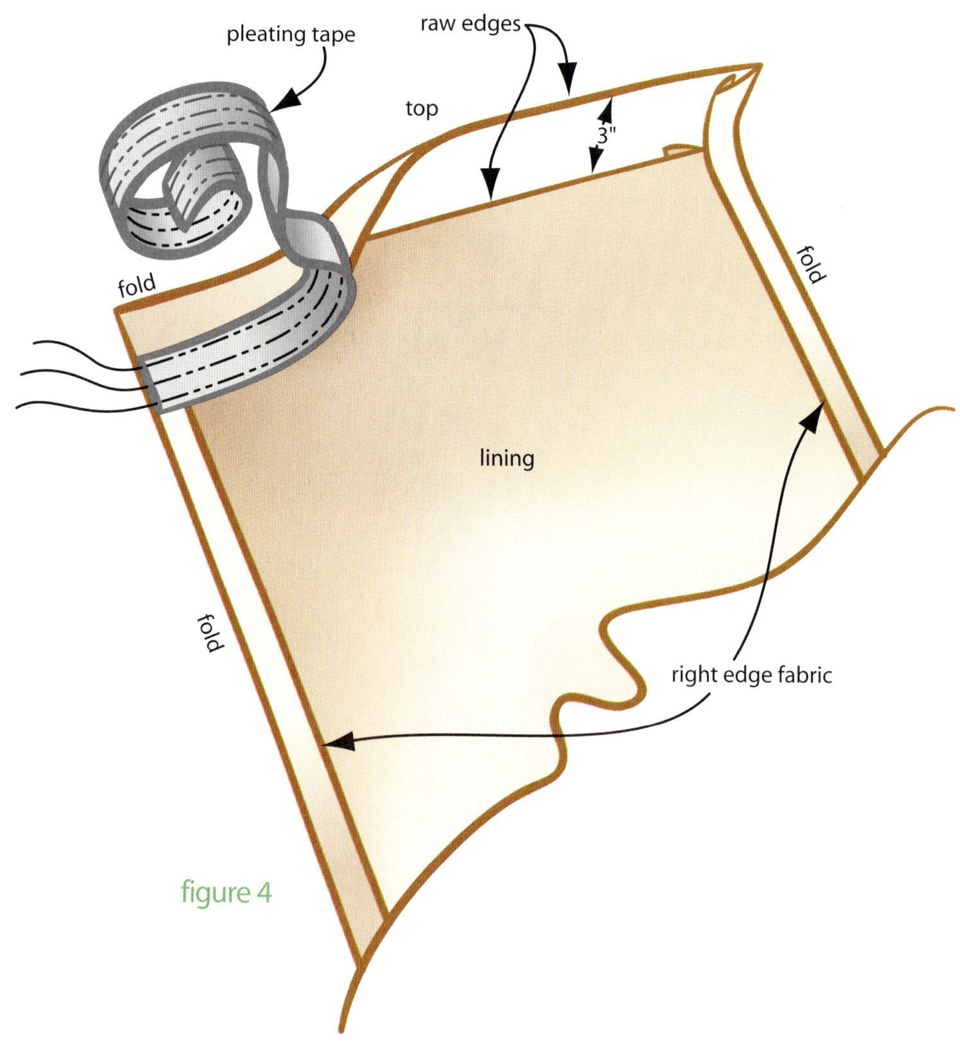

figure 4

6 To hem, turn under the bottom edge of the curtain front so it just meets the floor. To keep the lining edge free, fold the lining toward the top of the curtain and pin. Pin the curtain front along the hem fold. Remove the curtains from the rod. Press the fold, then open it. If necessary, trim the interlining even with the fold. Measure 6" below the fold and trim the excess. Turn the raw edge of the curtain front to meet the folded hem edge. Press. Refold the hem, making angle folds at the corners. Hemstitch the folded edges.

7 Remove the pins holding the lining out of the way. Turn under the lining so it is 1" shorter than the curtain front. Press. Measure 2" from the fold and trim the excess. Turn under the raw edge to meet the crease. Turn under the side edges 1/2". Press. Working from the wrong side, edgestitch the hem close to the folded edge. Hand-stitch the lining and curtain together below the side seams. Hang the curtains.

PLEATING TAPES

Pleating tapes make easy work out of formal or intricately pleated draperies. Choose from a number of different pleating styles. Traditional pinch pleats or triple pleats finish the curtains in the window treatment on page 110. Cartridge pleats, shirred or pencil pleats, and smocked pleats are other choices.

When selecting a pleated heading for your curtains, keep in mind that each style of pleat requires a specific fullness to achieve the look. The pleating tape manufacturers indicate how much tape to buy based on window width. For example, if a window measures 3 feet wide and the pleating tape style calls for three times the window width, you need to purchase 3 yards of tape. Purchase additional length to allow for placement of the pleats on the curtain heading. A good rule is to allow one more pleat section of tape for each curtain you will make. For a pair of curtains, allow two pleat sections.

Pleating tape is applied after the curtain panel has been hemmed on the side edges and the heading has been turned to make a finished edge. The combined width of the curtain panels before applying the pleating tape must equal the necessary length of tape. In this example, you have calculated that you need 3 yards of tape, so together the curtain panels should measure 9 feet wide. Halve this width to find the finished width of each panel in the pair. Following these specifications, the curtains will meet when drawn, covering the window completely.

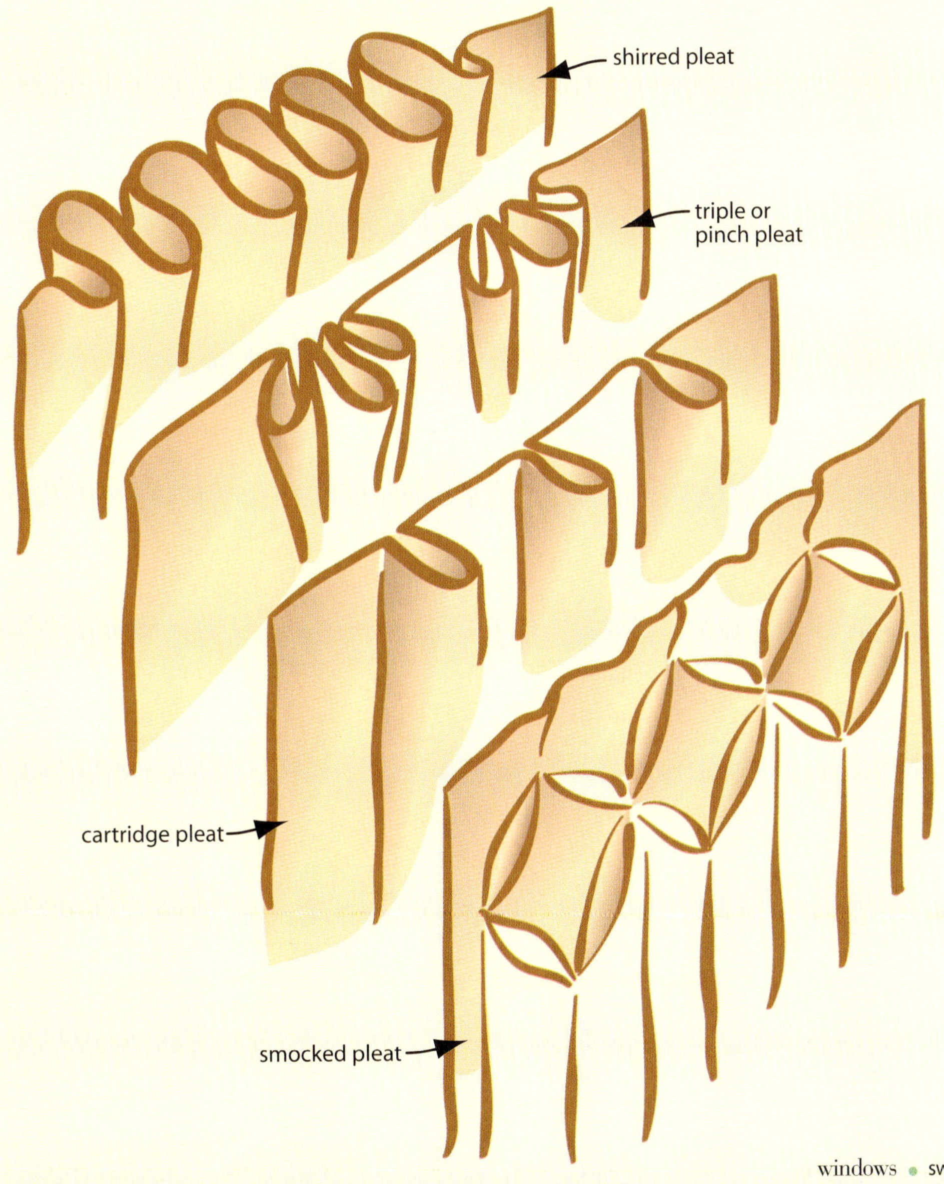

materials

1×6 pine board
2 (4") inside corner braces
4 (2") No. 8 wood screws, or wall anchors and 1¼" No. 6 wood screws
4 (1") No. 8 wood screws
Hook-and-loop fastener tape
Sheets of tissue paper
54"-wide decorator fabric*
54"-wide decorator lining fabric*
54"-wide interlining
6/32 filler cord
Decorator twisted cord
T-pins

tools

Electric drill and drill bits
Handsaw
Level

sewing tools

Sewing machine
Iron and ironing board
Fabric marking pen or pencil
Pins
Needles
Thread
Scissors
Tape measure
Liquid ravel preventer

(*Note: Yardage estimate does not allow for matching patterns. Compare cut size of panels to fabric design to find how much fabric you will need.)

skill level: advanced
time required: 2½ days

making the swag & jabot valance:

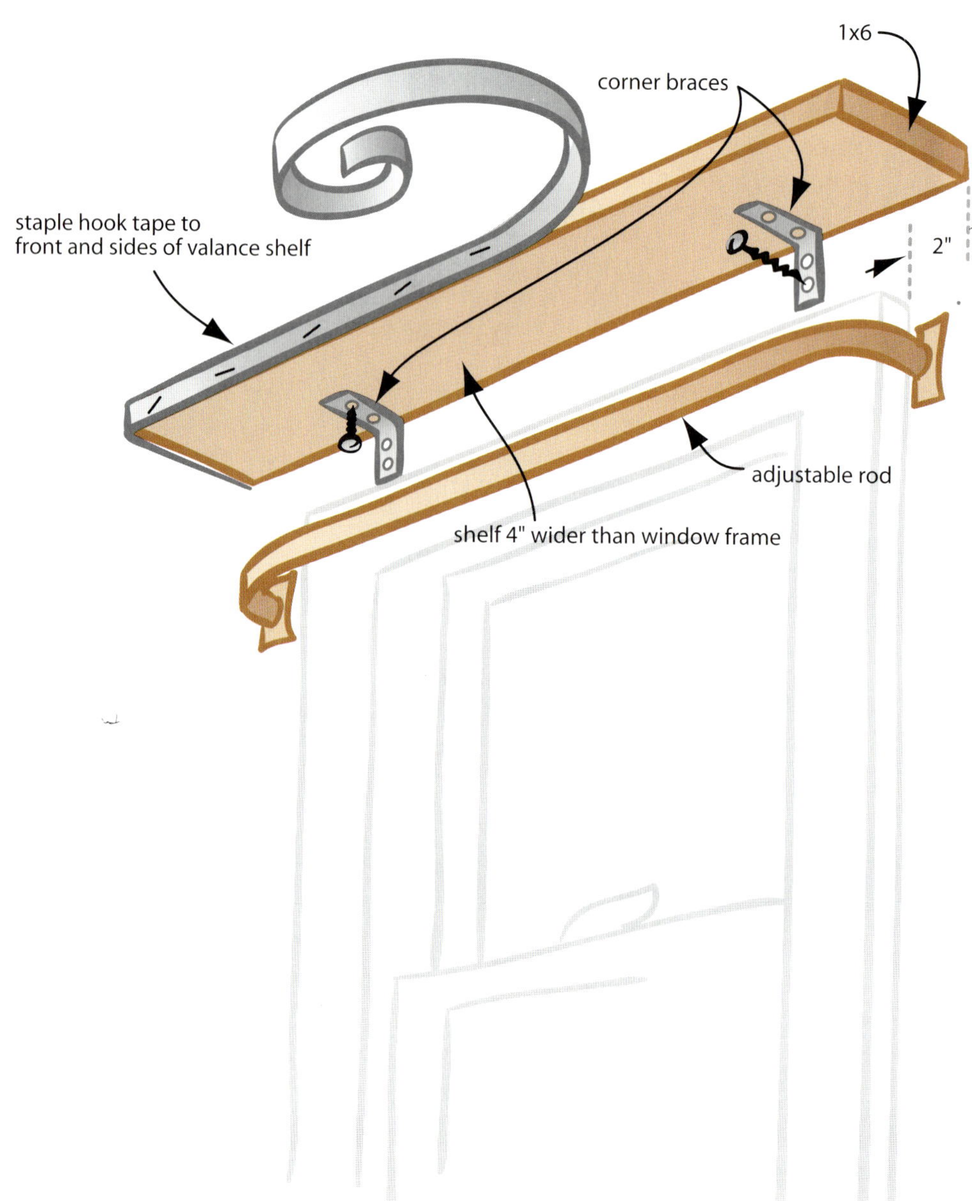

figure 1

1 Measure the window from side to side, including the placement of the adjustable rod for the curtains, and add 4". Cut the 1×6 to this measurement. Paint the board to match the wall or the lining fabric. Install 2 inside corner braces into the studs over the window with long wood screws. Center the 1×6 on top of the braces with the narrow edge facing into the room. Mark and drill pilot holes on the underside of the board through the screw holes in the braces and use short wood screws to attach the board to the braces. Separate the hook tape from the hook-and-loop fastener tape. Staple the hook tape to the ends and along the front edge of the valance shelf (see Figure 1). Set the loop tape aside.

2 Begin by working with several sheets of tissue paper to make each piece. The finished swag sections measure about 12". If your valance shelf measures about 36" from side to side, divide the shelf into thirds. If your window is wider, adjust the design to include 4 or 5 swag sections across the valance shelf and adjust the finished width of each swag section accordingly. To the finished width of each swag section, add 16" for the cut width of the swag paper pieces. Measure the desired valance drop from the top of the shelf to one-fourth the window height. Add 14" to this measurement (see Figure 2). From tissue paper, cut 3 pieces to this size.

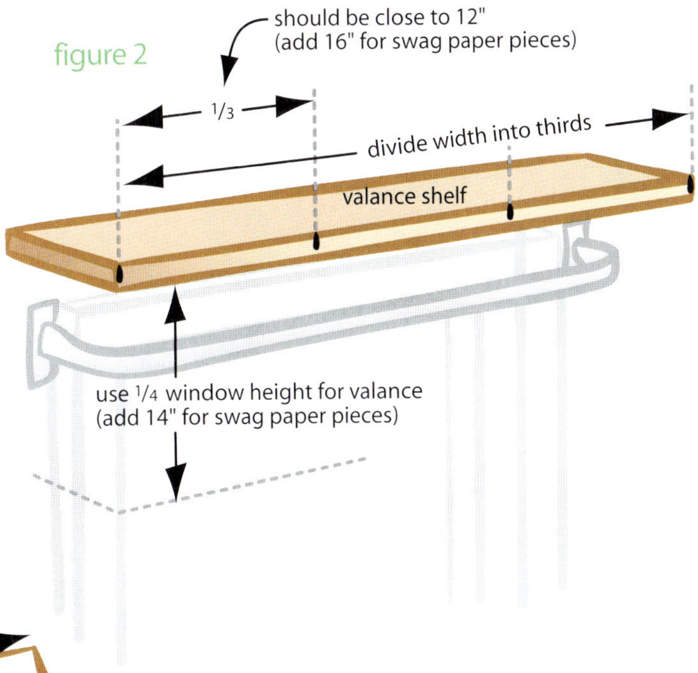

figure 2

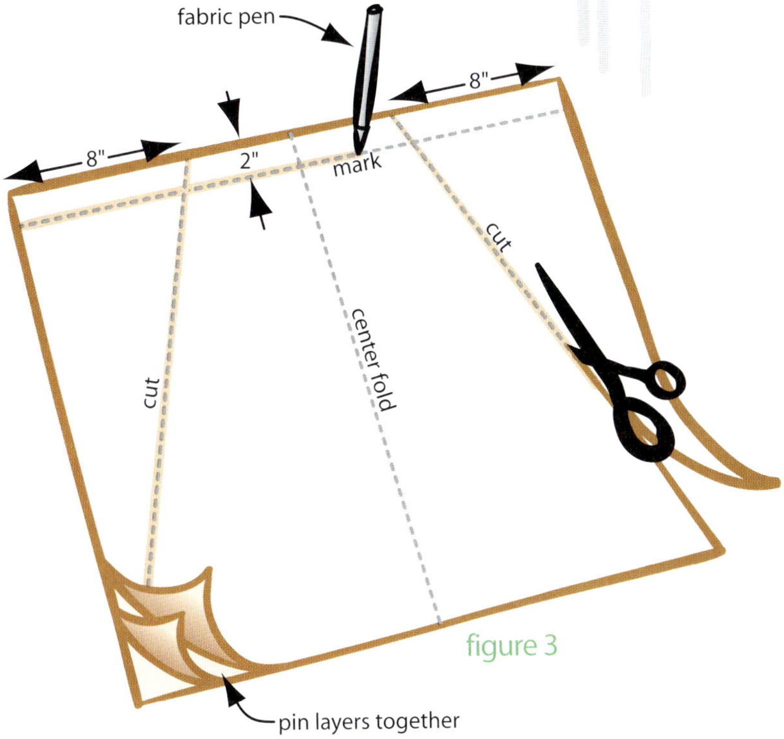

should be close to 12"
(add 16" for swag paper pieces)
1/3
divide width into thirds
valance shelf
use 1/4 window height for valance
(add 14" for swag paper pieces)

fabric pen
8"
8"
2"
mark
cut
center fold
cut
pin layers together

figure 3

3 With edges aligned, stack the swag paper pieces. On each piece, measure and mark a line 2" from top edge and pin the layers together. On the top edge, measure 8" from each corner. Mark a line on each side of the paper from this point to the bottom corner of the paper to make a trapezoid-shape swag piece (see Figure 3). Cut all layers on the marked line. Fold each piece from side to side, matching the angled edges. Crease the center fold, then open out the paper again.

4 Tape the pieces together along the angled sides. Working from the bottom edge of each panel toward the top, make 4 or 5 (2"-deep) accordion folds. Pin the folds in place and arrange the pleats individually, shaping the swags into soft folds. Use pushpins to secure the paper swags to the valance shelf, aligning the marked line at the top edge of the panels with the front edge of the valance shelf (see Figure 4).

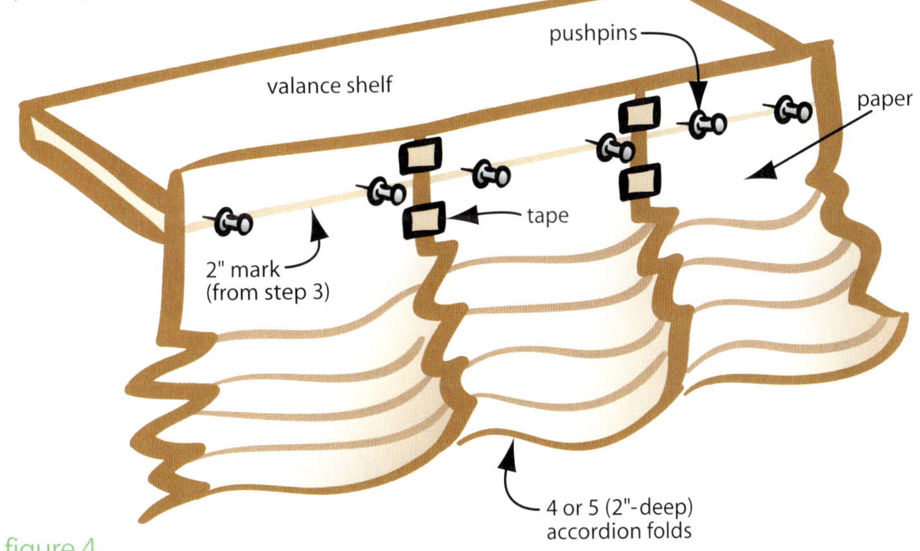

figure 4

making the swag & jabot valance (continued)

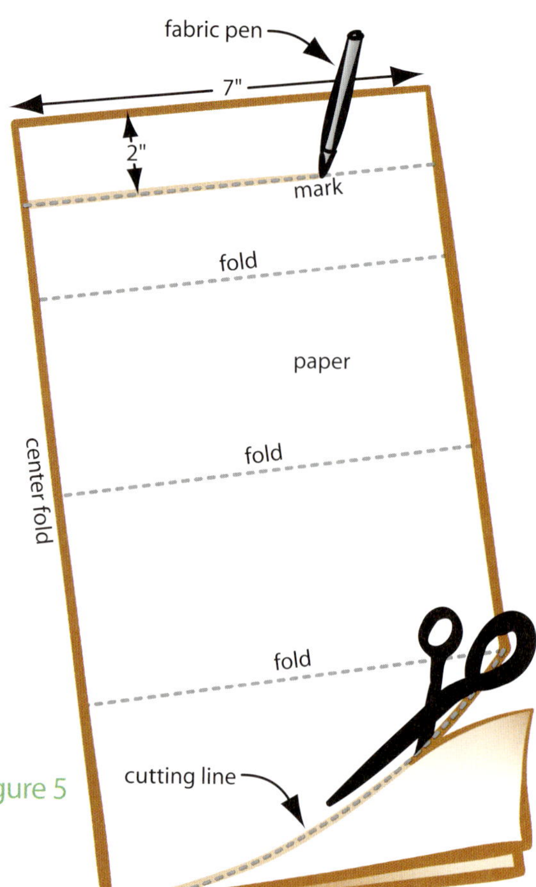

figure 5

5 From tissue paper, cut 2 pieces 14" wide by the desired valance length plus 2". On each piece, measure and mark a line 2" from the top edge. Stack and pin the papers together. Fold the pieces from side to side, matching the edges, and crease the center fold. Fold the stack from top to bottom, matching the edges. Fold again from top to bottom, dividing the length of the jabot piece into fourths. Open both top-to-bottom folds. Draw a curve in the bottom fourth of the jabot to the center fold. Cut on the marked curve (see Figure 5).

fabric pen
20"
2"
mark
small jabot paper section
center fold
jabot tail
cutting line
paper
cut 2

figure 6

6 For the jabot tails, cut 2 pieces 20"-wide by twice the desired length of the valance. Measure and mark a line 2" from the top edge of each piece. With edges aligned, stack the paper pieces. On one top corner of the stack, place one jabot paper section to use as a guide. Align the edges. Beginning at highest point in curved edge of the jabot piece, draw a line on the jabot tail to the opposite lower corner (see Figure 6). Remove the jabot piece. Cut the jabot tails on the marked line.

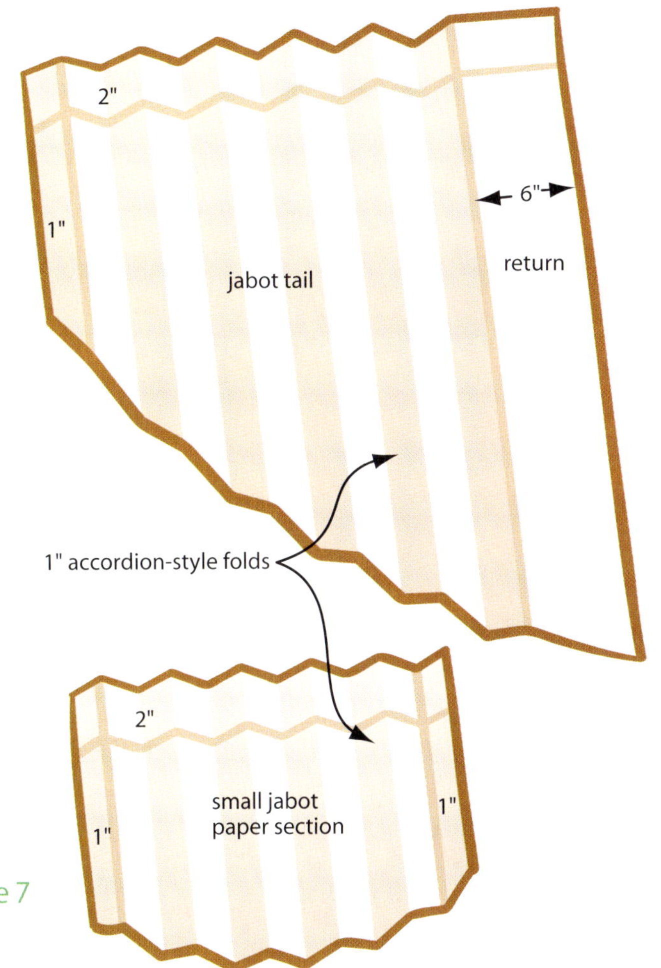

figure 7

7 Separate the jabot tails. Place the paper jabot tail pieces to mirror each other (see Figure 7). Fold the long outside edge of each jabot tail under 6" to form a return. Beginning at each short side of the jabot tails, turn under 1", then make additional accordion-style folds along the top edge up to but not including the return. On each paper jabot section, turn under 1" on each side edge. Accordion-fold the top edge of each piece between the folded side edges (see Figure 7).

MAKING ROSETTES

Decorative cord dresses up formal window treatments, such as this swag and jabot valance. To create the rope rosettes at the pleated neck of each of the jabot sections, follow these simple instructions:

- Starting at one end of the valance, pin the cord to the valance up to the first jabot.

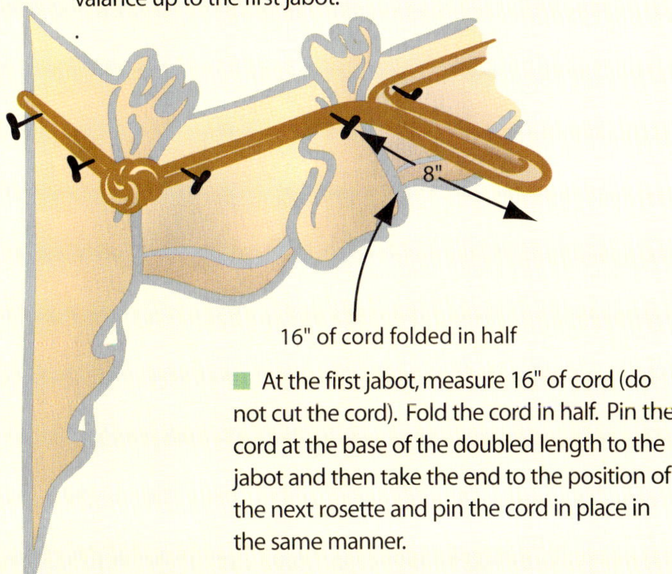

- At the first jabot, measure 16" of cord (do not cut the cord). Fold the cord in half. Pin the cord at the base of the doubled length to the jabot and then take the end to the position of the next rosette and pin the cord in place in the same manner.

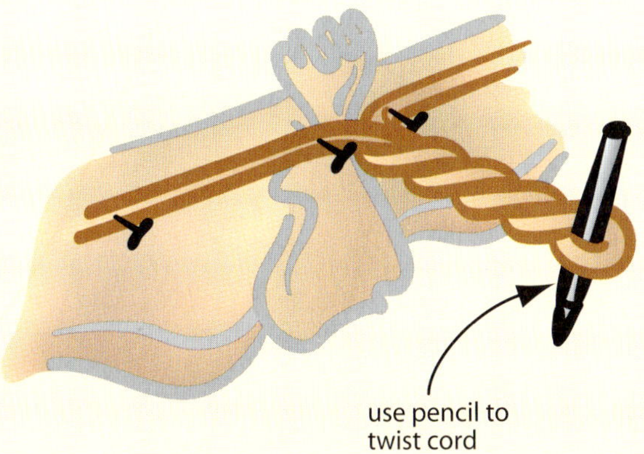

- Insert a pencil into the folded end of the double cord. Holding the base of the cord in your left hand, gently twist the pencil with your right to wrap the cord around itself along the doubled length. When the cord is twisted tightly, remove the pencil. Circle the end of the cord into a loose knot, resembling a rosette. Using a needle and thread, secure the rosette to the jabot with a few stitches.

- Make additional rosettes at each position in the same manner.

making the swag & jabot valance (continued)

8 Place the line marked at the top edge of each jabot tail and jabot piece along the side or front edge of the valance shelf. Using pushpins, temporarily hold the jabot tails and jabots in place (see Figure 8). Assess the overall look of the window treatment and the length of the valance. Note the scale of the swags and jabots and the length of the tails. If desired, adjust the design, cutting new swag, jabot, and jabot tail pieces from tissue paper and making them larger or smaller as needed.

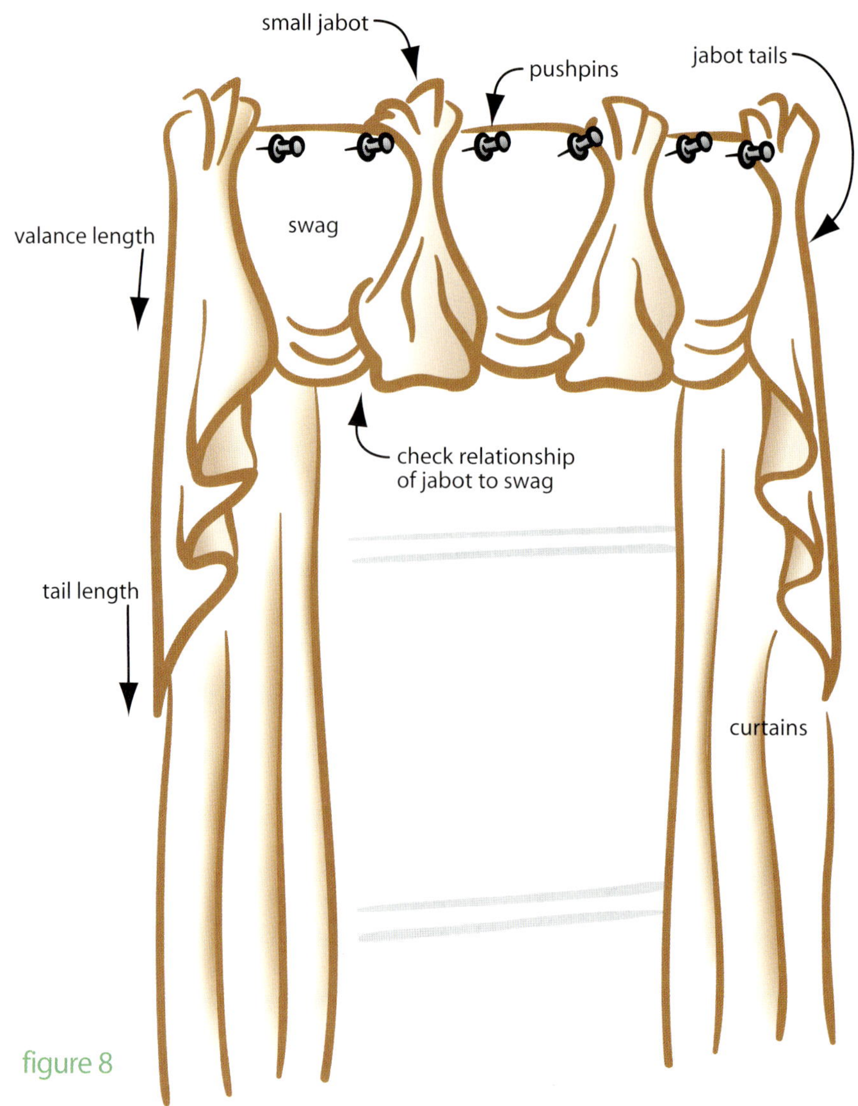

figure 8

9 When you are satisfied with the paper valance design, remove the pieces from the valance shelf. For welting, measure the edges of each jabot piece and each jabot tail piece and add 36": This is the amount of welting needed to trim the jabots and jabot tails (see Step 15). The swag panels do not have welting on the edges. Remove the pins from the pleats in the swag panels and cut the 3 sections of swag pieces apart along the taped sides.

10 Trim off the fabric selvages. Place the paper swag pieces on the right side of the fabric. Use the center fold to align the paper with the straight of the grain. Be sure to begin each panel at same point in the fabric design and to position each paper piece so the fabric motifs will show to best advantage. Pin the paper swag pieces in place. Measure and mark a 1/2" seam allowance around each paper piece. Cut each panel on the marked line. From lining, cut swag panels in the same manner.

11 On the right side of the fabric, place the paper jabot and jabot tail pieces. Be sure you have a left jabot tail and a right jabot tail. Use the side edges to place the paper on the straight of the grain. Place the pieces in the same manner as the swag panels to show the fabric motifs to the best advantage. Pin the paper jabot and jabot tail pieces in place. Measure and mark a 1/2" seam allowance around the paper pieces. Cut each jabot panel and jabot tail panel on the marked line. From the lining, cut the jabot and jabot tail panels in the same manner.

12 Pin the paper swag, jabot, and jabot tail pieces to the interlining. Cut out the interlining panels along the edges of the paper pieces. Match each interlining piece to one fabric piece. Lay the fabric panel wrong side up. Center the interlining on the wrong side of the matching piece. Using a needle and thread and working from the wrong side, tack the interlining to the fabric piece. Use tiny stitches that are barely visible on the right side of the fabric, and space the stitches 4" to 6" apart. Set aside the interlined panels and the lining pieces for the jabots and jabot tails.

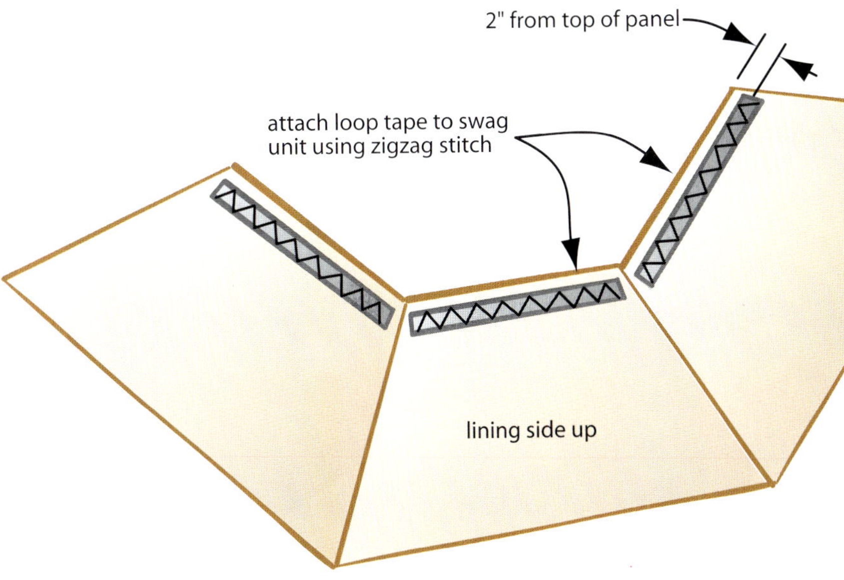

figure 9

13 With right sides together and raw edges aligned, pin the interlined swag panels together on the angled edges to make a 3-section unit. Using a $^1/_2$" seam allowance, stitch the edges together. Press the seams open. Stitch the swag lining together in the same manner. With right sides together and raw edges aligned, pin the interlined swag unit to the lining on all edges. Using a $^1/_2$" seam allowance, stitch all edges, pivoting at the corners and leaving a long opening in the top edge for turning. Clip the corners. Turn to the right side through the opening. Place the seams on the edge and press flat. Turn the raw edges along the opening to the inside and press flat. Using a needle and thread, stitch the opening closed by hand. Lay the swag panel lining side facing up. Measure 2" from top edge of panel. Cut a strip of loop tape to fit each section of the swag panel. Place the loop tape 2" from the top edge of the panel (see Figure 9). Using the wide and long zigzag setting on the sewing machine, stitch the loop tape to the swag unit.

14 Starting at the bottom of the swag unit, at each end of the unit and at each seam, turn under 2", then make 3 or 4 additional accordion-style folds, working toward the top of the unit. (The center of each panel will drape below the folds.) Pin the folds in place on the lining side of the unit. Arrange the pleats individually, shaping each swag panel into soft folds. Match the loop tape on the swag unit to the hook tape on the front edge of the valance shelf. Leave the pleats pinned in place until you are ready to attach the jabots and tails.

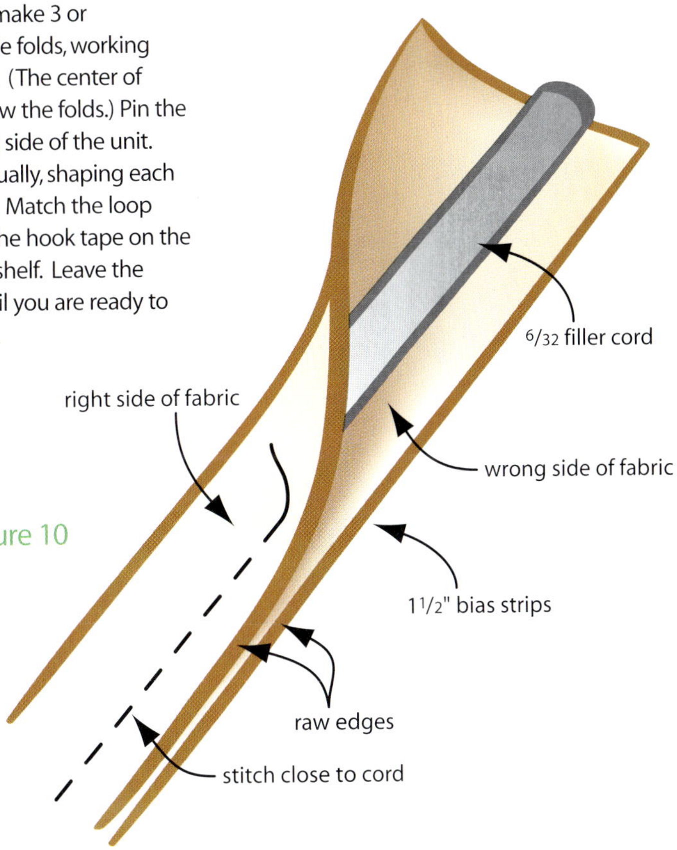

figure 10

15 To make the welting that outlines the jabots and jabot tails, cut enough $1^1/_2$" bias strips from the remaining fabric to make the length required for the edges of the jabots and jabot tails. Stitch the strips together at the short ends to make a continuous length. Fold the bias strip around the cord, matching the long raw edges. Using a zipper foot and long stitch length, baste close to the cord, encasing the cord in the fabric (see Figure 10).

making the swag & jabot valance (continued)

16 On the right side of each interlined jabot and jabot tail piece, pin the welting, aligning raw edges. Clip the welting's seam allowance at corners and around curves. Where the welting ends meet, overlap the ends 1" and cut the welting. Remove about $^1/_2$" of stitching from the fabric in each end of the welting to expose the cord. Cut the cord ends so they are flush, then refold the fabric over the cord, turning under $^1/_2$" on the top edge (see Figure 11). Using a zipper foot and long stitch length, baste the welting to the jabot piece. Pivot the stitching at the corners.

17 With right sides together and raw edges aligned, pin one interlined jabot piece to one jabot lining piece on all edges. Using a zipper foot, stitch the edges together following the basting for the welting. Pivot the stitching at the corners. Leave a long opening in one side edge for turning. Turn to the right side through the opening and place the welting on the edges. Turn the raw edges at the opening to the inside and press flat. Using a needle and thread, stitch the opening closed by hand. Repeat to make remaining jabots and jabot tails.

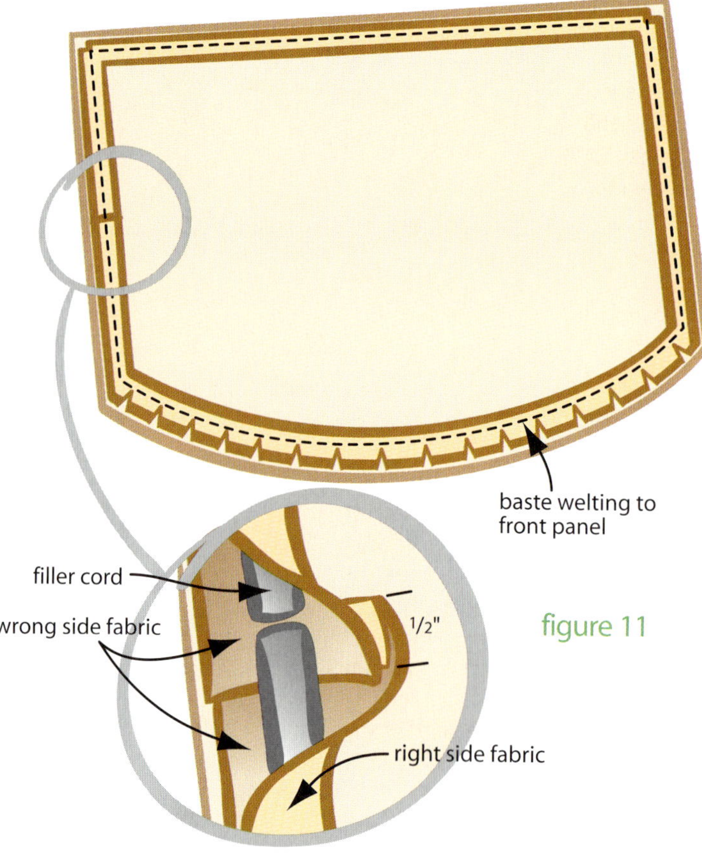

figure 11

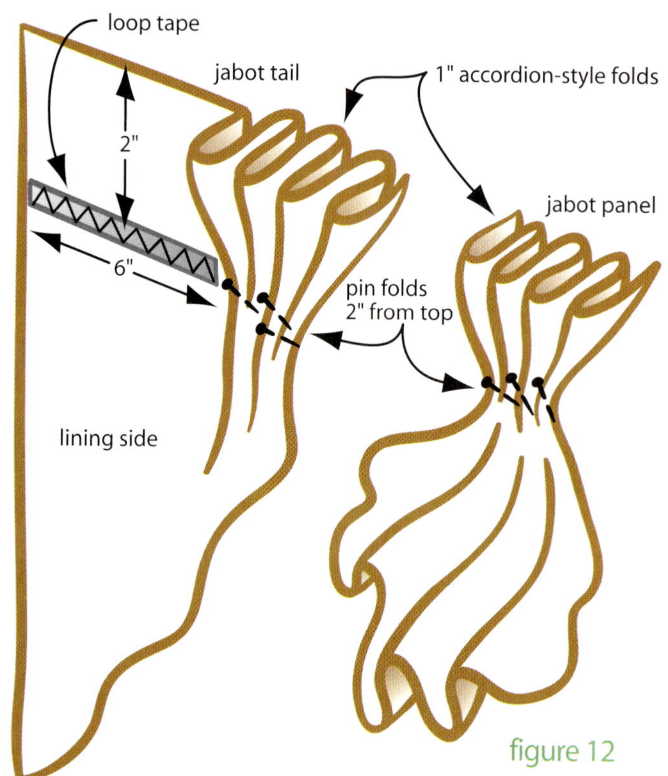

figure 12

18 On each jabot tail, measure 2" from the top edge. Place one of the 6"-long segments of loop tape 2" from the top edge of the piece. Using the wide and long zigzag setting on your sewing machine, stitch the loop tape to each jabot tail unit. Beginning at each short side of the jabot tails, turn under 1". Make additional accordion-style folds along the top edge to meet the loop tape (see Figure 12). Leave the loop-tape portion of the jabot tail free. Pin the folds 2" from the top edge of the jabot tail, forming a fan with pleats along top edge. On each jabot piece, turn under 1" on each side edge. Make accordion-style folds along the top edge between these first folds. Pin the folds 2" from the top edge of the jabot, forming a fan with pleats along the top edge.

19 Match the loop tape on the jabot tail with the hook tape on the ends of the valance shelf and pin the pleated section of the jabot tail to the swag unit. Pin the pleated jabots over the seams in the swag unit. Step back to look at arrangement of swags, jabots, and jabot tails. Adjust the pleats as desired.

20 When you are satisfied with the placements, remove the jabots and jabot tails. Using a needle and thread, stitch the pleats together by hand 2" from the top edge of the jabot or tail (see Figure 13). Remove the swag unit from the valance. On the lining side, use a needle and thread to tack the pleats in the lower portion of the swags. On the right side of the swag unit, stitch the pleats together in same manner. Place the jabot sections over the seams in the swag unit. Using a needle and thread, stitch the jabots to the swag unit by hand. Stitch the pleated section of the jabot tails to the swag in the same manner. Match the loop tape on the swags and jabot tails to the hook tape on the valance shelf to install.

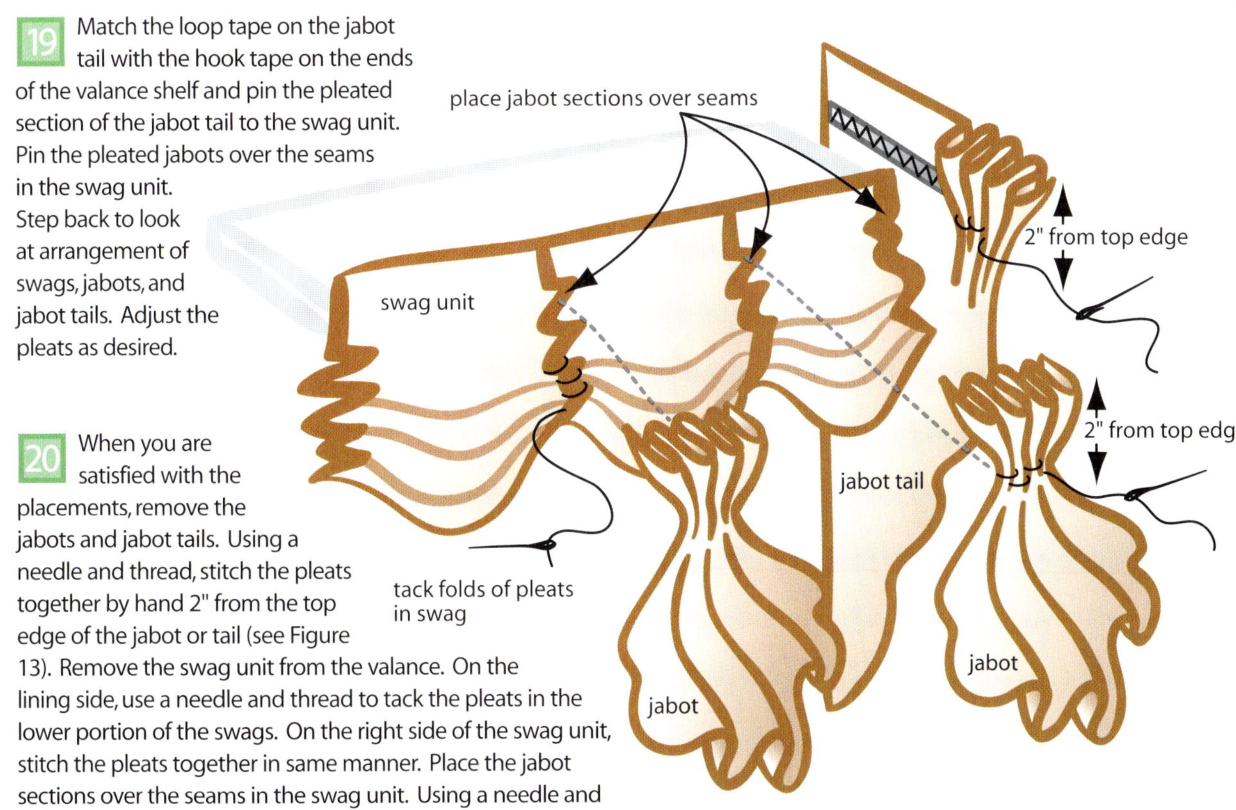

figure 13

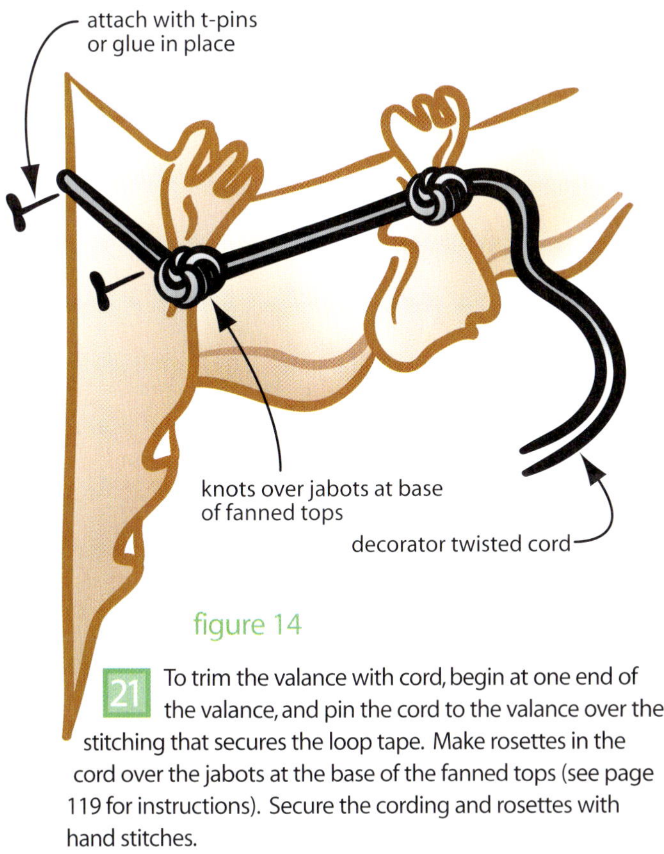

figure 14

21 To trim the valance with cord, begin at one end of the valance, and pin the cord to the valance over the stitching that secures the loop tape. Make rosettes in the cord over the jabots at the base of the fanned tops (see page 119 for instructions). Secure the cording and rosettes with hand stitches.

HOW TO KEEP A CORD FROM UNRAVELING

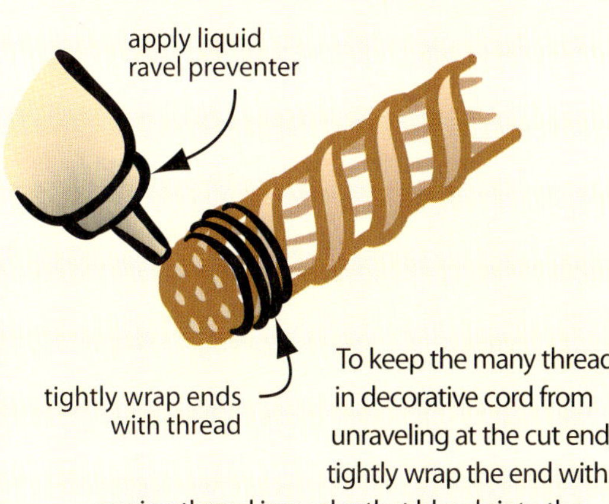

To keep the many threads in decorative cord from unraveling at the cut end, tightly wrap the end with sewing thread in a color that blends into the colors in the trim. Knot the thread ends, then trim the cord close to the wrap. Immediately apply a light coat of liquid ravel preventer to the cut end to seal together all cut threads. The sealant dries clear if applied sparingly. Overuse causes the product to dry as a white, filmy residue.

glossary

Baste: to hold pieces of fabric together temporarily with long, loose stitches, usually made by using the longest stitch length on your sewing machine; basting may be used as a guide for permanent stitches and removed after stitching permanently.

Bias: the diagonal of the weave or a line across the grain of a fabric, drawn at a 45-degree angle to the selvage edge; cloth cut on the bias will stretch, allowing a smoother fit around curves.

Bullion fringe: fringe made of gold or silver threads.

Cargill: a type of long, silky fringe used to trim draperies.

Casing: a pocket or channel into which a rod or dowel is inserted; it may be formed by parallel lines of stitching through two layers of fabric or by folding a single layer fabric to the desired depth and stitching along the edge.

Clip: to make snips or tiny cuts into the seam allowance, up to but not through the stitching, so the seam will lie flat. On a concave curve, make triangular notches to allow for flattening the seam easily.

Cornice: a wooden or metal box or band hung at the top of a window to hide the curtain mechanics; it may have a shaped crown or edge and may be covered with fabric or wallpaper for decorative effect.

Crosswise grain: the weft, or grain of the fabric going across the width of the fabric from selvage to selvage.

Cut: a length of fabric prepared for use in a sewing project. For example, to make a pair of curtain panels, you need two cuts of fabric for the pair.

Cut length: the measurement of a piece of fabric that includes allowances for hem, header, any gathers or pleats, and fabric repeat; the length to which you need to cut fabric before you begin sewing.

Cut width: the measurement of a piece of fabric that includes allowances for hems, gathers, or pleats; the width to which you need to cut the fabric before you begin sewing.

Dress pleats: the term refers to the technique of shaping and arranging pleats until you achieve the desired effect, then wrapping or otherwise binding them so the fabric develops a "memory" of the desired shape.

Edgestitch: to stitch close to the folded edge of the fabric with medium-length to short stitches.

Facing: a piece of fabric or nonwoven material stitched to the raw edge of fabric and then turned to the wrong side; it produces a stiffer, more substantial edging than simply hemming a raw edge; it is often incorporated into a design to conceal raw edges.

Fingerpress: using your fingers to press a crease or fold into fabric; the fold isn't as sharp or permanent as one made by pressing with an iron, but is sufficient to retain its shape.

Finish: to prevent unraveling on the raw edges of a seam allowance or to create a neat edge by zigzag-stitching, cutting with pinking shears, binding with seam binding, or treating with liquid ravel preventer.

Flat-fell seam: used for lightweight fabrics to create a finished seam on both the right and wrong sides of the fabric; one seam allowance is trimmed shorter than the other; the longer one is then folded and stitched over the trimmed allowance, encasing both the allowance and its raw edge; a double row of stitching shows on the wrong side of the fabric; on the right side, a line of topstitching parallels a conventional-looking seam. See page 74 for step by step instructions on making a flat-fell seam.

French seam: similar to flat-fell seams in that the seam allowances are enclosed, but the right side of the fabric looks like a conventional seam; the wrong side of the seam looks like a casing. No stitches are visible.

Gimp: flat braid or round cording used to trim curtains or upholstered pieces.

Hand of the fabric: a subjective description of the way a fabric feels, its weight and finish, its degree of crispness or softness, the amount of drape the fabric allows. The hand is often compared to a standard.

Heading: the top of a curtain panel or valance to which pleating tape, curtain hooks, tabs, ties, or drapery rings are attached.

Hem: a finished edge; an edge of the cloth that is folded over and stitched. Usually the hem is understood to be the bottom edge.

Hemstitch: worked by hand from the wrong side of the fabric, hemstitching secures a folded edge to the fabric by means of diagonal stitches. Draw the needle through the folded edge from underneath, pick up one or two threads of the flat fabric, then insert the needle in the folded edge and draw it through. Continue in this manner to secure the hem; the stitches should be nearly invisible from the front.

Hook-and-loop tape: a two-part fastening tape that has fuzzy material on one strip and plastic "teeth" on the other; one strip is stitched or adhered to each side of an opening or to two surfaces that will be applied to each other.

In-the-ditch: a line of stitching worked on the seam line from the right side of the fabric so the stitching disappears into the seam; stitch in-the-ditch to secure facings behind seams.

Interlining: a type of fabric made to be sandwiched between the main fabric and the lining; it enhances the curtain's insulating qualities, adds bulk and weight to the curtain, and improves the way it hangs and drapes.

Layout: the arrangement of fabric cuts or pieces on the original length of fabric; the plan by which pieces are arranged on the fabric to allow for matching patterns from curtain panel to panel or from piece to piece.

Leading edge: the edge of the curtain that falls toward the center of the window; the edge that will be pulled to draw the curtain closed.

Lengthwise grain: the grain of the fabric that runs parallel to the selvage edges.

Lining: backing fabric that protects decorator fabric from sunlight, improves the curtain's insulating qualities, and enhances the way the curtains hang. Lining fabric is usually a firmly woven, smooth-finish cotton. Lining fabrics may have added surfaces to provide additional insulating or light-blocking properties.

Liquid ravel preventer (seam sealant): a clear liquid adhesive applied to the cut edges of fabric or cording to prevent fraying.

Loop shade tape: a ready-made strip of twill or polyester netting that has loops attached; it is intended for use in making shades and blinds. Loops may be hard plastic rings or soft fabric loops.

Mounting board: a board, usually installed inside the window frame to support a blind or shade, or attached to studs outside the window frame to support a cornice.

Oriented: pertaining to the direction a fabric design should appear on each piece of a project: the selvage edge notes "up" or "top" of the design.

Panel: the curtain itself, not including valance or swag; a pair of curtains consists of two panels.

Pilot holes: starter holes for screws, made by drilling a short distance into the wood with a fine drill bit.

Pivot: leaving the sewing machine needle in the fabric, raise the presser foot, turn the fabric at a sharp angle, lowering the presser foot, and continue stitching. Pivoting at corners and points is necessary to make a crisp point on the finished piece.

Pleating tape: a ready-made band of twill or polyester netting into which a series of cords have been arranged. The band is fastened to the wrong side of a curtain panel or valance at the heading. The cords are drawn to create a pre-planned pleated effect. See page 115.

Puddle: a decorator term describing the way draperies are sometimes made longer than the measured distance from curtain rod to floor so the excess fabric can be folded under and arranged gracefully to suggest luxuriousness.

Repeat: the vertical length of a design or motif.

Return: the distance between the wall or window frame and the end of the curtain rod or the front of the curtain track.

Right side: the patterned, printed, or figured side of a piece of fabric. This is the side that is intended to show.

Rod pocket: a channel formed by two rows of stitching at the top of a curtain panel or valance into which a curtain rod can be inserted.

Roman shade cord: See loop shade tape.

Running stitch: a simple hand stitch worked from the right side of the fabric, made by taking two or three stitches on the needle at a time; stitches are worked in a straight line.

Seam allowance: the fabric between the raw edge and the seam line; usually 1/2 inch in home decorating projects.

Selvage: the edge of a piece of woven fabric, finished by the manufacturer to prevent unraveling; the selvages are cut off before you begin sewing. Selvages provide information as to the manufacturer, the colors in the fabric, and the direction of the design or pattern repeat.

Straight grain: the grain that runs the length of the fabric, parallel to the selvages.

Tassel fringe: a decorative trim that consists of a gimp or braid portion combined with a fringe comprised of tassels.

Tension: the balance between the bobbin and needle threads on a sewing machine; correct tension ensures a perfect stitch.

Topstitch: a line of stitching worked from the right side of the fabric to reinforce a seam and to make a decorative effect.

Turn under: to fold the edge of the fabric to the wrong side.

Understitch: to turn the facing and seam allowance straight out, extending from the fabric piece, and to stitch parallel to the seam (1/8 inch), catching the facing and the seam allowances in the stitching.

Valance: a fabric treatment hung at the top of curtains to hide the curtain fixture.

Whipstitch: to sew in small circles, catching the fabric as if to tack. Insert the needle through the fabric and bring it out, around the edge, and back through the fabric in the same manner; the effect is similar to the way the wire coils in a spiral binder.

Wrong side: the back of the fabric, not intended to be seen in the finished project.

resources

resources

Waverly fabrics and wallpapers shown in this book were available as of publication date. Please note that items may be discontinued without notice. If a fabric you like is no longer available, call consumer information at 800/423-5881.

Page 6:

Ottoman, scarf trim: Stockholm Stripe 647260; chair, pillows: Inga 664032; Nicholas Plaid 664022; coverlet, pillows: Baltic Brocade 664052; pillows, scarf: Hans 664062, Eugenia 664002; canopy: Greta 664072, Gustavian Stripe 664012; shades: Fredrick 663992; color Oyster. Sheers: Caprice/Cream 631302.

Page 12:

Wallpaper: Langston Stripe/Crimson 571123, Fairhaven/Rose 570923, Norfolk Rose Border/Rose 570860, Bows Jolie Border/Crimson 563666; sofa, chair cushion: Norfolk Rose/Rose 662510; piping: Country Fair/Crimson 662682; windows, pillow: Fairhaven/Rose 662623; upholstered chair, pillow, window shades: General Store/Crimson 662780; pillows: Fernwood Vintage/Crimson 662642.

Page 18:

Designer: Rhea Crenshaw, Rhea Crenshaw Interiors, Memphis, Tennessee; photographer, Emily Minton; stylist, Julie Azar; workroom: Unique Decor, Memphis, Tennessee. Wallpaper: Pantry Plaid/Blush 570961; valance, window seat cushion, Charade Vintage/Crimson 662550; shade and pillows: Country Fair/Citron 662687.

Page 24:

Designer, stylist: Catherine Kramer; photographer, Hopkins Associates. Walls: Waverly paints WP136 Snow White, colorwashed with WD303 Lichen. Roman shade: Limerick/White 647091; pillows, swag, and banding on shade: 664423; sofa: 664370; chair seats: Limerick/Ruby 647106; chair seat skirts and fabric picture mats: Check It Out/Cherry 664404; area rug: Limerick/Nile 647119, Limerick/Khaki 647096; solid pillows: Old World Linen/Daffodil 645606, Navy 645622.

Page 32:

Designer, stylist: Catherine Kramer; photographer, Hopkins Associates. Walls: Waverly paints: WT110 Buttercream, WP237 Azure Blue, WD238 Delft; overdoor valance: Parfait/Sky 663981; chair pads, napkins by Waverly.

Page 38:

Comforter: Just Leaves/Leaf 664161; shams: Just Leaves/Leaf 664161, with flange: Block Party/Celadon 664200; windows: Starlight/White 631310 with border Checkmate/Celadon 664210.

Page 42:

Window: Simple Stripe/Sage 664425 and Country Fair/Sage 647433; sofa, chair, pillows: Last Summer/Sage 664351; pillows: Field of Flowers 647423, Summer Stripe 664361.

Page 46:

Drapery, sofa: Lookout Mountain Vintage/Mulberry 662223; chair cushion, pillow, table skirt: Hillsdale Vintage 662600; pillows: Wall Street/Mulberry 662715, Pantry Plaid/Mulberry 662670, Grand Teton/Mulberry 662790.

Page 50:

Curtains: Parma/Copper 664523; chair: Lorenzo/Pewter 664443; canopy: Turino Stripe/Copper 664453; comforter, pillows: Firenze/Pewter 647503; pillows: Florin/Pewter 664493, Galileo/Pewter 664503; wallpaper: Vertical Strie/Natural 557390.

Page 54:

Photo courtesy of Better Homes and Gardens® Special Interest Publications® Quick and Easy Decorating™ Spring/Summer 1999. Walls, Waverly paint WT131 Camel; draperies: Boater Stripe/Jungle 630796; valance: Bremen/Golden 663912; chairs: Limerick/Topaz 647095 and Sandstone 647097, Ranger/Loden 608631; curtain rod: Kirsch, Inc., 800/528-1407.

Page 58:

Wallpaper: Sweet Violets Vintage Toss/Blush 571090; Langston Stripe/Violet 571120; border: Sweet Violets Vintage Border/Blush 570940; comforter, pillows: Sweet Violets Vintage/Blush 662490; piping: Country Fair/Sage 662686; chair: Old Lyme Vintage/Sage 662612; windows, pillow: Pantry Plaid/Blush 662671, Old Lyme Vintage/Blush 662611.

Page 66:

Curtains: Simple Stripe/Cobalt 664422; table skirt: Cherry Blossom/Cobalt 664381; table topper and slipcovers: Check It Out/Cherry 664404; wallpaper: Cherry Blossom/Cobalt 573931, Cherry Plaid/Cobalt 573951; border: Cherry Plaid Border/Cobalt 573941.

Page 70:

Wallpaper: Demitasse Companion/Lake 572211, Demi Check/Porcelain 572220, Demitasse Border/Lake 572201; chairs: Demitasse/Lake 663541; tablecloth: Perfection/French Blue 647207; table topper: Perfection/Buttercream 647198; trim: Wickerwork/Royal 660872.

Page 76:

Draperies: Spring Morning/Primrose 664790 trimmed in Seasons Texture/Spring 647480; chair and ottoman: May Flowers/Primrose 664860; pillow on chair: Seasons Texture/Spring 647480; sofa and pillows: Pretty Plaid/Primrose 664780; pillows on sofa: Spring Morning/Primrose 664790, Seasons Texture/Spring 647480.

Page 82:

Designer: Sally Draughon, Previews Interior Design, Macon, Georgia; photographer, Emily Minton. Draperies: Brilliant/Lemon 602123; table runner: Greenbriar Damask/Persimmon 631546; chair sesats: Chaplin/Straw 601105, Chaplin/Tomato 601102.

Page 88:

Designer: Rhea Crenshaw, Rhea Crenshaw Interiors, Memphis, Tennessee; photographer, Emily Minton; stylist, Julie Azar. Wallpaper: Camilla/Sage 572892; window shade: Castlebury/Stone 663711.

Page 98:

Draperies: Westbourne/Claret 663672; sofa, cushions: Lynnbrook/Topaz 663723; pillows on sofa: Easton Gate/Claret 663692; chair and pillow on sofa: Highgrove/Topaz 647243; pillow on chair: Prescott/Topaz 663685.

Page 104:

Designer: Rhea Crenshaw, Rhea Crenshaw Interiors, Memphis, Tennessee; photographer, Emily Minton; stylist, Julie Azar; workroom: Unique Decor, Memphis, Tennessee. Draperies, side chair seats, pillow trim: Hanover/Colonial 661080; sofa: Ranger/Maize 630002; armchair: Arcadia/Boxwood 601549.

Page 110:

Designer: Sally Draughon, Previews Interior Design, Macon, Georgia; photographer, Emily Minton. Draperies, bedspread, pillow shams: 661455; bed skirt, pillows, bench: 600723.

index